THE
HEIR

INSIDE THE (NOT SO) SECRET
NETWORK OF ALEX SOROS

MATT PALUMBO

Liberatio
Protocol

A LIBERATIO PROTOCOL BOOK
An Imprint of Post Hill Press
ISBN: 979-8-89565-321-0
ISBN (eBook): 979-8-89565-322-7

The Heir:
Inside the (Not So) Secret Network of Alex Soros
© 2025 by Matt Palumbo
All Rights Reserved

Cover Design by Jim Villaflores
Cover Photo by Tom Brenner / Getty Images News via Getty Images

Liberatio
Protocol Post Hill
PRESS

Post Hill Press
New York • Nashville
posthillpress.com

Published in the United States of America
1 2 3 4 5 6 7 8 9 10

Advance Praise for *The Heir*

"This is a meticulously researched look at Alex Soros that uncovers the next chapter of the Soros dynasty's grip on global affairs. It lays out how Alex is reshaping policy in his father's shadow. It's an essential read for anyone that wants to understand how the Soros network is operating post-George."

—Newt Gingrich, Former Speaker of the House of Representatives

"The dark spectre George Soros hung over America from Capitol Hill to rural Texas, to Harvard Yard, and to the battle-torn streets of the latest left-wing protest. That was simply the opening act. *The Heir* will have you realize the cancer we failed to cut out has metastasized."

—Steve Bannon, Former Trump Presidential Campaign CEO

"Matt Palumbo is fighting a David vs. Goliath battle."

—Sali Berisha, First Democratically Elected President of Albania

"People will have to think again who thought that once George Soros timed out, the deca-billion-dollar funding of attacks on Western values would subside."

—Lord Moynihan of Chelsea

"A must read for anyone who values truth."

—Carl Higbie, Host of Newsmax's *Frontline*

"A fearless and extensively reported investigation into one of the most influential—and controversial—dynasties in global politics."

—Jon Miltimore, Senior Editor at The American Institute for Economic Research

"Palumbo does a tremendous job outlining the new role Alex Soros has in financing the political operations of the left. If we thought George had significant tentacles across the globe, give Alex a decade."

—Joe Borelli, Former New York City Council Minority Leader

Also by Matt Palumbo

Fact-Checking the Fact-Checkers:
How the Left Hijacked and Weaponized the Fact-Checking Industry

The Man Behind the Curtain:
Inside the Secret Network of George Soros

Dumb and Dumber:
How Cuomo and de Blasio Ruined New York

Debunk This!:
Shattering Liberal Lies

Table of Contents

A Note on Style

When George Soros and Alex Soros are being spoken about together, I refer to them as "George" and "Alex." Generally speaking, in books like this a character is introduced by their full name first, and then their last name thereafter, so my informal use of their first names may appear unprofessional. But I felt that for this particular book, it would've been too confusing or awkward to write more formally.

Introduction

The world took notice when Alex Soros took the helm of the Soros empire of influence—not because it was unexpected, but because it marked a potential turning point in the most polarizing political legacy in modern politics.

George Soros built that empire to thrive in the shadows, within a labyrinth of funding and proxies that has shaped policy from Washington to Warsaw. Alex's rise flips that script: he's not just inheriting a machine but remaking it. This book peels back the curtain on that transition, tracing how a billionaire's son turned a whispered legacy into a public crusade, and why that shift matters now more than ever as the world tilts toward populism and skepticism of elite power.

George is a notorious billionaire whose wealth has toppled regimes and planted seeds in their ashes, infiltrated governments and media organizations, radically shifted public opinion without anyone knowing who was influencing them, destroyed judicial systems, and called you a conspiracy theorist for noticing. His legacy, like his influence, has always been the subject of debate.

And now the empire of influence is under new management.

When I started writing this book, I had planned for it to be a documentation of what happened since it was announced that Alex took over his father's Open Society Foundations (OSF), with the book starting in June 2023. It became immediately evident, while researching Alex's specific roles, that it was merely announced publicly that he'd be taking over the OSF in mid-2023; but he'd actually taken over specific parts of its operation before then. Alex has been the primary operator in Europe since at least 2015 and funding rogue district attorneys since at least 2022. It also became clear that I wouldn't be able to tell the story of Alex without explaining how George built some of the networks that Alex was inheriting, in order to provide valuable context.

Alex inherits the Soros machinery at a moment of declining popularity for the exact policies his father worked his whole life to promote. George's promotion of weak-on-crime policies and prosecutors were what finally made him a widely criticized household name; his promotion of DEI and racial guilt propaganda has shifted young men far to the right; and the unpopularity of his open borders agenda helped catalyze the rise of Donald Trump and populists in Europe.

George's political power, via his clout in legacy media, has been blunted as they have become increasingly irrelevant. Once shielded from criticism by major media accusations of anti-Semitism, exposing and criticizing all things Soros has gone mainstream in the age of "alternative media," where conservatives and moderates now dominate.

The Soros circle operated in the shadows for decades, but everyone is on to their game now. World leaders from Donald Trump to Nayib Bukele (El Salvador) to Recep Tayyip Erdoğan (Turkey) and Narendra Modi (India) have been quick to call George out.

But if Alex's behavior is any indication, he's doubling down on all of his father's causes.

A new king is in town, and he's keeping parts of his father's conglomerate on autopilot while cranking others into overdrive.

(Chapter 1)

Alex Takes the Reins

"My goal is to be the conscience of the world."
—GEORGE SOROS

"I'm more political than my father."
—ALEX SOROS

It was following a TV appearance on June 11, 2023, where I was discussing George Soros, that the news came through the wire that Alexander Soros was taking over his father's empire of influence, the Open Society Foundations. Just days prior, he'd met with Vice President Kamala Harris—a meeting that wasn't acknowledged by Harris on her public schedule.[1]

With that announcement, Alex laid claim to the most influential and destructive organization ever to infect US and global politics. George had given over $32 billion to the OSF since its founding, and Alex inherited a war chest with $25 billion.

As George aged, speculation had run rampant as to whom his replacement would be, and observers increasingly saw Alex as the obvious pick. This came amid rising attention in the media to Alex's political power and his constant visits to the Biden-Harris White House, amid his countless political adventures abroad, which he shared on his social media accounts.

---

[1] Matt Palumbo, "George Soros' Son Posts Photo of Meeting with VP Harris That Wasn't on Her Public Schedule," *Bongino,* June 7 ,2023. https://bongino.com/alexander-soros-posts-photo-of-meeting-with-vp-harris

He was standing next to the throne the whole time.

Alex was already in a high-ranking position before taking over the OSF, serving as deputy chair of the Open Society Global Board and as a member of the Open Society–US Advisory Board—a role in which, in 2020, he oversaw a $1.2 billion budget for the OSF.[2] In 2022, he'd been named the president of Democracy PAC, George's major campaign spending vehicle since 2019. That PAC was used to fund the campaigns of DAs with an "anything goes" attitude towards crime, which soon made headlines for destroying America's cities.[3] His involvement in European affairs dates back to at least 2015.

He already helped pull the strings; now he just officially directs the operation.

Alex quickly got to work. Shortly after taking over the OSF, Alex hosted an event in the Big Apple attended by House Minority Leader Hakeem Jeffries and other Empire State Democrats, such as Representatives Jerry Nadler, Gregory Meeks, Pat Ryan, and Ritchie Torres. Alex said the meeting was to strategize how to regain the congressional majority in 2024,[4] but we all knew it was to discuss what his leadership would mean for the future of the OSF, and for the funding of Democrats for decades to come.

Contrary to his father's elusive style of exerting power, which inspired my book on him, Alex (as CNN's only watchable pundit, Scott Jennings, puts it) "collects Democrats" the way his kids collect Pokémon cards. In what was practically a gift to me in writing this book, Alex has extensively documented his meetings with

2   "Alexander Soros." *Influence Watch.* https://www.influencewatch.org/person/alexander-soros

3   "Alexander Soros." *Discover the Networks.* https://www.discoverthenetworks.org/individuals/alexander-soros

4   Joe Schoffstall and Cameron Cawthorne, "Alex Soros Huddled with Top Democrats Shortly After Taking Over His Father's Nonprofit Empire," Fox News, June 19, 2023. https://www.foxnews.com/politics/alex-soros-huddled-top-democrats-after-taking-over-his-fathers-nonprofit-empire

leading Democrats, left-wing leaders, left-wing activists, foreign leaders, and more, on his X/Twitter, Facebook, and Instagram accounts. Through them, he has provided a useful trove of insight into his own network—and these are just the ones he shows.

Alex's takeover isn't just a handover of cash; it's a masterclass in rebranding power.

As the Capital Research Center's Parker Thayer has documented, internationally, that includes the heads of states of Albania, Austria, Barbados, Belarus, Canada, Croatia, Estonia, France, Kosovo, Latvia, Lithuania, Moldova, Montenegro, Netherlands, North Macedonia, Rwanda, Senegal, Serbia, the European Union, the Democratic Republic of Congo, Ukraine, and Zambia. These are all places where his father held sway, and Alex is continuing what his father started there.

Domestically, it includes the usual Democratic suspects, such as Joe Biden, Kamala Harris, Nancy Pelosi, Chuck Schumer, Adam Schiff, and Barack Obama, among many, many household names.[5]

Some on the left dislike the publicity from Alex and believe it could hurt them politically. But Alex says he must engage with certain people to promote an open society and believes being public helps to deconstruct the perception that his family is a shady cabal.[6]

Alex claims he posts his political activity to be transparent, to avoid the kind of "conspiracy theories" that surrounded his father; but that term has mostly just been used as a pejorative against critics. The executive director of the American Civil Liberties Union, Anthony Romero, believes that given Alex's comparative

---

5   Parker Thayer, "Alexander Soros, Electric Cars, and the Inflation Reduction Act: What to Expect from George Soros's Heir," Capital Research Center, June 28, 2023. capitalresearch.org/article/alexander-soros-electric-cars-and-the-inflation-reduction-act-what-to-expect-from-george-soross-heir

6   Roula Khalaf, "Alex Soros: 'These People Are Bullies. And You Fight Back,'" *Financial Times*, January 21, 2025. https://www.ft.com/content/fdde5d56-5dc1-4bd4-af43-b58ef969c1bb

openness, the right would be less likely to target him than they did his father.[7] I'll be the first to disagree.

As for his real motive? To paraphrase the movie *The Big Short*, he's not confessing, he's bragging.

Alex will claim to fear the left has gone *too* left on free speech, but he hasn't spent a dime fighting that issue since taking over. In one breath he says that, in the next he says that fire walls on free speech are needed, citing Germany as an example; "All anybody needs to do is pick up a history book to figure out why."[8]

He'll claim to disagree with his father on Israel—while funding the national embarrassment that was the pro-Hamas student encampments that sprouted following the October 7 massacre. And on the issue that helped solidify George as a household name— his funding of rogue district attorneys who launched skyrocketing crime rates in America's cities—Alex has funded, among others, a progressive prosecutor to defeat a *George*-funded prosecutor for being insufficiently left-wing (yes, really—see chapter three).

For as much as he wants to present himself as a fresh face, the apple didn't fall from the tree.

It doesn't even seem to have fallen at all.

THE EARLY LIFE OF ALEX SOROS

But first, who is Alex, anyway?

Born the fourth of five children, Alex enjoyed a luxurious childhood. He was raised in a fourteen-room estate in upscale Katonah, New York, and educated from K–12 at King Low Heywood Thomas (now "King School"), the elite Stamford private school

---

7   Ewan Palmer, "George Soros' Successor Says He Is 'More Political' Than His Father," *Newsweek*, June 15, 2024. https://www.newsweek.com/george-soros-son-alex-osf-1805787

8   Simon Van Zuylen-Wood. "The New Soros: With Trump on the Rampage, Alex Soros Takes Control of his Father's Empire. What Will He Do With the Influence?" *New York Magazine*, April 22, 2025. https://nymag.com/intelligencer/article/alex-soros-george-soros-foundation-democrats-trump-politics.html

where tuition for the 2024–25 semester ranges from $41,000 for kindergarten to $55,000 for grades 9–12.

While it became obvious in recent years that Alex would take his father's spot (and likely did years before the family officially announced it years later), a decade prior it would've seemed impossible, even to someone with a "fly-on-the-wall" view of his life.

Many believed Soros would never cede his control of the philanthropic enterprise while still alive. George also did not want any of his children to succeed him at the OSF; instead, he preferred the most competent person to take over.[9]

However, Alex, who was an "unlikely successor," earned his trust over time. Some sources say while George had been reluctant to hand over the nonprofit, he later said Alex had "earned it." Not everyone agreed; in a profile of Alex in the left-wing *New York Magazine*, journalist Simon van Zylen-Wood revealed that that "someone with deep Open Society Foundations ties" said that "the real story is that every single person who knows the family knows that Alex was exactly the wrong person to lead the foundation."[10]

Many had believed that Alex's elder half-brother, Jonathan Soros, would succeed his father at OSF, but George and Jonathan had a falling-out, with Jonathan leaving the operation in 2011.[11]

Jonathan also had assumed he would be selected to lead the organization, but was aware of his father's tendency to change his mind. "I always knew he could change his mind," Jonathan said.

9   Gregory Zuckerman, "George Soros Hands Control to His 37-Year-Old Son: 'I'm More Political,'" *The Wall Street Journal*, June 11, 2023. https://www.wsj.com/articles/george-soros-heir-son-alexander-soros-e3c4ca13

10   "The New Soros: With Trump on the Rampage, Alex Soros Takes Control of his Father's Empire. What Will He Do With the Influence?" *New York Magazine*.

11   Maggie Severns and Gregory Zuckerman, "The Soros Heir Who Is Everywhere This Election," *The Wall Street Journal*, March 11, 2024. https://www.wsj.com/politics/elections/alexander-soros-democratic-donor-2024-7811415b

Their management style also differed sharply, with George being more impulsive while Jonathan was analytical.[12]

Explaining why he parted ways with his son, Soros told the *Wall Street Journal* that he and Jonathan disagreed on "certain points," which were more evident, particularly to the young Soros, who preferred to chart his own course.

Although Jonathan was "disappointed," he said their business relationship ended in "pretty good terms," and he was not regretful. He disclosed that they remain friendly but not close.

Alex is now the only Soros who serves as a board member of the Soros Fund Management investment committee.[13] According to George, he and Alex "think alike" but still embrace "some different causes," with the younger Soros being "more political."[14]

Of Alex vision, OSF President Binaifer Nowrojee said after being appointed to the position she told him that she'd like to know it. "He didn't want some stone tablet where we kind of put it on a wall and say, 'Alex Soros said this; now, everybody must march.' That's exactly what an open society is not, so he was very loath to do that," she said.[15]

van Zylen-Wood was blunter; "In our last conversations, [Alex] made references to von Clausewitz, Thomas Jefferson, French pamphleteers, Lenny Bruce, Slavoj Zizek, the manosphere, the statue of Teddy Roosevelt outside the American Museum of Natural History, and the Compromise of 1877, but he did not put forward anything approximating a vision."[16]

---

12 "George Soros Hands Control to His 37-Year-Old Son: 'I'm More Political,'" *The Wall Street Journal*.

13 Parker Thayer, "Alexander Soros, Electric Cars, and the Inflation Reduction Act: What to Expect from George Soros's Heir," Capital Research Center, June 28, 2023. https://capitalresearch.org/article/alexander-soros-electric-cars-and-the-inflation-reduction-act-what-to-expect-from-george-soross-heir

14 "George Soros Hands Control to His 37-Year-Old Son: 'I'm More Political,'" *The Wall Street Journal*.

15 "The New Soros: With Trump on the Rampage, Alex Soros Takes Control of his Father's Empire. What Will He Do With the Influence?" *New York Magazine*.

16 Ibid.

Despite his own dabbles in what the Soros family considers to be philanthropy, Alex's reputation over a decade ago was what you'd expect from the son of one of the wealthiest men in human history: that of a "trust fund kid." In 2008 he made his public debut in the form of a *Cityfile* article showing pictures from Facebook of him at a party, which became a minor embarrassment for his family—and bolstered a "playboy" image for him.

In 2012, when Alex was just twenty-six years old, the *New York Times* interviewed him.[17] At the time he was profiled, he'd just received his master's degree at the University of California, Berkeley, and was working towards a PhD in history from UC Berkeley (which he received in 2018). He previously graduated with a history degree from New York University, where he roomed with entrepreneur Adam Braun, the brother of entrepreneur Scooter Braun.[18]

The *Times* highlighted Alex's claim to want a more low-key lifestyle, in contrast to his father's high-profile life. Such a juxtaposition between the two would prove ironic by the time Alex had risen to the helm. He had garnered a reputation of publicly boasting of his meddling, while his father had shied away from the spotlight and did his talking through his money more than his mouth.[19]

"I have the incentive of failing my own reputation," Alex was quoted as saying. "If I don't succeed, then I'm just another deadbeat lazy trust-fund kid."[20]

Alex was politically active at the time, with his key concerns including environmental issues, drug policy reform, and a vague

---

17 Alex Williams, "Alexander Soros Tries to Live Up to His Family Name," *The New York Times*, July 19, 2012. https://www.nytimes.com/2012/07/19/fashion/alexander-soros-tries-to-live-up-to-his-family-name.html
18 Ibid.
19 Ibid.
20 Ibid.

"protection of human rights," which can only be interpreted in the modern liberal sense (primarily, protecting abortion and LGBT rights). In his twenties, he traveled to remote parts of the Amazon rainforest to meet with indigenous leaders for the purpose of drawing public attention to their needs.

It's clear that there was an immense weight on Alex's shoulders to measure up to his father and the impact he'd had on the world. It was George himself who encouraged him (and his other children) to forge their own lives from an early age.

But the two didn't have the best relationship, early on.

"I was very angry at him, I felt unwanted," he told the *Times*. "[George] had a very hard time communicating love, and he was never really around." Alex still did enjoy the time they spent together, especially when it came to politics. From a young age, Alex sat in on conversations with Hillary Clinton, Nelson Mandela, and Bono. Alex said that meeting Mandela was *the* freedom story for him. "My father was more about how you get closed societies to become open, and my task within the foundation (after taking it over) is how do you renew open societies from within."[21]

According to Alex, his father's worldview and work were shaped by WW2 and the "postwar international order." Alex says of his father, "I joke around with him that he never saw a transition he didn't like."[22] A statement even more true, considering his backing of the transgender movement.

While everyone else his age was worrying about their math homework, Alex was building a Rolodex a lobbyist would kill for.

By his teens his relationship with his father began to blossom, with George tutoring him in Latin and debating about Karl Marx, implying that one of them defended Marx.[23] A nineteen-year-

---

21   "Alex Soros: 'These People Are Bullies. And You Fight Back,'" *Financial Times*.
22   Ibid.
23   "Alexander Soros Tries to Live Up to His Family Name," *The New York Times*.

old Alex started working part-time for the OSF from 2004 until 2006, while it was still called the "Open Society Institute."[24]

Alex says he always had a special bond with his father, and that when he would accompany him on trips in the early 2000s, George would call him his "apprentice," a reference to Donald Trump's hit show *The Apprentice*.[25] Neither could imagine the show's star would one day be the biggest enemy their ideology would ever encounter.

ALEX GETS POLITICAL

Alex started making political contributions in 2010 when he gave nearly $74,000 to Democrats that midterm election cycle, which was followed by Democrats suffering blowout losses. He complained about Republican rhetoric on social issues from the perspective of "the son of a Hungarian Jew who survived the Nazis."[26]

Alex slammed the Tea Party as a "movement of intolerance," despite its platform focusing on deregulation, limiting the size of government, reducing spending, and lowering the national debt and taxes. (No matter what the platform is of a right-wing movement, it'll nevertheless be smeared as "intolerant" or "racist," by default.)

Alex contributed over $400,000 to Democrats in 2012, and another $400,000 in 2014. Hilariously, *Politico* reported in 2015 that Alex had also donated to Friends of Democracy, a super PAC created by his half-brother Jonathan, who "has focused his political efforts on getting money out of politics."[27]

It was in 2016 that Alex truly upped the ante, contributing $1 million to a pro-Clinton PAC, and $4.5 million to Democrat

---

24   "Alexander Soros." *Discover the Networks.*
25   "Alex Soros: 'These People Are Bullies. And You Fight Back,'" *Financial Times.*
26   "Alexander Soros." *Discover the Networks.*
27   Ibid.

campaign committees, of which a PAC associated with Chuck Schumer was the largest recipient. He also supported Hillary Clinton, Russ Feingold, and Keith Ellison with the maximum contributions allowed by law.[28]

His sudden surge in spending coincides with when he became the chosen one.

Once George no longer wanted to travel beyond Europe anymore, Alex became his official representative and would report back to his father with notes from his meetings. On a trip to Latin America for his own work, he got a call that changed everything.

> This was in the spring of 2015, and I went to see him in London and I showed him all the pictures of Peru and the Amazon and being in Colombia, and then he said, 'can you come with me to Paris?' I basically never left."[29]

In terms of his "philanthropic" life, it was in 2011 that Alex joined the OSF's board. "He is playing a constructive role within the Open Society Foundations, but he is also striking out on his own," George said of his addition. The same year, in 2011, Alex and his brother Gregory launched Soros Brothers Investments, and Alex was a managing partner. Alex was also on the advisory board of Tau Investment.[30]

ALEX STARTS HIS OWN FOUNDATION

He set up his own shop the following year in the Alexander Soros Foundation (ASF) with the mission of promoting "social justice and human rights."[31] He even indicated he wanted it to be more extreme than his father's OSF and to focus on "more experi-

---

28   Ibid.
29   "Alex Soros: 'These People Are Bullies. And You Fight Back,'" *Financial Times.*
30   "Alexander Soros: Development Strategy," *Tau Investment.* https://tau-investment. com/team/alexander-soros
31   "Alexander Soros Tries to Live Up to His Family Name," *The New York Times.*

mental and perhaps controversial projects that larger mainstream foundations might not be able to take on."

The ASF's first grant was $250,000 to Bend the Arc: a Jewish Partnership for Justice—a left-wing group that would later call itself the "Jewish resistance," focusing on the Trump administration. He told *Forbes* magazine that he played a large role in creating the group itself.[32] The year of its founding, the ASF's largest recipient of funding was Pencils of Promise, which got $625,000. That group was founded by his best friend and former roommate, Adam Braun.[33]

The ASF was tiny by Soros standards, with assets under $1 million by 2017. By that year, most of its beneficiaries were environmental groups, the environment being a key cause of Alex from his youth until today.

From 2012–2021, the foundation gave $8.8 million, with nearly half (47 percent) given to "hardcore leftist" groups.

ALEX'S FAUX CONCERNS

Alex even attempted to express concern about the role of money in politics, a sentiment akin to Hunter Biden voicing concern about corruption in the Oval Office. "I detest the idea that money is speech, but if the other side is going to do it, you have to do it," he said, attempting to argue that his family's spending is only justified because other people spend money, too.

In 2018, Alex Soros was the fifty-second-largest political contributor in the United States, donating $2.9 million to campaigns and campaign organizations.[34] (Some concern!)

His largest donation since 2018 was a $2 million grant to the Senate Majority PAC, affiliated with Senate Minority Leader

---

32   "Alexander Soros." *Influence Watch*.
33   Ibid.
34   "Who Are the Biggest Donors? (2018 Cycle)," *OpenSecrets*. https://www.open
       secrets.org/elections-overview/biggest-donors?cycle=2018&view=fc

Chuck Schumer—whom he's met at least nine times since 2018. He's also given at least $130,000 to a PAC supporting Nancy Pelosi, whom he's also posted photos of himself with.[35] He's publicly declared himself a supporter of other members of the Democratic Party's progressive wing, including Gavin Newsom of the shrinking state of California (increasingly a fellow pretend-moderate).

Alex never gained any self-awareness in this regard. Following Donald Trump taking office, he expressed concern about the participation of billionaires in politics due to Elon Musk, and shared a tweet (in agreement) from Senator Schumer, claiming that "An unelected shadow government is conducting a hostile takeover of the federal government."

Meanwhile, Democracy PAC II, which is now controlled by (an unelected) Alex, gave $2.5 million to Schumer in 2023.[36] The duo also met at the 2024 DNC.[37]

The timing of the contribution was interesting; it was while Schumer had become increasingly irate over Musk's efforts to decimate USAID—the federal agency exposed as a liberal slush fund that had bankrolled and collaborated with OSF projects. Schumer gave remarks on the Senate floor decrying the supposed "illegal seizure of USAID," and laughably claimed that it would be illegal to close the agency.[38]

---

35   "Alexander Soros." *Influence Watch.*

36   Danielle Wallace, "Soros, Other Left-wing Billionaires Pour Tens of Millions into Schumer PAC in Bid for Dems to Hold the Senate," Fox News, August 8, 2023. https://www.foxnews.com/politics/soros-left-wing-billionaires-pour-tens-millions-schumer-pac-bid-dems-hold-senate

37   Jon Levine, "High-profile Democrats, Including Bill Clinton, Kiss Megadonor Alex Soros' Ring at DNC: 'In His Pocket,'" *New York Post*, August 31, 2024. https://nypost.com/2024/08/31/us-news/high-profile-democrats-including-bill-clinton-kiss-alex-soros-ring-at-dnc-in-his-pocket

38   "Leader Schumer Floor Remarks Condemning DOGE and the Trump Administration's Illegal Seizure of USAID, Putting American Security at Risk," *Senate Democrats* (press release), February 3, 2025. https://www.democrats.senate.gov/newsroom/press-releases/leader-schumer-floor-remarks-condemning-doge-and-the-trump-administrations-illegal-seizure-of-usaid-putting-american-security-at-risk

As if the irony needed another layer: as Alex was sharing Schumer's tweet, he had been recently profiled in a *Financial Times* interview that he pinned to the top of his X/Twitter profile; in it, they describe him as the "Elon Musk of liberals."[39]

THE ALEX SOROS SPHERE

Like his father, Alex is well represented on the boards of left-wing "philanthropic" groups and other spheres of influence.

Alex sits on the boards of Bard College, the Center for Jewish History, Central European University (CEU), the European Council on Foreign Relations, and the International Crisis Group.[40]

His mother, Susan Weber (divorced from George), founded the Bard Graduate Center, while George founded the CEU. After obtaining his PhD, Alex was a post-doc fellow at the Hannah Arendt Center for Politics and the Humanities at Bard College. He also boasts being an honorary fellow at the Institute for Advanced Study at CEU and was a visiting fellow at the Institute for Human Sciences in Vienna.

Like father, his politics are those of the typical progressive ideologue.

My friend Joseph Vazquez and his co-author Tom Olohan dug through Alex's social media to assemble a profile of him "in his own words"[41] following his takeover. In their assessment, his past comments prove that he's even more radically left-wing than his father.

Among their discoveries in going through Alex's social media archive is that he's obsessed with the issue of abortion. In his tweets, Alex has demonstrated a perplexing understanding of his-

---

39   https://x.com/JohnLeFevre/status/1882415071726653826

40   "Leadership," Open Society Foundations. https://www.opensocietyfoundations. org/who-we-are/leadership/alexander-soros

41   Joe Vazquez and Tom Olohan, "ALEX SOROS: In His Own Words," Media Research Center, July 13, 2023. https://www.newsbusters.org/blogs/business/ joseph-vazquez/2023/07/13/alex-soros-his-own-words

tory: he compared the Republican Party to the Confederacy for pushing for the repeal of *Roe v. Wade* and called its overturning "one of the worst days in American history" (I'm curious to know which events he thought were worse).[42]

Among Vazquez and Olohan's other findings was that Alex wants climate-change propaganda to infect all areas of education, and said teachers should insert it into their curriculum if they teach "history, global affairs, or science." Among his solutions for climate change include wealth redistribution.[43] In May 2024, the OSF promoted an article arguing that "degrowth communism" could save the planet.[44]

As has practically become cliché at this point, Alex has claimed that there were white supremacists in the (then) first Trump White House, and that Trump was putting Jews in danger "to stir up his white nationalist base"—which never materialized. Alex also backed the 2020 Black Lives Matter riots, which were exacerbated and enabled by the weak-on-crime policies of his father.

Alex blamed an increase in hate crimes on Trump, claiming that he "embraced white supremacy" throughout his life, campaign, and administration. During Trump's first year in office, whites were roughly 64 percent of the population but only 25 percent of all hate-crime perpetrators, so the media narrative of "racist white Trump supporters wreaking havoc" was always a fantasy. The entire net increase in hate crimes leading up to Trump taking office was due to an increase in hate crimes *against* whites. These are counter-narrative facts that not-so-coincidentally never made their way into any mainstream reporting on the "rise in hate crimes under Trump." [45]

---

42   Ibid.
43   Ibid.
44   https://x.com/OpenSociety/status/1796594516129988938
45   Matt Palumbo, *Debunk This! Shattering Liberal Lies* (New York: Post Hill Press, 2019), pp. 80–83.

Alex fully embraces the "everything is racist" mantra of the left, having claimed that COVID-19 led to an increase in "antisemitism [and] racism," and that in 2021 blacks had worse voting rights than in 1965. Bear in mind, 1965 was a time when several states had poll taxes and some had only a single-digit percent of the black population registered to vote.

Alex has advocated censorship through the Trojan Horse of "fighting disinformation," calling on Biden to take up that mantle. The OSF has spent over $80 million on leftist groups that placed pressure on Big Tech to censor speech prior to the 2022 midterms.[46]

To briefly sidetrack: OSF president Nowrojee has indicated that this pro-censorship stance will continue.

Nowrojee claimed while speaking in South Africa that there's a "crisis around freedom of speech at this moment"—but not in the sense we think of free speech. The internet and social media, which were touted as engines of democracy, have become engines of disinformation and dangerous misinformation."[47] In other words, her feigned concern for free speech will be used to justify censorship. She added:

> We are not naive about the fact that where power lies, and we also try to use our access to power, and our influence, to put those voices to center. We also have access to various governments that we work with and have the ability to have conversations with. We use that to raise the issues with like-minded governments that are willing and interested in meeting with us.

---

46   "ALEX SOROS In His Own Words," Media Research Center.
47   Muhammad Hussain, "Soros-founded OSF Won't and Can't Replace USAID in SA, Says First African Woman President," News 24, March 19, 2025. https://www.news24.com/news24/opinions/analysis/soros-founded-osf-wont-and-cant-replace-usaid-in-sa-says-first-african-woman-president-20250319

Then the true insanity comes: "I would argue right now, frankly, that the United States is probably more in need of democratic assistance than South Africa."

Back to Alex's social media. One of the pro-censorship groups he's praised is Global Witness, which was the ASF's second-ever donation recipient.[48] Alex has called them a perfect example of how "a little money can go a long way in philanthropy." He even held an advisory position at Global Witness.[49]

George was a fan, too. Before Alex sent OSF's climate spending into the stratosphere (more on this later in the chapter), Global Witness accounted for a plurality of their climate spending. The OSF gave the group a massive $28,007,350 in total funding between 2016 and 2023 alone.

Alex praised Joe Biden's botched Afghanistan withdrawal—a turning point in his presidency, when his polling turned net negative, never to recover. "President Biden and team carried out the largest airlift in US history! While we must do what we can to get remaining at-risk Afghans out, Biden and team deserve applause for what they pulled off!"[50]

He's retweeted calls to abolish the electoral college, endorsed legalizing prostitution as "the best way to protect the health and human rights of sex workers (prostitutes)," and pushed transgender propaganda.[51]

No stranger to hyperbole, Alex also predicted that a Trump win in 2024 would lead to "the end of democracy" or "civil war."

Like his father, he's kept alive the most insufferable accusation against those noticing his family's activities: that they're motivated by anti-Semitism.

---

48 Miguel Forbes, "Alexander Soros: Man on Fire," *Forbes*, January 25. 2016. https://www.forbes.com/sites/miguelforbes/2016/01/25/alexander-soros-man-on-fire

49 "Alexander Soros." World Economic Forum. https://www.weforum.org/people/alexander-soros

50 Ibid.

51 Ibid.

In a 2018 interview with *Ynetnews*, he said that "Since I was a child, I realized that—beyond all political reasons—the attacks against my father have an anti-Semitic tone. I read what they said about him in Hungary. They described him as the creator of an international Jewish plot. All the Elders of Zion and the Protocols in one man, in my father. They asked how dare this man come to central and Eastern European countries and dictate norms to them; who is this immigrant fighting against the discrimination of Muslims in America. They stepped up the attacks on him because they saw how influential he was."[52]

To give some context here about Alex's threshold for anti-Semitism: in the same interview, he claimed that Israeli Prime Minister Benjamin Netanyahu had ties to anti-Semites. Even the Jewish leader of Israel isn't free from the allegations.

ALEX CHIMES IN ON HIS FATHER'S INFAMOUS 60 MINUTES INTERVIEW

Alex has tried to argue against what he calls anti-Semitic conspiracy theories about his father, without ever addressing what underpins the so-called conspiracy theories. In a *New York Daily News* article, he weighed in on his father's infamous *60 Minutes* interview from 1998, after comedian Roseanne Barr referred to his father as a Nazi.[53]

In a tweet that put Chelsea Clinton on blast, Roseanne wrote (sarcastically), "Sorry to have tweeted incorrect info about you! Please forgive me!" before adding, "By the way, George Soros is a nazi who turned in his fellow Jews 2 be murdered in Germany

---

52   Nuhum Barnea, "Why They Hate George Soros," *Ynetnews*, April 25, 2018. https://www.ynetnews.com/articles/0,7340,L-5241290,00.html

53   Alex Soros, "Rosanne Barr's Lies About My Father George Are an Insult to All Who Survived the Holocaust," *New York Daily News*, May 29, 2018. https://www.nydailynews.com/2018/05/29/roseanne-barrs-lies-about-my-father-george-soros-are-an-insult-to-all-who-survived-the-holocaust

concentration camps & stole their wealth-were you aware of that? But we all make mistakes, right Chelsea?"

George was not a member of the Nazi Party or a Nazi himself, as would obviously never be allowed for a Hungarian Jew, but everything else Roseanne wrote was true. In what has become one of the most widely viewed clips of George among conservatives, during the 1998 interview Soros gave with *60 Minutes*,[54] host Steve Kroft asked, "My understanding is that you went... went out, in fact, and helped in the confiscation of property from the Jews."

A few fact-checkers have attempted to debunk the implications of this interview by stating that George merely tagged along instead of actively participating in the persecution, but he has no remorse even for doing that.

"I mean, that's—that sounds like an experience that would send lots of people to the psychiatric couch for many, many years. Was it difficult?" Kroft asked.

"Not, not at all. Not at all. Maybe as a child you don't...you don't see the connection. But it was—it created no—no problem at all," George said emotionlessly.

"No feeling of guilt," Kroft replied.

"No."

When asked how he couldn't sympathize with other Jews being persecuted, Soros sociopathically replied by noting the "humor" in how his behavior then is like his behavior in finance—and then employed the old "just following orders" defense (ironically, a favorite of the Nazis on trial at Nuremberg).

"Well, of course...I could be on the other side, or I could be the one from whom the thing is being taken away. But there was no sense that I shouldn't be there, because that was—well,

---

54   "Charlton Heston/50,000 White Farmers/George Soros," *60 Minutes*, December 20, 1998.

actually, in a funny way, it's just like in the markets—that if I weren't there—of course, I wasn't doing it, but somebody else would—would—would be taking it away anyhow. And it was the—whether I was there or not, I was only a spectator, the property was being taken away. So the—I had no role in taking away that property. So I had no sense of guilt," George said.

Assisting the Nazis with a gun to your head by no means makes one a Nazi, but it's George's callous, emotionless response that drew attention to his remarks. Even a psychopath would've had the self-awareness to at least pretend to be emotional about what he did, if he knew a national audience was listening. How many people would speak of the experience in Wall Street terms?

This leads us back to Alex: What does Alex have to say about all of this, in his defense of his father against those hyperbolically calling him a "Nazi"?

Absolutely nothing.

In his article purporting to correct "smears" about his father's activities in Nazi-occupied Hungary, he never even acknowledges his father's comments (viewed by tens of millions), which were solely responsible for the "smears" in question. You can hardly blame him—if people looked up the video, Alex would be facing the challenge of convincing people that they're hearing impaired.

He just says of Roseanne's comments that his father is "frequently targeted by malicious lies and wild conspiracy theories," then talks about how George survived the Nazis. He does give his side of the story, drawing from Michael Kaufman's 2002 biography of George: *Soros: The Life and Times of a Messianic Billionaire*:

> When Jews in his native Budapest were being rounded up and killed by the Nazis, my grandfather Tivadar Soros saved many lives including his own family by securing false identity papers and helping put Jews into hiding.

Among those he helped was the wife of an official of the Hungarian Ministry of Agriculture. In exchange, my grandfather asked the official to hide my father and pretend he was his godson. The official's duties included taking inventory of the estate of a Jewish family that had fled earlier under duress, and he took my then 13-year-old father with him. This story is also told in my grandfather's memoir of surviving the Holocaust, "Masquerade: The Incredible True Story of How George Soros' Father Outsmarted the Gestapo." George Soros did not collaborate with the Nazis. He did not help round people up. He did not confiscate anyone's property.[55]

Complicating his narrative are his own father and grandfather. In an interview with the *New Yorker* in 2001, George discussed being part of a Jewish council, which the Nazis formed to aid in administration, thus aiding in confiscation of property of Jews.

"This was a profoundly important experience for me. My father said, 'You should go ahead and deliver [the summonses], but tell the people that if they report they will be deported.' The reply from one man was 'I am a law-abiding citizen. They can't do anything to me.' I told my father, and that was an occasion for a lecture that there are times when you have laws that are immoral, and if you obey them you perish," George recalled.[56]

In his memoir that Alex mentioned, his grandfather Tivadar recalled the following:

My younger son, George, also became a courier. On the second day he returned home at seven in the evening.

---

55   "Rosanne Barr's Lies About My Father George Are an Insult to All Who Survived the Holocaust," *New York Daily News.*

56   Rebecca Mead, "A Soros Survivor's Guide," *The New Yorker*, October 7, 2001. https://www.newyorker.com/magazine/2001/10/15/a-soros-survivors-guide

"What did you do all day?" (Tivadar asked)

"Mostly nothing (George replied). But this afternoon I was given some notes to deliver to various addresses."

"Did you read what they said?"

"I even brought one home."

He (George) handed me a small slip of paper, with a typewritten message:

SUMMONS

You are requested to report tomorrow morning at 9 o'clock at the Rabbinical Seminary in Rökk Szilárd Street. Please bring with you a blanket, and food for two days

THE JEWISH COUNCIL

"Do you know what that means?" (Tivadar asked George)

"I can guess," he replied with great seriousness. "They'll be interned."[57]

Children are often good guessers. I wondered whether he knew what being interned meant. Did this child of mine realize that these people would be deported to Germany and very possibly murdered? I felt too ashamed of the world I had brought him into to enlighten him."[58]

---

57   Tivadar Soros, *Masquerade: The Incredible True Story of How George Soros' Father Outsmarted the Gestapo* (New York: Arcade Publishing, 2011), p. 17 (citing Kindle version).

58   Ibid., page 18.

Tivadar says he told George that the Jewish Council has no right to give people orders and that he wasn't to work there anymore. George replied, saying, "I tried to tell the people I called on not to obey"—but according to Tivadar, he said it with disappointment. "He was beginning to enjoy his career as a courier: it was all a big adventure."[59]

Similarly, the Michael Kaufman biography that Alex plugged came to a conclusion similar to Tivadar's: "*George had liked the excitement of being a courier* [emphasis mine], but he obeyed his father without complaint."

Soros would later cite this experience as a reason for disliking fellow Jews for being Nazi collaborators, even while exempting himself.[60] Remember, this is the guy you get called anti-Semitic for criticizing.

There hasn't yet been a single source recommended by Alex that bolsters his own narrative—quite the opposite. It's as if he just hoped no one would bother to do the work of reading them.

After his family was split up for their own safety, George went to live as "Sandor Kiss" with a man of German origin named "Baufluss," as arranged by his father. Baufluss was a friend of Tivadar, an official at the Ministry of Agriculture, and a Nazi collaborator who was tasked with inventorying confiscated Jewish estates. "He [George] even helped with the inventory," Tivadar admitted. Baufluss played the role of George's godfather, keeping him safe from Nazi persecution.[61]

---

59   Ibid.
60   *The Life and Times of a Messianic Billionaire*, p. 32. Quoted from David Horowitz and Richard Poe, *The Shadow Party: How Geroge Soros, Hillary Clinton, and Sixties Radicals Seized Control of the Democratic Party* (Nashville, TN: Thomas Nelson, Inc., 2006), p. 79.
61   Ibid (Shadow Party)., pp. 70–71.

Baufluss died anonymously in 1999, never publicly given credit for saving his life. His identity was later revealed in 2018 as Miklós Prohászka.[62]

> According to Istvan Stefka, a former neighbor of the Prohászkas in Budapest, after the War [George] Soros showed his gratitude by giving the family $20 per month [about $350 in today's money].

> "The money never went up, even as Soros became rich and inflation rose," Mr. Stefka said. "That caused some tension for Mr. Prohászka.

> "One day, [George] Soros came to Hungary for an event. He sent an invitation to Mr. Prohászka. However, he neglected to invite his wife. I remember Mr. Prohászka getting furious. He went to Soros' hotel and shouted at him, then slammed the door in his face."[63]

George did, at least, pay his Prohászka's medical bills when he got lung cancer later in life.[64]

George's relationship with Tivadar further demonstrated his own sociopathic behavior.

George himself said in an interview with the *New Yorker* that near the end of Tivadar's life, Tivadar agreed to an operation but wanted to die if his "personal integrity was invaded." Despite that happening in his operation, Tivadar decided he still wanted to live—which George said was a source of "disappointment to him." George said a few weeks later, of his own father, "I was

---

62   Jake Wallace Simons, "Revealed: The Hungarian 'Schindler' Who Saved George Soros from Nazi Death Squads During the Occupation by Hiding Him Behind a Cupboard," *Daily Mail*, November 26, 2018. https://www.dailymail.co.uk/news/article-6415189/Revealed-Hungarian-Schindler-hid-George-Soros-Gestapo-death-squads.html

63   Ibid.
64   Ibid.

there when he died, yet I let him die alone. I saw him, but I didn't touch him."[65]

To call George devoid of empathy would be generous to a man with negative empathy, and it's the cloth that Alex is cut from.

Given how truly bizarre it would be if I knew more about Alex's own father's early life than he does, I'm going to go out on a limb and assume he's knowingly misleading his audience.

ALEX SOROS REMAKES THE OSF

In the summer of 2023, the Open Society Foundations announced that it would reduce its workforce in Europe and reallocate much of its resources on the continent into a new operating model. According to Alex in an internal letter, the organization, under the new model, "will be better positioned to allow the robust civil society sector in many EU countries to move forward as we free resources and personnel to anticipate emerging threats from authoritarians across the region, and indeed, around the world."[66]

OSF staff was 1,700 in 2017, dropping to around 500 by 2024.

The focus of the OSF also underwent a major shift in Europe.

An internal OSF email from Alex said that "the new direction provides for the withdrawal and termination of large parts of our current work within the European Union, shifting our focus to other parts of the world." Even with the scale-back, Alex stated that the OSF will remain committed to its European "project"[67] He denied framing this move as a "withdrawal" from Europe, calling that interpretation misleading.

---

65   Quoted in Rachel Ehrenfeld, *The Soros Agenda* (Washington, DC: Republic Book Publishers, 2023), p. 40.

66   Paul Hockenos, "Why Soros Is Retreating from Europe," *Financial Times*, September 5, 2023. https://foreignpolicy.com/2023/09/05/soros-open-society-foundation-europe-retreat

67   "Soros Foundation to Limit EU Funding in New Strategy—Internal Email," *Reuters*, August 15, 2023. https://www.reuters.com/world/europe/soros-foundation-limit-eu-funding-new-strategy-internal-email-2023-08-15

"We are not leaving," he wrote in a *Politico* op-ed, explaining that they were shifting their priorities in Europe to focus on Ukraine, Moldova, and the Balkans.[68]

In other words, he's shifting his priorities away from Europe more generally, and into some of the most corrupt nations in Europe specifically. I have given entire chapters to some of these countries—Ukraine and Albania specifically—explaining George's historic role there, and what Alex now has in store for them.

George has wielded more authority in Ukraine than any other nation outside the United States, and in the age of war with Russia, where hundreds of billions of dollars are being flung around, Alex isn't going anywhere. What Ukraine was to George, Albania has become to Alex—a country where his father has already worked to fundamentally overhaul the nation's judicial system to benefit the same sort of left-wing actors Alex is publicly associating with there.

OSF'S ENVIRONMENTAL MISSION KICKS INTO HIGH GEAR WITH ALEX AT THE HELM

In the world of Alex Soros, it's the Greta Thunbergs of the world who are the true heroes.

Ahead of a ceremony with his ASF, Alex complained that environmental activists aren't being considered great heroes: "Nobody is really looking at environmental defenders as great heroes. People who defend their environments are, oftentimes, vilified because they are seen as crazy, anti-technology people."[69]

The common deranged behavior of environmental activists leaves no doubt who is to blame for that perception—whether

---

68   Alex Soros, "No Soros Retreat from Europe," *Politico*, August 31, 2023. https://www.politico.eu/article/no-soros-retreat-from-europe

69   "Alexander Soros Says Environmental Activists Should Be Considered 'Great Heroes,'" *Reuters*, November 5, 2015. https://www.reuters.com/article/business/alexander-soros-says-environmental-activists-should-be-considered-great-heroes-idUS3914853954

it be throwing paint at famous paintings, blocking highways and roads, gluing themselves to random objects and surfaces, spraying paint on landmarks, disrupting sporting events, chaining themselves to infrastructure, destroying property, or much, much more. Even the Unabomber thought those kinds of people were deranged.[70]

Under Alex's leadership, the OSF announced in July 2024 a $400 million commitment to support "economic and climate prosperity" in the "global south," which includes Latin America, Africa, the Middle East, Asia, and Oceania. The funds are, on paper, intended to support "green jobs" and an "equitable green agenda" to "reduce inequalities."[71] Whoever called environmentalists watermelons (red on the inside, green on the outside) was ahead of the curve.

In a Facebook post, Alex wrote that "The countries affected most by climate change should be the ones we're supporting the most," to justify one of the OSF's *single biggest investments ever.*"[72] (Emphasis added).

The Soros Economic Development Fund—the "impact investment arm" of OSF—committed $25 million in February 2024 to the alarmist "Allied Climate Partners (ACP)—a new and innovative public-private partnership focused on increasing the number of bankable climate projects in emerging markets and developing economies around the world."[73]

70   He dives into what he believes motivates this sort of behavior in the section of his manifesto titled "The Psychology of Modern Leftism."

71   "Open Society Foundations to Commit $400 Million to Support Economic and Climate Prosperity," Open Society Foundations, July 16, 2024. https://www.opensocietyfoundations.org/newsroom/open-society-foundations-to-commit-400-million-to-support-economic-and-climate-prosperity

72   https://www.facebook.com/Alexandersorospublic/posts/the-countries-most-affected-by-climate-change-should-be-the-ones-were-supporting/1068959197925261

73   "Open Society Invests $25 Million to Boost Global Climate Projects," Soros Economic Development Fund, February 27, 2024. https://www.soroseconomicdevelopmentfund.org/newsroom/open-society-invests-25-million-to-boost-global-climate-projects

The Media Research Center found that the OSF under George and Alex committed an enormous additional $193,895,617 between 2016 and 2023 in climate and environmental spending to 347 militant groups that push climate extremism globally at the grassroots and policymaking levels.[74]

After a year and a half with Alex in charge, that number ballooned to a whopping $618,895,617.

In addition to the $400 million commitment, the OSF also announced $25 million to boost global climate projects, bringing total spending that year to $425 million.[75] Grants are only listed on the OSF website up to 2023, so the total spending is obviously larger, but this total is all that's provable. This means that at least 69 percent of the OSF's climate spending since 2016 happened in 2024 on Alex's watch. This is a conservative estimate, because Alex's half-year in 2023 isn't included, as the grant data isn't broken out by month.

ALEX THE CLIMATE INVESTOR

Alex is the only Soros family member on the investment committee for Soros Fund Management, George's hedge fund and source of wealth. The exact date when he joined isn't known, but it was reported by the *Wall Street Journal* that he served on it when they announced he was taking over the OSF in 2023.

Alex's potential leverage within the fund can be seen in its Climate Action Strategy, which it's issued reports for in 2021–2023. Goals include "reducing carbon intensity per dollar invested" (the amount of carbon emissions created by companies they invest in, divided by the dollar amount invested); ending all new investments in fossil fuels by 2025; and divesting current invest-

---

74   Joseph Vazquez and Matt Palumbo, "Eco Kingpins: How the Soros Empire Funds and Steers the Global Climate Change Agenda," Media Research Center, April 22, 2025. https://newsbusters.org/blogs/business/joseph-vazquez/2025/04/22/eco-kingpins-how-soros-empire-funds-and-steers-global
75   Ibid.

ments that don't align with climate goals.[76] These metrics are the financial equivalent of virtue signaling when it comes to publicly traded stock, because the investment is simply shifting hands. Their best-case scenario would be to tank the price of a stock, but that has no impact on operations. For every one dollar in stock an oil company that Soros Fund Management sells, someone else has one dollar in that oil company's stock. No value is created nor destroyed.

Other goals are deliberately vague, such as "Taking an active role engaging companies and sectors to accelerate their climate transition business models," and "Investing in climate solutions."

As is always the case with leftism, the vaguer the details, the more likely the true agenda is being hidden. And as is always the case for all things Soros, there's politics and activism involved, too.

Aristate Capital argues that litigation related to "progressive" ESG (Environmental, Social, Governance) standards and goals can be a profitable "investment"—essentially becoming the environmentalist version of patent trolls—and it launched a fund backed by the Soros Economic Development Fund to realize that goal. The fund aims "to maximize proceeds for claimants and provide a return for investors and generate resources for more litigation," and they targeted an above-market-rate 20 percent internal rate of return.[77] Its "Aristata Impact Litigation Fund I" ended up raising £52 million, slightly exceeding its £50 million target.[78]

While it can't be conclusively linked to Alex, in 2021 Soros Fund Management invested $2 billion in the electric vehicle com-

---

76   "Climate Action Strategy, Soros Fund Management." https://sorosfundmgmt.com/wp-content/uploads/2025/04/ClimateActionStrategy.pdf

77   David Whitehouse, "ESG: Soros-backed Aristata Fund Aims to Turn ESG Litigation into Profitable Investment," Funds Europe, October 17, 2022. https://funds-europe.com/esg-soros-aristata-fund-esg-litigation-profitable-investment

78   "Impact Litigation Fund Targeting 'Justice Gap' Achieves £52m Final Close," *Impact Investor*, July 18, 2023. https://impact-investor.com/impact-litigation-fund-targeting-justice-gap-achieves-52m-final-close

pany Rivian, for a two percent stake in the company at $100 a share, representing potentially its biggest single investment ever.[79] As of this writing, Rivian trades under twelve dollars.

THE ALEX OSF-POST TRUMP'S SECOND WIN

What does the OSF have in store for the second Trump presidency?

In his first interview addressing the Trump presidency post-inauguration, Alex lamented the growing dominance of the "cool kids" table. Alex sat down for an interview with the *Financial Times* during inauguration week at Manhattan's Russ & Daughters cafe.[80]

Given the hefty sum he and his father set on fire that election cycle, it couldn't have been fun for either of them. Post-election, Alex doubled down on his fictitious opposition to money in politics while simultaneously doubling down on spending ungodly sums of money on politics.

In reality, the left has been massively outspending the right in presidential elections. Kamala Harris outspent Donald Trump in 2024, just as Biden outspent Trump in 2020, which came after Hillary Clinton outspent Trump in 2016, which followed Barack Obama (barely) outspending Mitt Romney in 2012, after massively outspending John McCain in 2008. George W. Bush did outspend John Kerry, so perhaps Alex was just thinking about two decades ago?

Alex's spending can't be considered in response to the elusive "right-wing money machine" when he's the biggest machine. Given the manufactured appeal of candidates like Harris, it's no surprise that she'd need more money to compete, while a candi-

---

79 Parker Thayer, "Alexander Soros, Electric Cars, and the Inflation Reduction Act: What to Expect from George Soros's Heir," Capital Research Center, June 28, 2023. https://capitalresearch.org/article/alexander-soros-electric-cars-and-the-inflation-reduction-act-what-to-expect-from-george-soross-heir

80 "Alex Soros: 'These People Are Bullies. And You Fight Back,'" *Financial Times*.

date popular despite a media onslaught, like Trump, can thrive on free publicity.

Nonetheless, Alex says he's ready to (not) put his money where his mouth is. "I'm happy to get money out of politics, let's go, let's do it tomorrow…campaign finance reform, and have it regulated like it is in Europe."

Perhaps he just sees it as a tit-for-tat game, where he'd be willing to stop spending if everyone else does, because it'll put him at a strategic disadvantage if only he withdraws. Liberals have been the big spenders as of late, so this reasoning is still questionable. Furthermore, a world with no future political spending would be one where he gets to maintain his web of contacts, garnered both by his, and his father's, past spending—putting up a new barrier to entry to anyone else seeking that kind of power.

Or maybe Alex just wants to avoid the embarrassment of losing a nearly $100 million bet in the future.

With the foresight of a teenager, Alex confessed that he viewed the election of Barack Obama as a rare "end of history" moment (in this case, "ending racism"). Obama's own actions would later guarantee the opposite, with race relations near the end of his tenure hitting lows not seen since Rodney King and the LA race riots.[81] The next (and the only other) moment Alex finds comparable was when he walked down a street in Rome and found himself beaming with joy, "just thinking how proud I was of my country," when he saw a pride flag flying outside the US embassy.

Of the new Trump era kicking off, Alex was ready to head straight to the principal's office:

---

81   "Views of Race Relations," Pew Research Center, June 27, 2016. https://www.pewresearch.org/social-trends/2016/06/27/2-views-of-race-relations

We have to know what we're dealing with. These people are bullies. And you fight back, you push back.... I hope Marx was right that first comes the tragedy and then comes the farce. I worry it'll be the other way around, that we'll look back at Trump's first term as farcical and this is going to be very bad and tragic for a lot of people.

To harken back to earlier in the chapter, it looks like Alex was the one defending Marx in his debates with his father. We can hope his plan goes the same way every other one has throughout history that was rooted in Karl Marx.

Of the OSF's future in the new Trump era, OSF President Binaifer Nowrojee reiterated that the organization will support the supposed human rights groups it traditionally has.[82]

These human rights groups, and others in the human rights sector that have relied on OSF funding, wait to see what the "reimagination under the leadership of the new board chair at Open Society Foundations [Alex Soros]" will mean for their funding. Nowrojee did not offer many details or specifics about where the OSFs funding will be allocated, outside of the $400 million already committed toward "green jobs and economic development."

One of these green projects will include a program that "focuses on environmental defenders" and "people who come under attack for defending resources" in countries in South America and Africa, according to Sharan Srinivas, a director of programs at OSF. This came after OSF "did a survey of what other donors are supporting and we [OSF] saw that this is where the gap is," according to Srinivas.

---

82   Thalia Beaty, "'A Reimagination Has Taken Place' Under George Soros' Son, Open Society Foundations President Says," *Washington Times*, December 10, 2024. https://www.washingtontimes.com/news/2024/dec/10/open-society-foundations-president-reimagination-t

One change will be that the OSF will be looking to offer shorter-term grants that should give grantees some flexibility in how they use the funds. But according to the Human Rights Funders, "When major funders adjust their priorities, it can have a ripple effect. Their decisions can dramatically impact the human rights movements they once supported, especially in regions where they've been a long-time champion," which shows that the changes at OSF are creating unease among human rights groups.

GEORGE REMAINS ACTIVE IN THE PASSENGER SEAT

George may have handed over his Open Society Foundations to Alex, but that didn't mark the end of his involvement in politics—far from it.

Ahead of the 2024 election, George, through Soros Fund Management, pulled off the acquisition of Audacy, granting him massive control over 200 radio stations in forty markets, allowing him to reach a combined audience of over 160 million. Soros purchased $415 million in debt in the company, granting him 40 percent control.[83]

It's key here that this was done through George's hedge fund, not through the OSF. Two years prior, Soros Fund Management took over eighteen Hispanic radio stations, including the influential Miami conservative Radio Mambi.[84]

Audacy is the second-biggest radio network in the country after iHeart, and broadcasts top conservatives including Sean Hannity, Mark Levin, Glenn Beck, and other household names.

---

83   Brooke Singman, "House Oversight Probes FCC's Expedited Approval of Soros Purchase Of 200+ Radio Stations Ahead of Election," Fox News, September 26, 2024. https://www.foxnews.com/politics/house-oversight-probes-fccs-expedited-approval-soros-purchase-200-radio-stations-ahead-election

84   Dana Kennedy, "Radio Stars Criticize George Soros-backed Move to 'Silence Conservative Hispanic Voices,'" New York Post, December 20, 2022. https://nypost.com/2022/12/20/inside-george-soros-backed-move-to-silence-conservative-hispanic-voices

Over 25 percent of ownership came from foreign sources. When such a large percentage of ownership will be from foreign sources, the FCC must determine whether "the public interest will be served by the refusal or revocation of such license." The national security review can take from three to six months, and national security agencies are brought in.

But not this time.

The Biden FCC expedited the required review of broadcast licenses, bypassing standard procedures and processes, resulting in the deal finalizing weeks before election day 2024. This came amid numerous Alex visits to the White House. According to FCC Commissioner Brendan Carr, the commission had never in its history signed off on the kind of shortcuts Audacy was granted, meaning that George was given special treatment.

Despite the handover of control to Alex, we're now dealing with a father-son business.

Power is seldom relinquished voluntarily, and only time itself was able to force George to give up some of it.

As for Alex, he's already admitted that he has more power in his current position than he'd have as head of state. When asked if he'd run for office, he admitted, "I wouldn't rule out anything but it's hard for me to see how I'm not in a more impactful position now."

That says it all.

Alex isn't just stepping into George's shoes—he's kicking down the door, trading shadows for floodlights. His takeover isn't a quiet handover, it's a bet that flaunting power can outmuscle the backlash George dodged for decades. George built an empire on whispers; Alex's is a shout.

Chapter 2

Alex Goes to Washington

The Alex Soros infiltration of Washington happened long before he was crowned the new king.

In addition to his father's decades-long meddling in our politics, Alex spent tens of millions backing Joe Biden and other Democrats in 2020,[1] including throwing $720,000 at the worst president of the twenty-first century. [2]

His $720,000 donation to Biden wasn't just a donation; it was a down payment on access.

Alex visited the White House dozens of times throughout the Biden presidency, making only two visits in 2021 before ramping them up during the rest of Biden's term. In 2023 his visits started making headlines in the *New York Post*, bringing knowledge of them to millions for the first time.

There was plenty to discuss.

THE SOROS INFILTRATION OF THE BIDEN WHITE HOUSE

The OSF forged numerous links with the Biden White House that started before he'd even been sworn in.

1   Maggie Severns, "Soros Pumps More Than $28 Million into Democratic Groups for 2020," *Politico*, April 10, 2020. https://www.politico.com/news/2020/04/10/soros-pumps-28-million-democratic-groups-2020-179367

2   Joe Schoffstall and Cameron Cawthorne, "Alex Soros Huddled with Top Democrats Shortly After Taking Over His Father's Nonprofit Empire," Fox News, June 29, 2023.   https://www.foxnews.com/politics/alex-soros-huddled-top-democrats-after-taking-over-his-fathers-nonprofit-empire

During the transition after the 2020 election, the incoming Biden administration assembled "transition review teams" that included people tasked with understanding the operations of specific government agencies, to help the administration "hit the ground running on day one." Seventeen team members directly served the OSF or other Soros-funded organizations.

Through them, the OSF was able to insert their ideology into the transition teams ranging from the State Department to the Consumer Financial Protection Bureau, United States Mission to the United Nations, Department of Defense, Department of Labor, Department of the Interior, Department of the Treasury, Federal Reserve, banking and securities regulators, National Security Council, Office of the US Trade Representative, and Department of Veterans Affairs.

Alex was well diversified.

Naturally, a handful of Soros lackeys made their way into the Biden administration.

Neera Tanden, a long-time confidante of the Clinton family and a former Obama aide, was president of the heavily Soros-funded Center for American Progress before becoming senior advisor to the president in May 2021. She was previously nominated to head the Office of Budget and Management, but had to withdraw as her past tweets came back to haunt her.[3]

Ron Klain, who served on the board of the Center for American Progress Action Fund, the group's lobbying arm, was Biden's first White House Chief of Staff.[4]

One less recognizable name was Sam Berger, who was a former "VP for Democracy and Government Reform" at the Center

3   Kyle Cheney and Kenneth P. Vogel, "Soros Regretted Supporting Obama in 2008, Clinton Emails Show," *Politico*, December 31, 2015. https://www.politico.com/story/2015/12/george-soros-hillary-clinton-barack-obama-217272

4   "Biden's Chief of Staff at Center of Controversy Over White House Budget Pick," *Washington Post*, February 25, 2021. https://www.washingtonpost.com/us-policy/2021/02/25/ron-klain-biden-neera-tanden-omb

for American Progress and became Biden's Director of Strategic Operations and Policy for his COVID-19 response team.

Only one attempted but failed to get in. A month after Biden's victory, OSF president Patrick Gaspard stepped down in his role and began lobbying labor leaders to support him becoming Biden's Labor secretary. Interestingly, Gaspard was still being quoted in internal documents days after stepping down. At the time, the Congressional Black Caucus PAC—which received campaign funding from George's daughter-in-law Jennifer Allan Soros[5] during the height of the Black Lives Matter uprisings in 2020—endorsed Gaspard, previously the US ambassador to South Africa under Barack Obama.

Likely due, in part, to the poor optics of picking someone so directly linked to George, Biden ended up nominating Boston Mayor Marty Walsh, a decades-long friend who also gained support from labor leaders, including the AFL-CIO's president. As we'll see, Gaspard would later plant his flag in the Biden White House in other ways.

While it didn't start making headlines until the third year of the Biden presidency, Alex racked up thirty visits to the White House, making visits every year. There were few visits in 2021, but they ramped up in 2022, signaling Alex was further expanding his domestic duties even before the handoff of power to him was official.[6]

Alex wielded greater influence than his father in the Biden administration. When George was awarded the Presidential Medal of Freedom by Biden, it was Alex who attended the award ceremony to pick it up.

---

5   Congressional Black Caucus Itemized Receipts Form. https://docquery.fec.gov/cgi-bin/fecimg/?202009199275280911

6   All archived Biden administration visitor logs: https://web.archive.org/web/20250117191047/https://www.whitehouse.gov/disclosures/visitor-logs

MAPPING ALEX'S WHITE HOUSE VISITS

As the meetings came under scrutiny when they started making news, it left millions wondering what, exactly, was Alex there to discuss?

Alex's White House visits aren't random photo ops, they're a calculated flex of soft power. Each handshake with Biden or Pelosi doubles as a message: the Soros network isn't just funding Democrats; it's shaping their priorities from the inside. In the words of an unnamed Biden official, Alex was "less interested in trying to twist arms than in cultivating power," and was seeking access to discuss issues.[7]

In a joint effort with *Newsbusters'* Joe Vazquez, we compiled a list of every single one of Alex's visits to the White House, and then sought to find what other politics events they correlated with. After weeks of work, we published it in a study called "Connecting the Dots,"[8] which quickly became the top article on their website. Posts referencing our findings drew over thirteen million views on X/Twitter, earning a reaction from Elon Musk himself.

There sure were a lot of cases of coincidences and "convenient timing," particularly when it came to climate-related events.

While it's impossible to prove causality, if there were no political events and policies correlating with Alex's many visits, it would lead to the question of what exactly the purpose of the meetings was. Are we to believe they were just making small talk? That's certainly what Alex would prefer.

---

7   "The New Soros: With Trump on the Rampage, Alex Soros Takes Control of his Father's Empire. What Will He Do With the Influence?" *New York Magazine.*

8   Matt Palumbo and Joseph Vazuez, "CONNECTING THE DOTS: Mapping Alex Soros's Growing Dominance in Washington," *Newsbusters,* February 18, 2025. https://newsbusters.org/blogs/business/matt-palumbo/joseph-vazquez/2025/02/18/connecting-dots-mapping-alex-soross-growing-dominance

KENYAN "CORRUPTION" AND A MEETING WITH THE BIG GUY

The most notable Alex meeting we uncovered in our research was with none other than President Biden himself, which happened as major foreign policy events were unfolding.

At 10:22 a.m. EDT on May 23, 2024, Biden gave remarks alongside Kenyan president William Ruto on the South Lawn,[9] where one of the main subjects was the two presidents' mutual fixation on fighting so-called climate change, one of Alex's key political obsessions.

Just after Biden's remarks with Ruto on May 24, 2024, White House visitor logs have Alex personally visiting with Biden at 6:15 p.m. the same day. Alex would also post Instagram photos[10] documenting his attendance at the state dinner that day at the White House in honor of Ruto, along with OSF president Binaifer Nowrojee, a human rights attorney from Kenya and the organization's first African president.

Alex once stated that one of his goals was to make climate-change fanaticism the twenty-first century's civil rights movement. "I also think that if environmental defenders become the Rosa Parks' and the Caesar Chavezes of the environmental movement, the movement will gain unprecedented traction," Soros told *Mongabay* magazine on October. 27, 2016.[11] We see this script play out in the Biden-Ruto meeting.

A highlight of the Biden-Ruto meeting—praised[12] by the Soros-funded[13] organization E3G—was that the two released a

9   "Remarks by President Biden and President William Ruto of the Republic of Kenya at Arrival Ceremony," The White House, May 23, 2024. https://bidenwhitehouse.archives.gov/briefing-room/speeches-remarks/2024/05/23/remarks-by-president-biden-and-president-william-ruto-of-the-republic-of-kenya-at-arrival-ceremony

10   https://www.instagram.com/alexsoros/p/C7XSQTCN7c-

11   Rhett Ayers Butler, "Recognizing Environmentalists Under Threat," *Mongabay*, October 27, 2016. https://news.mongabay.com/2016/10/recognizing-environmentalists-under-threat

12   "A New US-Kenya Climate Partnership," E3G, May 24, 2024. https://www.e3g.org/news/a-new-us-kenya-climate-partnership

13   "Funders and Partners," E3G. https://www.e3g.org/about/funders

fact sheet of shared initiatives on topics ranging from democracy to trade, but also included an "array of projects" under the header "Shared Climate Solutions."[14]

If that wasn't telling enough, E3G noted how Biden was prepared to use USAID, which constantly partners with the OSF directly or indirectly on projects, to accomplish his climate vision for Kenya:

> The White House also named specific climate projects in Kenya, including investments in hydropower and EV startups, promoting private and public clean energy adoption and increasing conservation. Utilizing USAID, the Development Finance Corporation, and a $60 million grant from the Millenium Challenge Corporation, the Biden Administration has put real weight behind the partnership with Kenya.

Right in line with the other absurd USAID projects that the Trump administration has since drawn attention to, in this case USAID was already seeking to spend $1.5 million on "empowering women to adapt to climate change in northern Kenya."

According to the USAID grant opportunity,[15] women in the region live in "traditionally patriarchal communities" and require training to join Kenya's fight against climate change. The funding announcement followed USAID's unveiling of its 2022–2030 climate strategy,[16] a $150 billion whole-of-agency approach to

---

14   "Fact Sheet: Kenya State Visit to the United States," The White House, May 23, 2024. https://web.archive.org/web/20250114155706/https:/www.white house.gov/briefing-room/statements-releases/2024/05/23/fact-sheet-kenya-state-visit-to-the-united-states

15   Kenya USAID–Nairobi Grant: "Empowering Women to Adapt to Climate Change in Northern Kenya." https://www.grants.gov/search-results-detail/348262

16   "Climate Strategy 2022-2023," USAID. https://web.archive.org/web/20230327 144643/https://www.usaid.gov/sites/default/files/2022-11/USAID-Climate-Strategy-2022-2030.pdf

achieving an "equitable world with net-zero greenhouse gas emissions." Included in the effort is a pledge to expand the "diversity, equity, inclusion, and accessibility of the climate workforce" through taxpayer-funded programs elevating gay, female, indigenous, and disabled climate activists.

Perhaps one of the reason Alex favors environmental causes, in addition to any actual concern for the environment, is because he can use the issue to easily create slush funds for all the other sorts of left-wing objectives he has.

According to the American Presidency Project, on the same day of Ruto's state visit, "The U.S. Department of Energy and Kenyan Ministry of Energy announced their intent to sign a Memorandum of Understanding in June in Nairobi intended to enhance bilateral collaboration and partnership in the development of clean energy, carbon management technologies, and decarbonization strategies."[17]

What made Alex's visit with Biden on the same day more than just a coincidental stroke of serendipity was the fact that the OSF has been heavily invested in Kenyan politics for decades. The Open Society Initiative for Eastern Africa (OSIEA) opened its doors in Nairobi in 2005,[18] where it's headquartered, and where Biden's DOE and the Kenyan Ministry of Energy would conveniently also sign their mutual Memorandum of Understanding.

They also absorbed the local climate groups in the area: from 2022–2022, the OSIEA's affiliate regional organizations "merged into the global structure" of the OSF.[19]

---

17   "Fact Sheet: Kenya State Visit to the United States," The American Presidency Project, May 23, 2024. https://www.presidency.ucsb.edu/documents/fact-sheet-kenya-state-visit-the-united-states

18   "Open Society Initiative for East Africa (OSIEA)," Grassroots Justice Network. https://grassrootsjusticenetwork.org/connect/organization/open-society-initiative-for-east-africa-osiea

19   "Africa." Open Society Foundations. https://www.opensocietyfoundations.org/what-we-do/regions/africa

The significance of Ruto's state visit was underscored by the fact that this was the first visit to the United States by an African leader in over fifteen years, and Biden would also subsequently designate Kenya a non-NATO ally.[20] Ruto fawned over Biden about the supposed importance of building global partnerships to fight climate change, which just means increasing regulations on energy producers.[21]

"We will have the opportunity to discuss and to have a conversation about building global partnership and leadership around the issues that pose challenges regionally, globally, and in countries like Kenya and many others: challenges of climate change, challenges of insecurity, challenges around debt distress," Ruto told Biden.

In November 2023, *Time* magazine named Ruto one of four Africans on its "climate leaders" list. In September, according to the BBC, Ruto "hosted the first ever Africa Climate Summit in Kenya's capital, Nairobi, which ended in a joint declaration demanding that major polluters commit more resources to help poorer nations."[22]

Alex himself shares this Marxist view. On November 18, 2021, he linked to a *Project Syndicate* article[23] by Soros ally Jeffrey Sachs[24] that called for taxing "high-income" countries at five dol-

---

20   "Ruto's State Visit Spotlights Kenya's Centrality to Africa–US Relations," Chatham House, May 22, 2024. https://www.chathamhouse.org/2024/05/rutos-state-visit-spotlights-kenyas-centrality-africa-us-relations

21   "Kenya Passes Law to More Closely Regulate Carbon Markets," *African Climate Wire*, September 4, 2023. https://africanclimatewire.org/update/kenya-passes-law-to-more-closely-regulate-carbon-markets

22   Gloria Aradi, "Kenya's President Ruto One of Four Africans on *Time Climate Leaders List*," *BBC*, November 17, 2023. https://www.bbc.com/news/world-africa-67447481

23   Jeffrey D. Sachs, "Fixing Climate Finance," *Project Syndicate*, November 15, 2021. https://www.project-syndicate.org/commentary/fixing-climate-finance-requires-global-rules-by-jeffrey-d-sachs-2021-11

24   Joseph Vazquez, "Parroting Chinese Propaganda? Soros Crony Claims COVID-19 Originated from U.S. Lab," *NewsBusters*, July 12, 2022. https://www.newsbusters.org/blogs/business/joseph-vazquez/2022/07/12/parroting-chinese-propaganda-soros-crony-claims-covid-19

lars per ton of CO2 and directing the funds to "low-income" and "lower-middle-income" countries. "#UN Climate Change Conference 26 dropped the ball on climate financing to stem loss and damage from the climate emergency. Jeffrey Sachs offers a compelling solution," Alex captioned his tweet on the article.[25]

Ruto isn't shy about showcasing his extremism on the eco-activist front, either. "In October 2023, he called for the eviction of people living in the 380,000-hectare Mau Forest," BBC reported. "While some environmentalists hailed the move as critical to safeguarding the forest, some human rights lawyers said the government illegally evicted the Ogiek indigenous community which has inhabited the land for generations to profit from carbon offsetting schemes."[26]

This kind of activism runs parallel with Alex's brand, given the Soros dynasty's dedication[27] to bullying businesses away from fossil fuels through fanatical environmental, social, and governance (ESG) strategies.[28] In an op-ed for *The International Journal on Human Rights*, Alex said "the real heroes of the environmental movement" are the "indigenous peoples that have peacefully lived off their land for hundreds, even thousands of years, and who are under threat from organized criminals, multinational corporations, and other entities seeking to turn a profit off their land." According to Alex, this profit-seeking all happens "at the expense of livelihoods of indigenous peoples living in harmony with mother earth."[29]

25   https://twitter.com/AlexanderSoros/status/1461414116636209157

26   Gloria Aradi, "Kenya's President Ruto One of Four Africans on *Time Climate Leaders List*," BBC, November 17, 2023. https://www.bbc.com/news/world-africa-67447481

27   Jeffrey Clark, "Now What? Soros Group Vows to Bully Businesses with Woke ESG Strategy," *NewsBusters*, May 2, 2022. https://newsbusters.org/blogs/business/jeffrey-clark/2022/05/02/now-what-soros-group-vows-bully-businesses-woke-esg

28   Tom Olohan, "Shellenberger to Tucker: Soros and Bloomberg Promote 'Anti-Human Death Cult,'" *NewsBusters*, December 5, 2023. https://newsbusters.org/blogs/business/tom-olohan/2023/12/05/shellenberger-tucker-soros-and-bloomberg-promote-anti-human

29   Alex Soros, "The Real Heroes of the Environmental Movement," *Sur International Journal on Human Rights*, March 2017. https://sur.conectas.org/en/real-heroes-environmental-movement

Just six days after Soros meeting with Biden during Ruto's state visit, the OSF released a report[30] on how one of its grantees' initiatives, the Global Media Index for Africa,[31] sought to shed "light on the global news media reporting on Africa." The Index, said OSF, indicated *"a need to significantly improve coverage on Africa in terms of more progressive narratives."* (Emphasis added.)

Just as the OSF was calling on the media to improve "progressive" coverage of Africa, Alex was there to help produce it.

Kenya was one of the case studies in the "media index," used to analyze how positively news stories were covering political "transition" in the country.[32] The overall goal was to try to nuke largely accurate perceptions about Africa as a continent in perpetual crisis, "characterized by wars, famine, poverty, disease, and corruption."[33]

Biden and Alex both shared a mutual interest in actively promoting their mutual ally Ruto's image as some kind of saintly hero of leftist utopianism on climate change and other issues.

How can we properly interpret this? Democrat Senator Chris Murphy wrote in an October 1, 2024 item for *Foreign Policy* magazine that Ruto returned home from his state visit with Biden "facing nationwide protests over a proposed bill to raise taxes" to pay down debt his government "accumulated mostly through deals with China that were riddled with dubious terms and kickback arrangements."[34]

---

30   Ruth Omondi, "Changing Global News Coverage of Africa Is About Acknowledging the Continent's Rightful Place in the World," Open Society Foundations, May 30, 2024. https://www.opensocietyfoundations.org/voices/changing-global-news-coverage-of-africa-is-about-acknowledging-the-continent-s-rightful-place-in-the-world

31   "Global Media Index for Africa 2024," Africa No Filter. https://africanofilter.org/documents/Global-Media-Index2024.pdf

32   Ibid.

33   "Today's Armed Conflicts," Geneva Academy of International Humanitarian Law and Human Rights. https://geneva-academy.ch/galleries/today-s-armed-conflicts

34   Chris Murphy, "Kenya's Anti-Corruption Protests Are a Wake-Up Call for Washington," *Foreign Policy*, October 1, 2024. https://foreignpolicy.com/2024/10/01/kenya-protests-corruption-us-national-security-good-governance

"The protests were largely led by Kenya's youth, who recognized that there's one thing preventing their country from reaching its full potential: corruption." As Murphy noted, "Kenya's former auditor general estimated that around half of the country's debt can likely be attributed to corruption. It's no wonder that Kenyans are angry."

And it's no wonder Alex and Biden needed to help clean up Ruto's image.

CLIMATE COINCIDENCES

As explained in the first chapter, climate change has been the top issue for Alex, who was a former member of the advisory board of leftist group Global Witness, which he joined in 2011.[35]

Global Witness, in their words, focuses on "natural resource-related conflict and corruption and associated environmental and human rights abuses." The group boasts that it works to "hold companies and governments to account for their destruction of the environment, their disregard for the planet and their failure to protect" human rights.[36] Part of its anti-fossil-fuel vendetta includes campaigns to "tackle the spread of division, hate and disinformation on digital platforms." This is another way of admitting that it fights to get Big Tech platforms like Facebook, X (formerly Twitter), and YouTube to censor speech according to what Global Witness determines should and should not be allowed.[37]

---

35   "Global Witness Welcomes Landmark U.S. Effort to Curb Corruption and Promote Transparency," press release, Global Witness, September 20, 2011. https://web.archive.org/web/20240519030112/https://www.globalwitness.org/en/archive/global-witness-welcomes-landmark-us-effort-curb-corruption-and-promote-transparency

36   "About Us," Global Witness. https://www.globalwitness.org/en/about-us

37   Joseph Vazquez, "Soros Gave $17.6M to Lefty Group Pushing Facebook, TikTok to Censor So-Called Election Disinfo," NewsBusters, October 27, 2022. https://www.newsbusters.org/blogs/business/joseph-vazquez/2022/10/27/soros-gave-176m-lefty-group-pushing-facebook-tiktok-censor

In 2017, environmentalist groups were the biggest beneficiaries of funds from his groups.[38] On his personal website AlexSoros. com (that now redirects to the OSF), the first article he lists as having ever published (back in 2014) was on environmental activists in Peru protecting the Amazon rainforest, which Alex himself has visited.[39]

So it should come to no surprise that climate-related policy announcements correlated with more of Alex's White House visits than any other subject. In fact, nearly two-thirds of all Alex's meetings connected with an environmental-related announcement or policy change from the Biden administration.

Meeting Date	Alex Met With	Following Biden Admin Policy Actions
July 29 and 31, 2024	Phil Gordon, National Security Advisor to the Vice President (July 29) and Katharine Reilly, Advisor to the Chief of Staff (July 31)	Fifteen days before this meeting, Alex Soros announced on Instagram $400 million from OSF to fight climate change in the Global South.[40] In August, Biden engaged with international partners on climate initiatives and investment in renewable energy projects.

38   "Alexander Soros Foundation." *Influence Watch.*
39   "Writing." *AlexSoros.com* https://web.archive.org/web/20230201220344/https:/alexsoros.com/writing
40   https://www.instagram.com/alexsoros/p/C9gVyhWRuED

Meeting Date	Alex Met With	Following Biden Admin Policy Actions
May 24, 2024	Amos Hochstein, Deputy Assistant to the President and Senior Advisor for Energy and Investment, and Jake Sullivan, National Security Advisor	On May 22, 2024, the Biden administration's Bureau of Land Management made a significant move by shutting down federal leases in Wyoming's Powder River Basin, a major coal-producing area, which was described as one of the biggest attacks on America's energy industry. On May 29, 2024, the Biden administration proposed expanding tax credits for solar and wind energy projects to include a broader range of clean energy technologies, such as nuclear fission and fusion.
March 27, 2024	Alia Schechter, Advisor to the Counselor to the President	The EPA issued new regulations that day, and the following day, Biden issued executive orders on climate change.

Meeting Date	Alex Met With	Following Biden Admin Policy Actions
September 13, 2023	Sofia Carratala, Policy Advisor—Domestic Policy Council (and former Soros-funded Center for American Progress Executive Policy Associate)	On September 6, the White House announced it would be canceling legal-issued leases for drilling in the Arctic,[41] which it completed on September 13.[42]
March 29, 30, and 31, 2023	Nina Srivastava, Associate Director for Domestic Personnel in the Presidential Personnel Office (March 29), Jon Finer, Deputy National Security Advisor, (March 30), and Amanda Sloat, Special Assistant to the President and Senior Director for Europe, National Security Council (March 31)	On March 29, Biden gave remarks alongside leftist Argentinian President Alberto Fernandez, when they discussed their climate change agenda. Around this time, on March 22, Alex was tweeting about "key climate indicators."[43] Also of note to these dates, on another subject: Biden spoke about reaffirming support for Ukraine on March 29 (read more in chapter five).

Alex's eight-year, $400 million investment in Global South "green" jumpstart projects notably happened on the heels of his hobnobbing at the May 2024 White House state dinner held in honor of Ruto.

41   "Biden Administration Disregards Congress, Attempts to Cancel ANWR Leases," press release, Office of (Alaska) Governor Mike Dunleavy, September 6, 2023. https://gov.alaska.gov/biden-administration-disregards-congress-attempts-to-cancel-anwr-leases

42   Tom Klein, "Biden Cancels Controversial Oil and Gas Leases in the Arctic," The Wildlife Society, September 13, 2023. https://wildlife.org/biden-cancels-controversial-oil-and-gas-leases-in-the-arctic

43   https://x.com/AlexanderSoros/status/1639075393285263360

OSF president Nowrojee told the Associated Press that the goal of this multi-million-dollar pledge—one of OSF's "single biggest investments ever," and its first major commitment since an internal restructuring—was to force industries in Brazil, Mexico, South Africa, Senegal, Malaysia, and Indonesia toward transitioning to "clean energy."[44]

"The idea of free markets cannot solve everything, particularly it cannot solve the climate crisis," she said, speaking from OSF's offices in Washington. Alex then touted Nowrojee's statement across his social media accounts.

On February 8, 2023, Alex met with Mariana Adame, advisor to the counselor to the president; with Jon Finer on February 9; and with Jordan Finkelstein, special assistant to the president and chief of staff to the senior advisor to the president, on February 10. This series of meetings surrounded Biden's February 10 meeting with Brazil's leftist President Lula da Silva, an ally of the Soros family. In a *Project Syndicate* op-ed, George called the election of Silva "crucial," as Brazil is "on the front line of the fight against climate change." Soros said "Lula must protect the rainforest" and "promote social justice. He will need strong international support because there is no pathway to net-zero emissions if he fails."[45]

During their meeting in the Oval Office, Biden and Lulu talked about the "climate crisis" and Biden's commitments to Brazil. Lulu also called for stronger global governance to address the climate issue—another desire of Alex.[46] The month before,

---

44   Thalia Beaty, "Soros' Open Society Foundations Say Their Restructuring Is Complete and Pledge $400m for Green Jobs," Associated Press, July 16, 2024. https://apnews.com/article/osf-george-soros-alex-soros-climate-change-green-economy-6f234035efdc3fa840b1f070e60ea091

45   George Soros, "Global Warming, Hot Wars, Closed Societies," *Project Syndicate*, February 16, 2023. https://www.project-syndicate.org/commentary/global-warming-war-and-geopolitical-rivalry-by-george-soros-2023-02

46   "Remarks by President Biden and President Lula da Silva of Brazil Before Bilateral Meeting," The White House, February 10, 2023. https://bidenwhitehouse.archives.gov/briefing-room/speeches-remarks/2023/02/10/remarks-by-president-biden-and-president-lula-da-silva-of-brazil-before-bilateral-meeting

Alex had met at Davos with Lulu's minister of the environment and climate change. [47]

Later that year, in August, Alex paid for five far-left members of Congress to take a trip to Latin America to meet leftist politicians there, including advisors of Lulu.

The reps in question were Alexandria Ocasio-Cortez (of course), Maxwell Frost, Greg Caesar, Joaquin Castro, and Nadia Velazquez. Alex footed the bill for their thousands of dollars in travel, lodging, and meals. Ocasio-Cortez's "domestic partner," Riley Roberts, even joined the all-expenses-paid trip.[48]

Their tour included meeting with Colombian president Gustavo Petro, Chilean president Gabriel Boric, and advisors to Brazil's Luis Ignacio Lula da Silva—all of them Soros allies. This happened after the trio were elected the year prior in a shift back to socialist leadership in Latin America.[49]

Petro was a former member of the terrorist organization FARC, and his son was charged with corruption for taking cash from drug traffickers and funneling it to his presidential campaign.

Brazil's Lulu had personally met with Alex earlier in the year to discuss OSF's activities there.

The purpose of the trip was billed as "strengthening diplomatic relations," and members of the OSF accompanied the delegation at dinners and meetings, according to congressional financial disclosures.[50] Not so coincidentally, as the *Free Beacon*'s Chuck Ross points out, the meeting happened after the Biden administration had expressed displeasure with Lulu's administra-

---

47   "After Acts in Brasilia, Soros Ngo Wants Lula Da Silva to Lead 'Global Alliance,'" *The Rio Times*, January 18, 2023. https://www.riotimesonline.com/brazil-news/brazil/after-acts-in-brasilia-soros-ngo-wants-lula-da-silva-to-lead-global-alliance

48   https://disclosures-clerk.house.gov/gtimages/MT/2023/500026961.pdf

49   Chuck Ross, "Soros Funded House Democrats' 'Socialist Sympathy Tour' to South America, Records Show," *Washington Free Beacon*, September 7, 2023. https://freebeacon.com/democrats/soros-funded-house-democrats-socialist-sympathy-tour-to-south-america-records-show

50   https://disclosures-clerk.house.gov/gtimages/MT/2023/500026921.pdf

tion for embracing America's enemies, including China, Russia, and Venezuela. In other words, Alex was trying to mend tensions between his allies.

And it worked.

Meeting Date	Alex Met With	Following Biden Admin Policy Actions
12/1/2022	President Joe Biden,* Jon Finer, Mariana Adame, and Nina Srivastava *Likely, Alex's attendance at the State Dinner may be getting misleadingly coded as this	State Dinner on South Lawn for French President Emmanuel Macron attended by President Biden on this day On December 12, Biden's Department of Agriculture announced an additional $325 million for "climate-smart commodities."[51]
10/6 and 10/14/ 2022	Kimberly Lang, Executive Assistant to the National Security Advisor Jon Finer (10/6) and Mariana Adame (10/14)	On October 7, the EPA announced new regulations aimed at reducing methane emissions from the oil and gas industry. On October 10, the Department of Energy announced a $3 billion investment in domestic

51   "Biden-Harris Administration Announces an Additional $325 Million in Pilot Projects Through Partnerships for Climate-smart Commodities, for Total Investment of $3.1 Billion," press release, US Department of Agriculture, December 12, 2022. https://www.usda.gov/media/press-releases/2022/12/12/biden-harris-administration-announces-additional-325-million-pilot

Meeting Date	Alex Met With	Following Biden Admin Policy Actions
		battery manufacturing to support electric vehicles. Then on October 13, the Department of the Interior announced the approval of new wind energy projects off the Atlantic coast, aiming to increase renewable energy production. Alex tweeted on October 6 an article about how the EU's lending arm urged leaders not to backslide on climate targets.[52]
10/29/2021	Madeline Strasser, advisor to Chief of Staff Ron Klain	On November 2, at a climate conference, the administration announced a methane emissions reduction plan and made a commitment to end deforestation by 2030. Ahead of this meeting, on October 28, Alex tweeted, "The climate crisis and unstable property rights are leading to more and more homes being lost, especially among Black families in the US South."[53]

52   https://twitter.com/AlexanderSoros/status/1579864794907414528
53   https://twitter.com/AlexanderSoros/status/1453740489069395975

In another instance of climate coincidences, on December 11, 2024, the US Department of Defense announced that it was combatting climate change "as a security concern" for Africans.[54]

"U.S. officials are listening and responding to those concerns," Maureen E. Farrell, the Biden administration's deputy assistant secretary of defense for African affairs, said in a Defense Department statement. She cited Somalia as a "climate-stressed area" where, they claim, groups like al-Shabaab (an al-Qaeda affiliate) see upticks in recruitment due to increased tensions over droughts.

Just one day before this announcement, the International Crisis Group, a Soros-funded foreign policy NGO, released a report on *Fighting Climate Change in Somalia's Conflict Zones*.[55] George and Alex Soros are both currently on the group's board of trustees,[56] and back in 1994, Open Society Institute provided seed money that help set up the group.[57] "George was in from the beginning, and he truly jump-started the organization," the International Crisis Group said in an anniversary publication celebrating fifteen years in operation.[58] In 2000, an "extraordinarily generous" $2.5 million matching grant made by Soros primed the pump for the group to go global. Open Society Institute continues to give $2 million annually.

Once Alex took up the mantle, funding ramped up. In August 2022, Open Society Foundations gave the group a $20 million

54   Jim Garamone, "DOD Dealing with Climate Change as a Security Concern for Africans," US Department of Defense, December 11, 2024. https://www.defense.gov/News/News-Stories/Article/Article/3997856/dod-dealing-with-climate-change-as-a-security-concern-for-africans

55   *Fighting Climate Change in Somala's Conflict Zones*, (Brussels, Belgium: International Crisis Group, December 10, 2024). https://www.crisisgroup.org/sites/default/files/2024-12/316-fighting-climate-change-somalia.pdf

56   "Board of Trustees," International Crisis Group. https://www.crisisgroup.org/who-we-are/board-trustees

57   "History." International Crisis Group. https://archive.is/E1iQt

58   *Fifteen Years on the Front Lines, 1995–2010* (Brussels, Belgium: International Crisis Group, 2010). https://www.crisisgroup.org/sites/default/files/fifteen-years-on-the-frontline.pdf

grant for researching issues fueling political violence, "like climate injustice," and expanding its network of activists operating in conflict-affected countries, particularly in the Global South.[59] Alex, in response to the funding pledge, praised the group's work.

It wasn't just Alex, either. While the Soros network maintained its most direct control through Alex, his pawns were also out there.

In 2023, the *New York Post* highlighted how past or present leaders at the OSF had racked up thirty-three private White House meetings in under two years.[60]

Tom Perriello, the executive director of the OSF-US, accounted for the majority (seventeen) of the meetings, having met with the chief of staff for the White House's Office of Political Strategy and Outreach, the associate director of strategic outreach, and even having a sit-down with John Podesta. He met most with Kimberly Lang when she was a national security advisor executive assistant. Perriello would land himself a job in the Biden administration late in the game: in February 2024, he was appointed the US envoy for Sudan by Biden.

The previously mentioned (non-) Labor Secretary Patrick Gaspard made ten visits, one of which was with White House Deputy Chief of Staff Jen O'Malley Dillon, whom Alex praised as Kamala Harris's pick for her 2024 presidential campaign manager.[61] Gaspard ended up at the Center for American Progress, a common employer of Soros delegations in the White House.

Fast-forward to 2024. Soros-backed digital strategist Tara McGowan racked up nearly twenty White House visits, just by

59   "$20m Grant Aims to Combine Local Voices and Global Expertise to Reduce Human Suffering," press release, International Crisis Group, April 25, 2022. https://www.crisisgroup.org/global/20m-grant-aims-combine-local-voices-and-global-expertise-reduce-human-suffering

60   Rich Calder and Matthew Sedacca, "George Soros' Army of Lieutenants Get Easy Access to Biden White House," *New York Post*, April 15, 2023. https://nypost.com/2023/04/15/george-soros-army-of-lieutenants-has-easy-white-house-access

61   https://x.com/AlexanderSoros/status/1815542166929961419

April.[62] In the 2024 election cycle, the Alex-led OSF donated $15 million to Courier Newsroom, which she founded. Courier operates eleven "local news" outlets, primarily in swing states, and does not disclose its political alignment directly in its political stories and coverage. McGowan, in a 2019 internal memo, explicitly outlined how Courier's role was to help Democrats get elected.[63]

Of note, McGowan is dating the Senator Chris Murphy, which he's refused to address.[64]

After the senility of Biden became impossible for even the media to ignore following his first and only debate with President Trump, we were all left to wonder who really was in charge all those years.

It certainly wasn't Joe.

Alex wasn't set to let his clout in the White House shrivel away—and with his fortune and connections, he didn't think it would.

GOLIATH VS. DAVID: ALEX TAKES ON TRUMP

Alex remained bullish on Joe Biden the entire election cycle. He addressed the World Economic Forum in Davos in January 2024 and cautioned against the assumption that Trump's victory in the 2024 election was inevitable.[65]

62   Joe Schoffstall and Cameron Cawthorne, "Founder of Soros-funded 'Propaganda' News Network Has Visited Biden's White House Nearly 20 Times," Fox News, April 2, 2024. https://www.foxnews.com/politics/founder-soros-funded-propaganda-news-network-visited-bidens-white-house-nearly-20-times

63   Robert Schmad, "Soros Gave Record Cash to Pro-Democratic 'Local News' Network That Spent Millions Influencing 2024 Election," *Washington Examiner*, December 5, 2024. https://www.washingtonexaminer.com/news/investigations/3249950/soros-record-cash-local-news-network-influence-election

64   Aubrie Spady, Andrew Mark Miller, and Julia Johnson, "Dem Senator Refuses to Address Relationship with Founder of Soros-funded 'Propaganda' News Network," Fox News, March 20, 2025. https://www.foxnews.com/politics/dem-senator-refuses-address-relationship-founder-soros-funded-propaganda-news-network

65   Elliot Smith, "Alex Soros Says a Trump Win Is a Done Deal for the Davos Elite—But They're Always Wrong," CNBC, January 19, 2024. https://www.cnbc.com/2024/01/19/alex-soros-says-davos-wrong-to-think-trump-win-is-a-done-deal.html

Hopefully, no one placed any bets based on his advice.

Biden was still the Democrat nominee, and his historically awful debate performance was still months away, as was the (first) attempted assassination of Donald Trump that energized his base—and signaled that Democrats had no path to victory besides homicide.

"In Davos, Donald Trump is already the president," Alex told the audience, which had been spared from a Greta Thunberg speech that year. "That's a good thing, because the Davos consensus is always wrong." The Davos consensus is indeed always wrong, and he managed to argue against the one exception.

Alex said the quiet part out loud on Trump's candidacy; admitting that his only options in 2024 are to wind up in power or prison. Those were options Democrats created with their unprecedented lawfare campaign against him, only to have it blow up in their faces. Most Republicans and Independents always saw the cases against Trump as politically motivated. Even in a media environment where the average voter is being fed a heavily liberal perspective on Trump's legal troubles, they still chose Trump over the alternative.

Previously, following Trump's conviction in Manhattan DA Alvin Bragg's bogus "hush money" case, Alex opined that Democrats should refer to Trump as a "convicted felon" at every opportunity—a strategy that Biden, NPR, MSNBC, and seemingly every left-wing pundit on social media relished. Were they getting their instructions from Alex himself? "Repetition is the key to a successful message and we want people to wrestle with the notion of hiring a convicted felon for the most important job in the country![66] Alex explained, unintentionally paraphrasing Hitler.

---

[66]   Julia Johnson, "Soros Heir Urges Democrats to Hammer Trump As 'Convicted Felon at Every Opportunity,'" Fox News, May 31, 2024. https://www.foxnews.com/politics/soros-heir-urges-democrats-hammer-trump-convicted-felon-every-opportunity

He was so enthusiastic to craft that narrative, because his family funded the events that would lead to it.

In 2021, George donated $1 million to the Color of Change PAC, which supported DA Bragg. Another son of George, Jonathan Soros, also donated directly to Bragg's campaign. In an attempt to deny this clear link, liberal fact-checkers attempted to argue that Soros didn't really fund Bragg; he just funded a PAC (that had announced their desire to back Bragg days before Soros donated to them). This one degree of separation was enough for fact-checkers like the *Washington Post's* Glenn Kessler to further make themselves into laughingstocks by trying to argue that this didn't count as Bragg being Soros-backed. *PolitiFact*, a subsidiary of a group that George donated $300,000 to, also tried to make this argument.[67]

Bragg also received substantial support from the New York Justice & Public Safety PAC and the state's Working Families Party, both beneficiaries of Soros money.[68]

Alex's specific predictions for what was to come grant some relief that he doesn't have his father's political acumen, at least not yet. Alex, predicting that Trump's "extremism" would be considered toxic, thought Biden had a "pretty good" map, where he'd hold Arizona and Georgia. In reality, by the time the votes were counted, the election was tighter in deep-blue New Jersey than it was in swing-state Arizona. Alex also predicted that Wisconsin would be the most pivotal state in the election, because by winning it, Biden would win Pennsylvania and Michigan, too. Once again Alex was right about the importance of Wisconsin as a bellwether, but in the opposite direction.

---

67 Matt Palumbo, "Media 'Fact Checkers' Lie to Defend Alvin Bragg," *New York Post*, April 17, 2023. https://nypost.com/2023/04/17/media-fact-checkers-lie-to-defend-alvin-bragg

68 "Justice for Sale: How George Soros Put Radical Prosecutors in Power," Law Enforcement Legal Defense Fund, June 2022. https://www.policedefense.org/wp-content/uploads/2022/06/Justice_For_Sale_LELDF_report.pdf

Compared to the 2020 election cycle, the direct political donations of the Soros network to candidates notably shifted in the 2024 election cycle under the new stewardship of Alex Soros. Most notably, the Soros-founded Democracy PAC, despite having $125 million earmarked for its use, only spent $67.5 million between January 1, 2023 and Election Day 2024. This is significantly less than the $81.5 million spent by the super PAC during the 2020 election cycle, when George was at the network's helm.[69] Of course, direct spending on candidates isn't the only way to tip the scales in an election—add in solely the $15 million that Alex funneled to the propaganda outlet Courier Newsroom, and spending exceeds the 2020 cycle.

Alex also pledged $50 million toward a plethora of leftist causes to be spent over the following three years, particularly to "increase civic engagement" among "Black women and younger women of color." The overturning of *Roe v. Wade* was used as a rallying cry and the activists celebrated a handful of anti-abortion measures going down in flames at the state level.[70] Among the groups benefitting from the $50 million include Planned Parenthood, Run for Something, Alliance for Youth Action, and Power Rising.[71]

Run for Something helps candidates who "are pro-choice, pro-universal health care, pro-LGBTQ equality, pro-criminal justice reform." The Alliance for Youth Action advertises its support for "Restorative Justice," "Economic Justice," "Climate Justice,"

---

69   Robert Schmad, "Soros PAC Significantly Cut Spending During 2024 Election Cycle," *Washington Examiner*, December 9, 2024. https://www.washingtonexaminer.com/news/investigations/3254541/soros-pac-cut-spending-2024-elections

70   "Open Society Foundations to Invest $50 Million to Support Civic Engagement of Women and Youth," media release, Open Society Foundations, December 5, 2023. https://www.opensocietyfoundations.org/newsroom/open-society-foundations-to-invest-50-million-to-support-civic-engagement-of-women-and-youth

71   Tom Olohan, "Soros Family to Flood Youth Organizations with Cash Ahead of 2024 Election," *Newsbusters*, December 8, 2023. https://newsbusters.org/blogs/business/tom-olohan/2023/12/08/soros-family-flood-youth-organizations-cash-ahead-2024

and "personal bodily autonomy," while Power Rising is a member of the "Black Women's Leadership Collective"; it has supported incompetent candidates like Stacey Abrams and pushed for Ketanji Brown Jackson to join the SCOTUS.[72]

But all the money in the world wouldn't make a difference in the presidential campaign. Even with the entire deck stacked against him, Trump would handily defeat Harris after having raised "only" $464 million to her $1.2 billion.[73]

Alex Soros's questionable political acumen already established, the political equivalent of the Hindenburg disaster was still no deterrent to him. On July 10, 2024, just weeks after the presidential debate between Trump and Biden, Alex took to X to try and regain Democratic support behind his puppet in the White House. "Let's stop running against ourselves and run against the existential threat that is Donald Trump! Biden-Harris 2024!"[74]

The message came amid growing public concerns from the Biden-friendly press over Biden's cognitive ability and the soundness of his candidacy in the 2024 presidential race—the key word being "public." Everyone in the media was aware of these issues the whole time. The concern wasn't over Biden's mental state; it was that the jig was up, and the public *knew* about Biden's mental state. CNN's Jake Tapper had blasted guests for daring to suggest Biden was suffering mental decline, then later had the gall to write a book on the coverup. If anything, Biden's declining mental fitness was positive for the progressives around him pulling the strings, like Alex.

Ten days after Alex called for Democrats to unite around the man who gave him easy access to the White House, Biden

---

72   Ibid.
73   "2024 Presidential Race." OpenSecrets. https://www.opensecrets.org/2024-presidential-race
74   Andrew Stanton, "Joe Biden Gets Support from George Soros' Son Ahead of Key Press Conference," *Newsweek*, July 11, 2024. https://www.newsweek.com/george-soros-joe-biden-donald-trump-election-alex-soros-warning-1923871

dropped out of the race via Twitter and immediately endorsed Kamala Harris, effectively propelling her to be the nominee. Any fears Alex may have had that he'd need to get his foot in the door of the administration of whoever would replace Biden would were immediately laid to rest, and he'd enthusiastically endorse Harris. For him, Harris was the perfect replacement, because she too was someone he could control.

Alex joined several other "Democratic heavyweights" at the private home of Vice-President Harris on his twenty-first visit with the Biden-Harris administration, this visit being less than two weeks before Alex took over as the public face of the OSF.[75] A week later, Alex posted a photo of the two to his Twitter. "Great to catch up with Madame Vice President, Kamala Harris!" Alex wrote in a tweet accompanying the photo. The meeting wasn't acknowledged by Harris on her public schedule.[76]

At the 2024 Democratic National Convention the month after Biden was ousted, Democrat leaders lined up for the chance to meet Alex. Many of their photographs with him were taken from the Skybox at the United Center of Chicago, where some of the party's most elite donors paid up to $5 million to be included. Alex and Huma Abidin took a photo with vice presidential candidate Tim Walz, whom Democrats picked because they thought he'd project masculinity.[77] "Walzified! Walzpilled!" an equally masculine Alex gushed.[78] To those not terminally online, "Walzpilled"

75   Chuck Ross, "Kamala Harris Hosted Soros Scion and Supermodel 'Roommate' at Private Residence," *Washington Free Beacon*, September 1, 2023. https://freebeacon.com/biden-administration/kamala-harris-hosted-soros-scion-and-supermodel-roommate-at-private-residence

76   Matt Palumbo, "George Soros' Son Posts Photo of Meeting with VP Harris That Wasn't on Her Public Schedule," *Bongino*, June 7, 2023. https://bongino.com/alexander-soros-posts-photo-of-meeting-with-vp-harris

77   Jon Levine, "High-profile Democrats, Including Bill Clinton, Kiss Megadonor Alex Soros' Ring at DNC: 'In His Pocket,'" *New York Post*, August 31, 2023. https://nypost.com/2024/08/31/us-news/high-profile-democrats-including-bill-clinton-kiss-alex-soros-ring-at-dnc-in-his-pocket

78   https://x.com/AlexanderSoros/status/1826783810878672942

was supposed to be a reference to being "red pilled," from the movie *The Matrix*.

Others that Alex met with included Hillary Clinton, Eric Swalwell, and Ruben Gallego. On the second day of the convention, he met up with Barack Obama and Nancy Pelosi. Alex has donated over $600,000 to Pelosi and her Democratic Congressional campaign committee since 2010. He also gave his quote, stamp of approval, unquote, to Texas Representative Jasmine Crockett, whom he blessed as a rising star (we can only hope).[79]

Still other top Democrats that Alex met with included Transportation Secretary Pete Buttigieg, Arizona Senator Mark Kelly, North Carolina Governor Roy Cooper, and Pennsylvania Governor Josh Shapiro. He also met with Representative Hakeem Jeffries, the Democrat House minority leader, and Senate Majority Leader Chuck Schumer. George has given Majority PAC over $5.5 million just since 2016. In the 2022 midterms, he gave $175 million to Democrats, and at least another $60 million to Democrats in 2024.[80]

A month after the Biden shakeup, Alex would meet with Tim Walz at his (Alex's) NYC home,[81] further confirming that his easy access wouldn't be subject to change if Harris-Walz were to lead the next administration.

Given the reputation that George had built for the Soros name, due to the chaos in America's cities he's funded through rogue DAs, Walz couldn't have been a better candidate and complement to Harris.

79   "High-profile Democrats, Including Bill Clinton, Kiss Megadonor Alex Soros' Ring at DNC: 'In His Pocket.'" *New York Post*.
80   Ibid.
81   https://x.com/AlexanderSoros/status/1838662515124789692

Walz allowed rioters to burn and loot Minneapolis in 2020, just as DAs backed by the elder Soros did—and then refused to prosecute those rioters. Approvingly, his wife Gwen said that during the riots, she kept her windows open to she could smell the "burning tires,"[82] and their daughter tipped off rioters to let them know that the National Guard wasn't coming, helping further fuel the violence.[83]

Harris herself encouraged the unrest by boosting a "bail fund" in a never-deleted tweet: "If you're able to, chip in now to the Minnesota Freedom Fund to help post bail for those protesting on the ground in Minnesota."[84] Among those freed through the Freedom Fund after Harris advertised it included a man who committed a murder a week later; a serial DUI offender who crashed and killed a passenger after being freed; and a serial arsonist who then went on to try to burn down a mosque—among many others.[85]

The Soros empire has funded countless pro-open-borders groups, including NGOs that provide legal services to illegal immigrants, and Alex's backing of Walz shows none of those commitments have changed. As governor, Walz signed legislation to give illegals state-funded healthcare, driver's licenses, and free college courtesy of the North Star Promise scholarship program—a full tuition-free ride to public Minnesota universities—while he

---

82   Olivia Land, "Tim Walz's Wife, Gwen, Said She Kept Windows Open During George Floyd Riots to Smell 'Burning Tires,'" *New York Post*, August 7, 2024. https://nypost.com/2024/08/07/us-news/gwen-walz-said-she-kept-windows-open-during-george-floyd-riots-to-smell-burning-tires

83   Michael Lee, "Walz Slammed For 'Hesitating' to Send in Guard as His Daughter Tipped Off Rioters Via Social Media," Fox News, August 7, 2024. https://www.foxnews.com/politics/walz-slammed-hesitating-send-guard-his-daughter-tipped-off-rioters-via-social-media

84   Megan Palin and Isabel Vincent, "Kamala Harris-backed Bail Fund Set Loose Criminals Who Went on to Be Hit with Murder, DUI Death and Arson Charges," *New York Post*, August 22, 2024. https://nypost.com/2024/08/22/us-news/kamala-harris-backed-bail-funds-fails-continue

85   Ibid.

hiked taxes on residents despite the state's $17.5 billion surplus.[86] Meanwhile, Harris vowed to create an amnesty program for them, claiming they've "earned a pathway to citizenship." What exactly did they do to "earn" it? Enter the country illegally.[87]

Since at least the late 1990s, the OSF has argued in favor of extending voting rights to convicted felons, claiming that it's racist (of course) that we don't. And naturally Walz supports that, too, and signed a law to grant the franchise to 55,000 of them. Harris would love to go even further: she once entertained the possibility of allowing felons to vote from prison, in addition to funding their sex-change surgeries.[88]

As crazy as allowing felons to vote is, it's perfectly sane from the perspective of Democrat leaders making political calculations. A study in the *Annals of the American Academy of Political and Social Science* found that in New York, roughly 62 percent of convicts are Democrats, and 9 percent Republicans. In New Mexico, the split was 52 percent Democrat to 10 percent Republican, and in North Carolina it was 55 percent Democrat to 10 percent Republican.[89]

Studies aside, the racial demographics of prisoners are consistent with this kind of voter registration, and common sense suggests that if felons voting were somehow a benefit to Republicans, it wouldn't be the case that 100 percent of politicians pushing for it were Democrats.

---

86   Torey Van Oot, "Minnesota Budget Surplus Updated To $17.5 Billion," *Axios*, February 27, 2023. https://www.axios.com/local/twin-cities/2023/02/27/minnesota-budget-surplus-17-billion-2023

87   Matt Palumbo, "Alex Soros' Dinner Date with Tim Walz Reveals Who'll Pull the Strings in a Harris White House," *New York Post*, September 25, 2024. https://nypost.com/2024/09/25/opinion/soros-walz-dinner-date-reveals-who-pulls-dems-strings

88   Ibid.

89   Paul Bedard, "Jail Survey: 7 in 10 Felons Register as Democrats," *Washington Examiner*, January 1, 2014. https://www.washingtonexaminer.com/news/washington-secrets/1390328/jail-survey-7-in-10-felons-register-as-democrats

JUDGMENT DAY

Fast-forward just a few short months, and the day before the election, Alex was confident. "Blue wave??" he wrote in response to a Tweet predicting Harris would take Michigan by 2 percent and Pennsylvania by 3 percent.[90]

Harris would then go on to lose every single swing state and the popular vote, with the election being called for Trump despite many analysts expecting days to pass without a winner officially announced. Trump became the first Republican to win the popular vote since 2004, with 2,630 counties turning more Republican and only 301 more Democratic. Every single swing state has swung right since 2020, and Trump outperformed or tied his 2016 swing-state results in five out of the seven.[91]

Despite national polling to the contrary, Harris advisors say her internal polling never once had her ahead.[92] Yet she was still an improvement over Biden, whose internal polling showed Trump winning over 400 electoral votes against him.[93]

As bad as things were for Democrats, the election results were more Democrat-leaning than public opinion among voters, as the Democrat Party-linked research firm Blue Rose Research embarrassingly discovered.

While almost all polls are of likely voters (for obvious reasons), polls of non-likely voters constantly showed Trump leading that demographic by double digits, sometimes +20 or higher.

90   https://x.com/AlexanderSoros/status/1853596119223189921
91   Henrik Pettersson, Byron Manley, Zachary B. Wolf, and Matt Stiles, "America's Red Shift: See the Counties Where Trump Boosted His Share of the Vote," CNN, November 2, 2022. https://www.cnn.com/interactive/2024/11/politics/vote-shift-trump-election-dg
92   Sam Woodward, "Kamala Harris Advisers: Internal Polling Never Showed VP Ahead," *USA Today*, November 27, 2024. https://www.usatoday.com/story/news/politics/elections/2024/11/27/kamala-harris-advisers-internal-polling/76626278007
93   Juliann Ventura, "'Pod Save America:' Biden's internal Polling Showed Trump Winning 400 Electoral Votes," *The Hill*, November 8, 2024. https://thehill.com/homenews/campaign/4981792-pod-save-america-bidens-internal-polling-showed-trump-winning-400-electoral-votes

In other words, it's a guarantee that whatever amount Trump won by understated his true popularity.

Blue Rose Research calculated that Trump would've won by 4.8 points, or nearly three times as much as the 1.4-point margin he won by, had everyone turned out to vote. (If 2024 had 2022 levels of turnout, their model says Harris would've led the popular vote by 0.6 percent, though that likely still would've resulted in a Trump electoral victory.)[94]

This also blows out of the water any claims from liberals that "voter suppression" causes them to lose elections. That can't possibly be the case when Democrats would lose by even greater margins with 100 percent turnout.

After a completely bombing his 2024 election predictions twice—first, that Trump would lose to Biden, and then that he'd lose to Harris—Alex decided he was qualified to explain *why* Trump won.[95]

Taking to social media, Alex described Donald Trump as a "super candidate" whose appeal was underestimated by Democrats, without mentioning that he was one of those Democrats. Alex recognized that Trump outperformed Republicans nationwide, meaning this wasn't just a shift to the right or to the Republican party. The 2024 election represented a shift to Trumpism.

To close out the eventful year, Alex made some final donations to what would become the "resistance."

Through his Democracy PAC he donated $250,000 to Ben Wikler's campaign to become the next DNC chairman (he lost).

94   Matt Palumbo, "Democrat Research Firm: Trump Would've Crushed Harris by Even More with 100% Voter Turnout," *Silverloch*, March 19, 2025. https://silverloch.com/democrat-research-firm-trump-wouldve-crushed-harris-by-even-more-with-100-voter-turnout

95   Rich Calder, "Dem Megadonor Alex Soros Explains Why 'Super Candidate' Trump Won," *New York Post*, November 16, 2024. https://nypost.com/2024/11/16/us-news/dem-megadonor-alex-soros-explains-why-trump-won-and-tells-his-own-party-to-make-huge-shift

Wikler is the current chair of the Wisconsin Democratic Party and was once a senior advisor at the Soros-backed Moveon.org.

That made the Soros family one of two top contributors to Wikler, along with former Jeffery Epstein associate Reid Hoffman who also gave $250,000 a few days after, which account for nearly 70 percent of Wikler's funding.[96] With that backing, Wikler was seen as the frontrunner for party chair; but he ended up losing to Ken Martin, coming in second place with 30 percent of the vote.

Alex did manage to rack up one victory for himself that year.

Closing out the year, on December 18, 2024, Alex held his engagement party in New York to former Hillary Clinton aide Huma Abedin. Soros proposed to Abedin in July of 2024, writing in an Instagram post that the couple "couldn't be happier, more grateful, or more in love."[97]

The party, hosted at the home of *Vogue* executive director Anna Wintour, was attended by many high-level Democrat donors, media personalities, and celebrities. Abedin's former boss, Hillary Clinton, attended with Bill Clinton. Also attending were Joe Scarborough and Mika Brzezinski of MSNBC, whose network hired Abedin as a contributor in 2022; actors Adrian Brody and Georgina Chapman; and mogul Barry Diller and his wife, fashion designer Diane von Fürstenberg.[98]

When she was Hillary's deputy chief of staff, Abedin acted as her point person, gatekeeping access to the then-secretary of state. Power brokers genuflected to her in hopes of earning time with Clinton. According to emails obtained by Judicial Watch,

---

96   Chuck Ross, "DNC Chair Candidate Reveals Massive Donations from George Soros, Reid Hoffman on Eve of Vote," *Washington Free Beacon*, February 1, 2025. https://freebeacon.com/democrats/dnc-chair-candidate-reveals-massive-donations-from-george-soros-reid-hoffman-on-eve-of-vote

97   Andrew Mark Miller, "Alex Soros and Huma Abedin Hold Star-studded Engagement Party at Anna Wintour's Home: Photos," Fox News, December 19, 2024. https://www.foxnews.com/politics/alex-soros-and-huma-abedin-hold-star-studded-engagement-party-at-anna-wintours-home-photos

98   Ibid.

even Hillary's director of policy planning, Anne-Marie Slaughter, had to appeal to Abedin to pass along documents. "I hope you can get this to the Secretary—I've sent it to everyone else," Slaughter once emailed Abedin.[99]

ALEX IN THE NEW TRUMP ERA

For Alex, the real battle began once Trump took office, and his subsidiaries mobilized to attack Trump's policies, particularly his agenda on mass deportations. Alex has also been going after Elon Musk, triggered by the sight of another billionaire wielding such power.

Among the most notable policies of Trump to be blocked by a leftist judge was when Trump deported hundreds of Venezuelan Tren de Aragua members to El Salvador, a country that has gone from being one of the most violent on the planet to having a homicide rate about a third of America's in just a few years by cracking down on gangs.

On January 20, his first day in office, Trump signed an executive order initiating the process to designate various drug cartels and transnational gangs, such as Tren de Aragua, as Foreign Terrorist Organizations. It was a move by Trump that only a leftist could have a problem with.

US District Judge James Boasberg, a Biden-appointed Democrat donor, issued an order to block the deportations Trump authorized under the Alien Enemies Act of 1789, but the gang members were already in international waters. El Salvador's President Nayib Bukele mocked the judge, posting to his X account, "oopsie...too late," after he issued the order, and Trump has called for the judge to be impeached.

---

99   Benjamin Wallace-Wells, "The Real Scandal of Hillary Clinton's E-Mails," *The New Yorker*, August 12, 2016. https://www.newyorker.com/news/benjamin-wallace-wells/the-real-scandal-of-hillary-clintons-e-mails

Democracy Forward, the American Civil Liberties Union (ACLU), and the ACLU of the District of Columbia successfully challenged the deportations on legal technicalities. They then asked a federal court to investigate whether the Trump administration violated the judge's order.

To the surprise of few, these groups are tied to the Soros network. The largest grant George had given to the ACLU was $50 million in 2014 (out of a budget that year of $133 million), to push to reduce jail sentences, with the goal of reducing the US prison population 50 percent by 2020.[100]

Democracy Forward, which has also been targeting the operations of Elon Musk's DOGE, lists several clients and partners that are Soros-funded. This includes Color of Change, which got a $3 million grant from the OSF on Alex's watch, after receiving nearly $1.5 million in 2018–2019.[101] Other groups that Democracy Forward lists as clients and partners include the Center for American Progress (of which a number of top members have worked in the Biden administration) and National Immigration Law Center. Hundreds of thousands of dollars in funding also has gone to UnidosUS, Common Justice, and the Catholic Legal Immigration Network.

Also on his first day in Office, President Donald Trump issued an executive order to end birthright citizenship, to take effect after thirty days.[102] About 250,000 anchor babies are born in the US

---

100   Erik Eckholm, "A.C.L.U. in $50 Million Push to Reduce Jail Sentences," *The New York Times*, November 6, 2014. https://www.nytimes.com/2014/11/07/us/aclu-in-dollar50-million-push-to-reduce-jail-sentences.html

101   John Binder, "Soros-linked Network Behind Lawsuit Attempting to Stop Trump from Deporting Illegal Alien Gang Members," *Breitbart*, March 7, 2025. https://www.breitbart.com/politics/2025/03/17/soros-linked-network-behind-lawsuit-attempting-stop-trump-deporting-illegal-alien-gang-members

102   "Protecting The Meaning And Value Of American Citizenship," *The White House*, January 20, 2025. https://www.whitehouse.gov/presidential-actions/2025/01/protecting-the-meaning-and-value-of-american-citizenship

every year (and it's been higher in the past—390,000 in 2007),[103] automatically granting them US citizenship despite their parents not having it.

America's birthright citizenship policy is based on a dubious interpretation of the 14th Amendment, one of the reconstruction amendments crafted to protect the rights of blacks. Native Americans weren't granted citizenship until 1924, so interpreting the 14th Amendment as meaning that everyone born on US soil was to be automatically granted citizenship is nonsensical.

The Soros network is behind a lawsuit trying to preserve our anchor baby policy through the group CASA Inc. and the indirectly linked Asylum Seeker Advocacy Project, both of which are representing pregnant illegal aliens planning on delivering children who sued to block the order.

CASA took $2.23 million from the Open Society Foundations from 2016-2023.[104] Meanwhile, the Open Society-US's Soros Justice Fellowships, which, in their words, "fund outstanding individuals to undertake projects that advance reform, spur debate, and catalyze change on a range of issues facing the US criminal legal system," has previously funded a then-policy director for the Asylum Seeker Advocacy Project as an "Advocacy Fellow."[105]

In March, Trump revoked the legal status for 532,000 migrants Biden flew into the US interior from Cuba, Haiti, Nicaragua, and

---

103   Jeffrey S. Passel, D'Vera Cohn and John Gramlich. "Number Of U.S.-born Babies With Unauthorized Immigrant Parents Has Fallen Since 2007," *Pew Research Center*, November 1, 2018. https://www.pewresearch.org/short-reads/2018/11/01/the-number-of-u-s-born-babies-with-unauthorized-immigrant-parents-has-fallen-since-2007

104   John Binder. "Soros-funded Group Behind Lawsuit Trying To Preserve Anchor Baby Policy," *Breitbart*, April 18, 2025. https://www.breitbart.com/politics/2025/04/18/soros-funded-group-behind-lawsuit-trying-preserve-anchor-baby-policy

105   "Soros Justice Fellowships: Leidy Perez-Davis," *Open Society Foundations*, https://www.opensocietyfoundations.org/grants/soros-justice-fellowships?fellow=leidy-perez-davis

Venezuela through a controversial "mass humanitarian parole" program. Trump requested that they self-deport afterwards.

While Biden granted them legal status with the stroke of a pen, the Obama-appointed Judge Indira Talwani decided that Trump can't revoke it with the stroke of a pen and ruled in April that each migrant must have their case received individually. This is clearly impossible and would take hundreds of years to complete.

The groups Human Rights First and Justice Action Center sued the Trump admin to challenge the Trump admin's ability to cancel Biden's bogus parole program and make them eligible for deportation. In 2023, under Alex, the Human Rights First received a $450k grant from the OSF, while under George, Justice Action Center received nearly $6.2 million from 2016-2021.[106]

Also in March, President Trump ordered the elimination of the DHS' Office for Civil Rights and Civil Liberties, which has been criticized as a bureaucratic obstacle to deportations. The Biden administration packed the office with bureaucrats with pro-open borders views.

Trump's order was challenged by the leftist legal firm Democracy Forward, which is representing several non-governmental organizations, including the Urban Justice Center, to try to block the office from being closed. Both Democracy Forward and Urban Justice Center have financial ties to the OSF—Democracy Forward's clients have received millions from the OSF, while the Urban Justice Center has received nearly half a million in grant money.[107]

---

106 John Binder. "Soros-Linked Network Behind Lawsuit Attempting to Stop Trump from Deporting Illegal Alien Gang Members," *Breitbart*, March 17, 2025. https://www.breitbart.com/politics/2025/03/17/soros-linked-network-behind-lawsuit-attempting-stop-trump-deporting-illegal-alien-gang-members

107 John Binder. "Soros-linked Groups Sue To Stop Trump From Eliminating DHS Civil Rights Office For Migrants," *Breitbart*, April 25, 2025. https://www.breitbart.com/politics/2025/04/25/soros-linked-groups-sue-to-stop-trump-eliminating-dhs-civil-rights-office-migrants

In May, two Soros-linked NGOs are sued to stop Trump's reforms for the Unaccompanied Alien Children (UAC) program, which represent a new effort to deport unaccompanied minors to end human trafficking of migrant children into the US. The reforms were issued in February. The NGOs are the National Center for Youth Law and Democracy Forward.[108]

Just months into Trump's second term, Alex's network has tried to smear the United States as a nation regressing, due to his wildly popular policies.

One so-called "human rights" group that you've never heard of before, called CIVICUS, made headlines on March 10 for adding the United States to a "global human rights watchlist." In fact, it is just another leftist advocacy group.

Based in South Africa (not exactly a bastion of human rights), the group claimed that "civic freedoms" were threatened under Trump. Specifically, they complained that Soros-aligned goals were being undermined—that "the new administration slashed federal funding for organizations supporting people most in need, dismantled USAID, and reversed progress on justice, inclusion, and diversity."[109]

Their criteria for what degrades "human rights" were set up to give liberal publications something to write about. And they ate it up.

"US added to international watchlist for rapid decline in civic freedoms," read *The Guardian*'s headline. *The Independent* chimed in: "US added to human rights watchlist for 'narrowing' freedom and now ranks near Serbia and Congo"—with zero self-awareness

108 John Binder. "Soros-Linked Groups Sue to Stop Trump's Migrant Child Trafficking Crackdown," *Breitbart*, May 9, 2025. https://www.breitbart.com/politics/2025/05/09/soros-linked-groups-sue-to-stop-trump-migrant-child-trafficking-crackdown

109 "Monitor: Tracking Civic Space." CIVICUS. https://monitor.civicus.org/watchlist-march-2025/USA

about how their headline itself exposes the absurdity of the criteria. A casual Google search reveals that media in India, Morocco, Ireland, and more were thrilled the pick up the story, portraying an America in decline under Trump. Even countries that ranked worse on CIVICUS's rankings hopped on the bandwagon.

For groups like CIVICUS, the justification always comes after the conclusion. They were always going to find some way to generate a negative headline about Trump, and then just work backward from that conclusion to anything he did. By contrast, they put out an entire report in 2021 praising the United States for electing Kamala Harris the first female VP, so it's no mystery where their political bias lies.

On purpose, no one in legacy media bothered to report on who funds the group. Just look at their donors. The *Washington Examiner*'s Robert Schmad quickly discovered:

> The Open Society Institute and the Foundation to Promote Open Society, for instance, gave $1.8 million to the group between 2020 and 2023, according to tax filings. Both of those organizations are part of a network of nonprofit groups funded and controlled by the Soros family. The Soros family has long played a key role in financing both the Democratic Party and the broader progressive movement.[110]

Part of this spending was on Alex's watch.

The Soros machine has been literally attacking Team Trump while they're at it.

---

110   Robert Schmad, "Soros and Liberal Megadonors Behind Nonprofit Group That Added US to Human Rights Watchlist," *The Washington Examiner*, March 11, 2025. https://www.washingtonexaminer.com/news/investigations/3344047/george-soros-megadonors-behind-nonprofit-us-human-rights-watchlist

Leftist activists have taken "direct action" against Elon Musk's assets and the property of anyone owning a product he created. This has ranged from leftists vandalizing Tesla cars, to attacking dealerships and charging stations. The goal was to punish those who own his cars, to discourage sales, and to increase the costs to insure them.

Before Musk's entrance into right-wing politics, his consumer base was more left-leaning. Since then, some have tried to reinvent Passover by putting stickers on their cars reading, "I bought this before I knew he was awful" or "I bought this before I knew he was a Nazi" on them. (The latter would be way funnier on a Volkswagen or a Ford.) Others have decided to protest by selling their Teslas, even though that doesn't change the number of Tesla cars on the road.

As the left's jihad continued, Musk took to X to accuse Soros-funded groups of being behind them. "An investigation has found 5 ActBlue-funded groups responsible for Tesla 'protests': Troublemakers, Disruption Project, Rise & Resist, Indivisible Project and Democratic Socialists of America," Musk wrote.[111]

Naturally, the OSF denied the claims in a statement. "We do not direct, coordinate, or dictate the strategies or activities of the organizations we support.... Our grantees operate independently and are expected to do so in full adherence to U.S. law." The latter statement reveals how they can claim plausible deniability: they can just create standards they know will be broken by the groups they fund, and then once they are violated, they say it doesn't count, because of their standards. You can't give money to an arsonist, tell him not to start fires with it, and then be surprised when he uses it to start fires.

Musk was basing the "Soros-funded" claim on the fact that the five groups causing mayhem have raised money on the Democrat

---

111   https://x.com/elonmusk/status/1898369343399899218

fundraising platform ActBlue, which Soros has contributed to. However, that doesn't mean his money went to any specific groups of the thousands that fundraise there. Nonetheless, one of the five groups he listed, Indivisible Project, has received millions in direct funding from the OSF—to the extent that it's practically a wholly owned subsidiary of OSF itself.

Not only is the heavily Soros-funded Tides Foundation a funding partner of Indivisible Project; as the *New York Post*'s Isabel Vincent uncovered:

> Indivisible Project has been almost entirely financed by Soros's Open Society. It is coordinating a cross-country protest against Musk, empowering "grassroots" affiliates to "stop the Trump-Musk coup," according to its website.
>
> The group took in more than $7.6 million from Open Society between 2017 and 2023. It was originally set up in 2016 to protest the election of Donald Trump.
>
> Indivisible Action's anti-Musk activities include posting a toolkit on its website for a "Musk or US March Recess" demonstration planned for next week during the government's spring break. The toolkit includes graphics for signs reading: "GTFO Musk" and "Fire Elon Musk."[112]

Andrew Padilla, the Indivisible Project's former policy director, used to work for the National Immigration Law Center, which was funded by grants from Soros, and was also a consultant for the Soros-funded UnidosUS.

---

112   Isabel Vincent, "Here Are the Five Radical Leftist Groups Protesting Elon Musk— One of Which Received $7.6m from George Soros," *New York Post*, March 12, 2025. https://nypost.com/2025/03/12/us-news/radical-anti-elon-musk-group-received-7-6m-from-george-soros

George has offered Alex an assist through the radio networks he owns via his hedge fund.

A news station owned by Audacy, the network he purchased under suspicious circumstances, helped unmask the identities of undercover ICE agents in a bid to help illegal aliens and put agents in personal danger.

As Joe Vazquez reported:

> [The Audacy owned] KCBS 740 AM elevated the insane unmasking of ICE agents from the leftist Rapid Response Network, which fights against deportation initiatives during the January 26 edition of KCBS Radio Weekend News.

> But to make matters worse, anchor Bret Burkhart gave exact descriptions of the vehicles the ICE agents were reportedly using, including specific locations. NewsNation confirmed January 27 that the agents were conducting an operation in that area around that time, meaning their cover was potentially blown.[113]

> Even in a supposed political retirement, the "man behind the curtain" remains active.

Soros money played an indirect role in the riots that erupted in June in response to ICE raids in Los Angeles.

The LA-based Coalition for Humane Immigrant Rights (CHIRLA) was a main instigator in the protests, and had received millions of dollars in grants from the State of California, and a $450,000 grant from the Department of Homeland Security

---

113   Joe Vazquez. "BETRAYAL: Soros-Controlled Station Unmasks Vehicles of 'Undercover' ICE Agents in San Jose," *NewsBusters*, January 27, 2025. https://www.newsbusters.org/blogs/business/joseph-vazquez/2025/01/27/betrayal-soros-controlled-station-unmasks-vehicles

to provide "citizenship education and training" under the Biden administration.[114] They also received $500,000 from the Tides Center, which manages the fiscal sponsorship services of the Tides Foundation, in 2023.[115]

The Tides Foundation (a major "pass through" for the OSF) and its associated groups, the Tides Center and Tides Advocacy took $66,438,520 from the OSF from 2016-2023 (the years the OSF has made grants public on their website). Earlier data is harder to track, but Influence Watch totaled $22.4 million to the Tides Foundation specifically from 1998-2018 (they didn't break out the data by year so I couldn't remove 2016-2018).[116]

A more direct role was played in financing the "No Kings" protests against Trump's military parade celebrating the army's 250th birthday too, which occurred as the LA riots were still ongoing. Those protests were organized by the aforementioned Soros-funded Indivisible Project.

---

114   Chris Nesi. "Some LA Migrant Protests Fueled by Taxpayer-funded Group With Dem Ties—Another With CCP Link," *New York Post*, June 8, 2025.https://nypost.com/2025/06/08/us-news/some-la-migrant-protests-fueled-by-taxpayer-funded-group-with-dem-ties-another-with-ccp-link

115   "Tides Center: Full Text of 'Full Filing' for Fiscal Year Ending Dec. 2023." https://projects.propublica.org/nonprofits/organizations/943213100/202412739349300301/full

116   "Tides Foundation," Influence Watch. www.influencewatch.org/non-profit/tides-foundation

Chapter 3

The Soros Agenda on Crime Continues

Alex has continued his father's funding of radical progressive on all fronts: from backing progressive prosecutors who bring crime and destruction across America, to aligning with all other aspects of his father's agenda of social disorder when it comes to promoting anti-police groups like Black Lives Matter and BLM-adjacent groups, or his decades-long mission of promoting drug use wherever he can.

The chapter "George Soros Goes Local" in my book on George, *The Man Behind the Curtain*, quickly became the longest chapter—tragically because that's where he's had the most impact. It's almost become the case again, because even as George Soros-backed prosecutors are being ousted from office, Alex is rushing to replace them.

It was estimated that as of January 2023, before handing off his empire to Alex later that year, George had spent $40 million on getting seventy-five rogue DAs in place. In terms of his return-on-influence, it was the best money he'd ever spent.[1] In local races that attracted scant funding, Soros would drown his preferred candidate in money, virtually guaranteeing victory for them. Contrary to his "coin flip" record in presidential races,

---

1   Matt Palumbo, "George Soros Spent $40m Getting Lefty District Attorneys, Officials Elected All Over the Country," *New York Post*, January 26, 2023. https://nypost.com/2023/01/22/george-soros-spent-40m-getting-lefty-district-attorneys-officials-elected-all-over-the-country

which draw so much money that it's virtually impossible for one person to move the needle, he found he literally could buy elections at the local level. One in five Americans, and half of those living in the nation's most populous cities, were living in an area run by a Soros DA, or one who shared his ideology.

With exceptions in the single digits, the DAs are all cut from the same radical cloth. They regularly make public statements portraying criminals as the "real victims" of their own behavior, opposing cash bail, opposing the death penalty, portraying crimes like shoplifting as being done solely for the purpose of survival and necessity, depicting cops and the concept of enforcing laws as racist, claiming the criminal justice system is inherently racist because it "disproportionately impacts" certain demographic groups (that disproportionately commit crimes). These are among the beliefs of the far-left that guide the decision-making of Soros DAs.

The "before and after" results are the same for virtually all these prosecutors. When they take office, immediately so-called "quality of life" crimes, such as graffiti, panhandling, unlicensed street vending, and various vice offenses are legalized and practically encouraged. In some cities, penalties have been lowered and police have been handcuffed in their ability to enforce the law, which has de facto legalized crimes like shoplifting.

While they are leftist extremists at their core, many of these DAs will use moderate rhetoric when politically convenient, such as portraying their agenda on the campaign trail as simply not wanting to prosecute "victimless crimes," or "not put people in jail for smoking marijuana." After election day, voters quickly get mugged by reality—and criminals. Violent criminals are released without bail, quickly reoffend, and are then given endless "second chances," such as the chance to participate in a "diversion program" that keeps them outside of jail—or, in the "worst case scenario" for the criminal, given a laughably lax plea deal that reduces or even eliminates any meaningful punishment.

The DAs themselves leave no doubt that these policies are out of empathy for the criminal class and disdain for those who contribute productively to society.

Consider the case of Contra Costa County DA Diana Becton, who had never served as prosecutor before and—paving the path for Biden spokesperson Karine Jean-Pierre—read through a binder of statements during the selection process after her predecessor resigned amid scandal. *RedState*'s Jennifer Van Laar obtained a document from Becton's office in August 2020 called "Looting Guidelines," which listed factors for when looting was *acceptable*. One circumstance where looting would be A-OK with her office was if the theft was committed for "personal need," essentially legalizing looting for anyone claiming poverty. The kind of people who would be fine with looting for "personal need" are the same people who are willing to stretch the definition of "personal need" to anything, as long as the looter is from a demographic on the left's preferred "victim" hierarchy.[2]

Writer Auron MacIntyre once brilliantly observed that when it comes to the left's sociopathic behavior, politics is about "rewarding your friends and punishing your enemies"—behavior for which Becton provides a case study.

Among the crimes Becton refused to prosecute were misdemeanors, which included vandalism. But when a white couple was accused of painting over a Black Lives Matter mural, do I even need to tell you that suddenly graffiti became a crime, in this one specific case? The two were hit with three misdemeanor charges, including a hate crime charge, vandalism, and possession of tools to commit vandalism.[3]

---

2   Matt Palumbo, *The Man Behind the Curtain: Inside the Secret Network of George Soros* (New York: Post Hill Press, 2022), pp. 108–109.

3   Ibid., p. 110.

For the progressive prosecutor and their enablers, being "weak on crime" doesn't mean being weak on crime for everyone; it means being weak on crime for whomever the left sees as part of a protected "victim" class, namely: leftists, people of color (except Asians, for some reason), drug users, the homeless, and shoplifters.

As one would expect, whenever DAs with this philosophy have taken power, their elections were, without exception, followed by an explosion in violent crime, sometimes more than doubling homicide rates. In some cases, the data get murky when it comes to property crimes like shoplifting, because the de facto legalization of shoplifting has made it completely pointless for vendors to report crimes to the police. What's the point in calling the police, sometimes waiting hours for them to show up, only to be told each time that there's nothing that can be done? The best-case scenario is for a police report to be filed—and then for nothing to happen.

San Francisco is home of a statistic as insane as its voting habits—a figure that demonstrates just how understated shoplifting is in areas with a Soros DA. The now-former DA Chesa Boudin, a Marxist who had never tried a case before, showed no interest in prosecuting shoplifting. Practically every day on social media a video was going viral showing someone walking into a retailer, packing a garbage bag with stolen products, and then leaving without resistance—or any consequences thereafter.

The evidence for how out of control shoplifting had gotten wasn't just anecdotal. Barely two years after Boudin was sworn in, Walgreens was reporting theft rates *five times the national average* at its San Francisco stores.[4]

---

4   Evan Symon, "5 More Walgreens Closed in San Francisco Over City's Retail Crime Wave," *California Globe*, October 13, 2021. https://californiaglobe.com/fr/5-more-walgreens-closed-in-san-francisco-over-citys-retail-crime-wave

And the true extent of the shoplifting explosion was muted in the statistics by the nonenforcement.

In September 2021, a single Target store in the city started using an automated system to report every single shoplifting incident that month to the San Francisco Police Department. Previously, most incidents went unreported. As a result, *the rate of shoplifting doubled that month...for the entire city*.[5] If a single store reporting 100 percent of its shoplifting incidents can double the rate of shoplifting *in the entire city*, imagine how understated the true rate of shoplifting has been in a city home to over 800,000 people.

Other DAs in the Soros sphere became household names, too. One was Chicago prosecutor Kim Foxx (who was pictured with Alex Soros in 2019 at a fundraiser for weak-on-crime prosecutors).[6] Foxx attempted to help failed actor and musician Jussie Smollett escape legal consequences after he starred in one of the most obviously faked hate crimes of all time. Then there was St. Louis prosecutor Kim Gardner, who persecuted homeowners Mark and Patricia McCloskey after a photo of the couple that went viral; it showed them standing outside their home with firearms after a group of Black Lives Matter protesters broke into their gated community and began threatening them.

It's generally the case that if a local politician has become a household name, they've royally screwed up, and coverage of the worst-of-the-worst Soros Das—like Boudin, Foxx, and Gardner—has sunk many of them.

---

5   Dominick Reuter, "Shoplifting Numbers for All of San Francisco Doubled in September After One Target Location Changed the Method It Uses to Report the Crime," *Business Insider*, December 1, 2021. https://www.businessinsider.com/san-francisco-shoplifting-numbers-doubled-after-store-changed-reporting-method-2021-12

6   https://www.facebook.com/photo/?fbid=1201089130053434

George-backed prosecutor Marilyn Mosby lost in the Democrat primary for State's Attorney of Baltimore and was later sentenced to a year of house arrest for perjury and mortgage fraud convictions. Foxx decided against running for reelection after her defense of Smollett, a national laughingstock, made her one, too. Gardner resigned after Missouri's AG moved to have her forcibly removed.

One DA was too crazy even for San Francisco (the nation's finest minds still trying to figure out to this day how that's possible). Chesa Boudin was recalled in 2022 with 55 percent voting in favor of his removal—this in a city where Trump got under 13 percent of the vote. Making the matters more humiliating for Boudin, George Soros tried to escape embarrassment by denying he had ever funded Boudin. After the conservative publication *The Post Millennial* reported on Boudin getting crushed, they received an email requesting a correction. The email read, "I am a representative of Justice & Public Safety PAC, the political action committee primarily funded by George Soros. Mr. Soros has not—*directly or indirectly*—backed or supported or contributed to Mr. Boudin."

The representative then included a link to an incomplete list of prosecutors or DAs that Soros has directly or indirectly supported from the website *Influence Watch*, noting that Mr. Boudin isn't on the (incomplete) list. *Influence Watch* is owned and operated by the Capital Research Center, which has described Boudin as among those that have "benefitted indirectly from Soros's contributions to organizations that opposed his recall," and pointed out that Soros and his allies were trying to obfuscate the flow of money.[7]

---

7   Parker Thayer, "Rise of the Soros 'Prosecutors,'" *Organization Trends, Capital Research Center,* June 13, 2022. https://capitalresearch.org/article/rise-of-the-soros-prosecutors

George's funding isn't always direct, and he often deploys his cash through a tangled web to give himself plausible deniability—such as through the Tides Center, Fair and Just Prosecution, the Brennan Center, Safety and Justice, and the Vera Institute for Justice (from which Boudin received $620k in backing).[8]

Furthermore, internal communications that the Media Research Center obtained through FOIA requests showed that Boudin had 508 communications ("defined as emails, virtual meetings, in-person meetings, conversations, etc.") with the Soros-backed Fair and Just Prosecution organization in an eighteen-month period.[9] Three other Soros-backed DAs sit on the board of Fair and Just Prosecution.

Given what it takes to be too crazy even for San Francisco, it's not hard to see why Soros would try to save face.

Boudin personally blamed Republicans, practically an endangered species in San Francisco, for his ouster. Racism was also blamed, but that accusation is practically a formality in progressive politics.

It didn't end there.

Overall, from 2022–2024, at least twenty-one George Soros-backed DAs were ousted and replaced by prosecutors that the Law Enforcement Legal Defense Fund rates as "tough on crime,"[10]

---

8   "Justice for Sale: How George Soros Put Radical Prosecutors in Power," Law Enforcement Legal Defense Fund, June 2022. https://www.scribd.com/document/577278421/Justice-for-Sale-LELDF-Report

9   Tim Kilcullen, Joseph Vazquez, Tom Olohan, and Dan Schneider. Law & Disorder: How the Soros Machine Directs & Controls Prosecutors Across America to Implement His Leftist Agenda, MRC Special Report (Washington, DC: Media Research Center, 2024). https://cdn.mrc.org/static/pdfuploads/Soros+Report_FINAL_PAGES.pdf-1723215421233.pdf

10   Ray Lewis, "21 Soros-linked DAs Replaced by 'Tough-on-crime' Prosecutors Since 2022, Report Finds," CBS Austin, December 3, 2024. https://cbsaustin.com/news/nation-world/21-soros-linked-das-replaced-by-tough-on-crime-prosecutors-since-2022-report-finds-the-law-enforcement-legal-defense-fund-district-attorney-kim-foxx-marilyn-mosby-george-gascon

and twenty-seven were removed from office in some manner or weren't running for reelection.[11]

Overall, 126 Soros backed prosecutors have held office at some point, according to the most recent list from the Media Research Center. Prior estimates were lower because they identified dozens of Soros-backed prosecutors from the early 2000s that had gone under the radar.

The backing of some of the craziest prosecutors came as George was funding chaos during the George Floyd racial hysteria of 2020. The OSF exploited the "racial justice" narrative, helping it go global by directing $220 million towards that goal seven weeks after Floyd's death in police custody while overdosing on fentanyl. Alex endorsed the move, declaring: "This is the time for urgent and bold action to address racial injustice in America. These investments will empower proven leaders in the Black community to reimagine policing, end mass incarceration, and eliminate the barriers to opportunity that have been the source of inequity for too long."[12]

The "fact checkers" were quick to rally to the Soros's defense, assuring their readers that this in no way meant they were funding the chaos. "They had never given money to groups for the express purpose of organizing protests with the movement," wrote *PolitiFact*, as if OSF were ever going to write "wreak havoc" as a line item.[13]

---

11   "Law & Disorder," Media Research Center.
12   "Open Society Foundations Announce $220 Million for Building Power in Black Communities," press release, Open Society Foundations, July 13, 2020. https://www.opensocietyfoundations.org/newsroom/open-society-foundations-announce-220-million-for-building-power-in-black-communities
13   Emily Venezky, "No, George Soros and his foundations do not pay people to protest," *PolitiFact*, June 1, 2020. https://www.politifact.com/factchecks/2020/jun/01/candace-owens/no-soros-and-foundation-do-not-pay-people-to-protest

ALEX TAKES OVER THE GEORGE SOROS AGENDA ON CRIME
Alex was already funding similar activism on his own accord.

The Alex Soros Foundation has given nearly $1.5 million between 2015–2021 to a defund-the-police group called Make the Road New York, a sum equal to nearly a fifth of all their total operation expenditures. Alex celebrated them as a "fantastic" group "making a positive impact." The group used Floyd's death to push for defunding the NYPD and taking police out of schools. They complained that then-Mayor Bill DeBlasio's plan to cut $1 billion from the NYPD's budget wasn't enough. At this time, Alex was tweeting about the need for "real police reform and racial justice."[14] "Real" reform meant defunding.

The 2020 riots were the most expensive on record in the nation, costing $2 billion according to insurance claims—which are major underestimates because 40 percent of small businesses have no insurance, and of those that do, 75 percent are underinsured.[15] At least twenty-five people were killed during the summer of chaos,[16] a number greater than the number of unarmed black people killed by police that year.

The OSF had previously funneled $33 million to far-left groups that wreaked mayhem in Ferguson, Missouri, in 2015, as part of the Michael Brown riots that followed a justified police shooting.

---

14   Joe Vazquez and Tom Olohan, "Meet the New Boss," Media Research Center, 2023. https://cdn.mrc.org/static/pdfuploads/Soros+Printed+Digital+Report_FINAL. pdf-1699558535143.pdf

15   Brad Polumbo, "George Floyd Riots Caused Record-Setting $2 Billion in Damage, New Report Says. Here's Why the True Cost Is Even Higher," Foundation for Economic Education, September 16, 2020. https://fee.org/articles/george-floyd-riots-caused-record-setting-2-billion-in-damage-new-report-says-here-s-why-the-true-cost-is-even-higher

16   Lois Beckett, "At Least 25 Americans Were Killed During Protests and Political Unrest in 2020," The Guardian, October 31, 2020. https://www.theguardian.com/world/2020/oct/31/americans-killed-protests-political-unrest-acled

Both the Mike Brown and George Floyd riots had a national impact in changing how police respond to black offenders. There was talk in the media of a "Mike Brown Effect" or "Ferguson Effect" in 2014—that police might stop policing as aggressively in fear that they'd have to use lethal force, and then become the subjects of a national Two Minutes Hate. There was an increase in crime in America's cities post-Mike Brown, yet it would look like a blip compared to the George Floyd Effect, which was amplified by the Soros-backed prosecutors who enabled it and cheered on the carnage.

The cultural shift pushed by these sorts of prosecutors, and their enablers in the liberal (and often Soros-linked) media, was particularly pronounced concerning patterns of policing caricatured with stereotypes—such as the widespread belief that there's a "driving while black" phenomenon. While driving fatalities per mile driven by race have been relatively similar ever since statistics have been collected, police really did start relaxing traffic enforcement on black drivers in the post-Floyd years. This Floyd Effect of inhibiting police also led to a general decline in law enforcement in urban centers. The result was an explosion in auto fatalities and homicides among blacks.

If we compare the first forty-three months of the Floyd Effect (June 2020 to December 2023) to the same time frame a decade prior (June 2010 to December 2013, so that the Michael Brown effect isn't included in this comparison), we find that total motor vehicle deaths were up 9 percent among whites during the Floyd Effect period—but soared nearly 80 percent among blacks.[17] For decades prior to this period, whites often had a slightly higher per capita car accident death rate than blacks, but that ended in June 2020 and has never reversed.

---

17   Steve Sailer, "The Fast and the Curious," *Taki's Magazine*, July 31, 2024. https://www.takimag.com/article/the-fast-and-the-curious

CDC: Motor Vehicle Accident Death Rate by Month
Notice impact of Ferguson Effect (2015-17) and Floyd Effect (2020-2023)

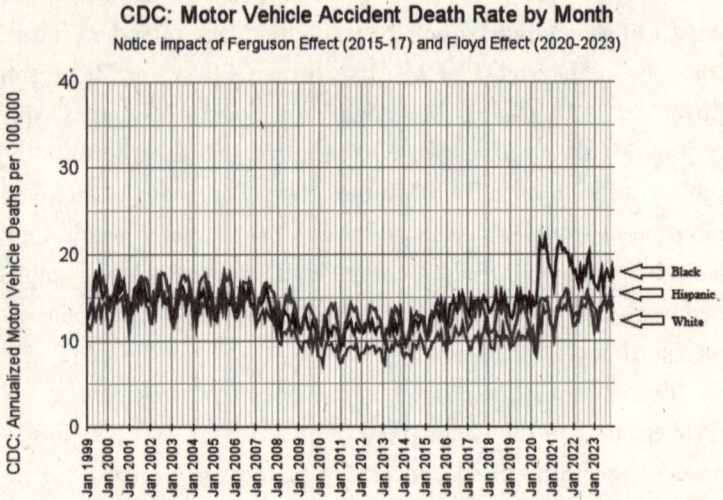

Copyright © 2025 Steve Sailer

In the two charts, compare the CDC death counts for black homicides and motor vehicle accidents for 2020–2022 with the corresponding counts from 2018–19. If the previous lower rates had been maintained, we can estimate an additional 36,042 blacks died due to the Floyd Effect, which inhibited policing. As Steve Sailer quantifies it: "It's very similar to American deaths in the Korean War of 36,516, and more than five times the total deaths in the Iraq and Afghanistan Wars combined."

CDC: Homicide Victimization Rate by Month: 1999-2023

Notice impact of 9/11, Ferguson Effect (2015-17), and Floyd Effect (2020-23)

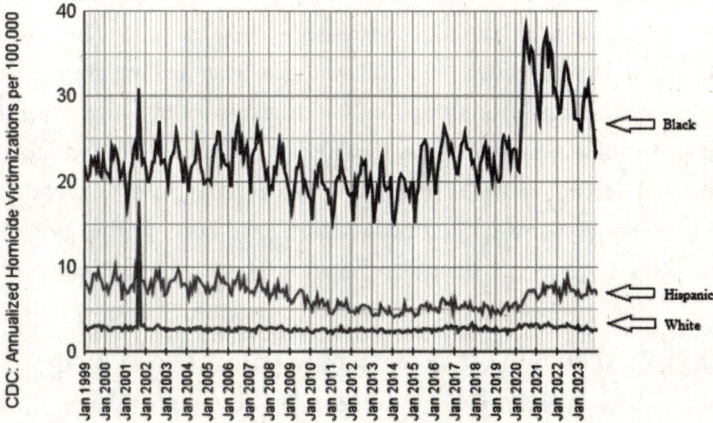

CDC: Annualized Homicide Victimizations per 100,000

Black

Hispanic

White

Copyright © 2025 Steve Sailer

It was a high price to pay to attempt to reduce police killings of unarmed blacks, of which there were 135 from 2015–2020. Given the average rates of auto and homicide deaths of blacks over that time frame, it would take 1335 years of zero police killings of unarmed blacks just to make up for the increases in death caused by de-policing for just two years.

Don't expect any social justice warrior to learn their lesson from this, of course. A report in Harvard's School of Public Health headlined "Racial Disparities in Traffic Fatalities Much Wider Than Previously Known" overlooks it being "wider than previously known" because it's a new phenomenon. Instead, inevitably, the report blames it on "structural racism within the US transportation system."[18]

---

18 "Racial Disparities in Traffic Fatalities Much Wider Than Previously Known," Harvard T.H. Chan School of Public Health, June 9, 2022. https://hsph.harvard.edu/news/racial-disparities-traffic-fatalities

As always, the hammer finds its nail.

The funding of rogue DAs is the ultimate test for Alex to prove that he's different from his father—and it's a test he failed.

In addition to helping fundraise for these sorts of DAs, Alex took over Democracy PAC in 2022 and has been fielding even more rogue prosecutors ever since. By 2025, the Soros family investment in progressive prosecutors had ballooned to nearly $118 million, with 30 percent of the country now living under a Soros prosecutor.[19] George Soros-backed prosecutors have been getting ousted, but Alex is replacing them—and they're more extreme than ever.

(ALEX) SOROS DA TAKES DOWN (GEORGE) SOROS DA

Not only is Alex ramping up the spending to replace the ones that have been ousted, but he's also running new candidates against candidates formally funded by his father that haven't turned out crazy enough—of which there only seems to be one so far.

There's no better illustration than in the 2024 Harris County, Texas, district attorney race, where a showdown between old Soros money and new Soros money showed that Alex is a force to be reckoned with.

The candidate Alex backed is Sean Teare, who received over $2 million from him.[20] Even with the major financial edge, Teare barely squeaked out a victory, defeating his Republican opponent 50.8 percent to 49.2 percent.[21]

But the Republican opponent wasn't the main target of Alex's money—it was the formally George-funded incumbent, Kim Ogg, in the Democrat primary.

---

19   "Law & Disorder," Media Research Center.

20   Amelia McKenzie, "George Soros Funds Harris County District Attorney Challenge," *Texas Scorecard*, March 4, 2024. https://texasscorecard.com/local/george-soros-funds-harris-county-district-attorney-challenger

21   "Sean Teare." *Ballotpedia*. https://ballotpedia.org/Sean_Teare

Teare easily defeated Ogg, who was Soros-funded to the tune of $500,000 in 2016. The primary was a blowout election for Teare, and surprisingly, in a singular rarity for a Soros DA, Ogg had drawn the ire from leftists and local Democrats for *not* pushing a lenient-enough criminal justice reform agenda.[22]

Initially Ogg had seemed on board. She declared herself part of the "national reform movement" and dropped nearly 1,800 charges against 654 protesters during the George Floyd riots. But leftists whined that she didn't apologize for the rioters being charged in the first place. This gave her an early wakeup call as to the kind of insufferable leftists her progressive policies had to placate. Early on, she implemented other soft-on-crime policies, such as increasing the number of violent offenders released on personal recognizance bonds. Not surprisingly, this was followed by an increase in crime.

But unlike other Soros DAs, she didn't deny or rationalize the rise in crime. Instead, she reversed course, turning against soft-on-crime policies and the bail reform movement, a key Soros priority. Teare slammed Ogg for breaking her campaign promises to decriminalize drug possession, and he called for more "second chance" programs, which Ogg didn't create because they always turn into "third chance" and "fourth chance" and fifth chance" (ad infinitum) programs.

Of the many Soros DAs I covered in *The Man Behind the Curtain*, Ogg's section was the shortest in length. She had notably never made any comments demeaning towards police, expressed empathy with criminals, or claimed that racism was responsible for so-called inequities in the criminal justice system. There was

---

22   Holly Hansen, "Harris County District Attorney Kim Ogg Ousted by Democratic Challenger Sean Teare," *The Texan,* March 6, 2024. https://thetexan.news/elections/2024/harris-county-district-attorney-kim-ogg-ousted-by-democratic-challenger-sean-teare/article_e3e52b10-dbd9-11ee-a665-4ba292a96605.html

no "burn down the system" rhetoric. This was a key difference between Ogg and the other DAs that George funded: the others had long histories of making truly insane public statements, and George was investing in them to continue behaving the same way they always did. Ogg was a bet on the corrupting power of money.

It was just a few months after my manuscript headed to the publisher that Ogg blasted bail reform for the first time, which Teare used as a point of attack.[23] In turn, somewhat ironically, Ogg blasted Teare for being Soros-funded (which she no longer was).[24] But for the Democrats voting in the Harris County primary, being Soros-funded was a plus, and Teare handily defeated Ogg with 75 percent of the vote.

Whatever relationship Ogg ever had with George was short-lived, and that experience set something off in her to the point where she was seeking revenge on his other picks while in office. Ogg opened a corruption investigation into the Soros-funded Harris County Judge Lina Hidalgo, a move that was among the reasons she was admonished by the local Democratic Party, and primaried amid allegations she wasn't liberal enough.

Ogg has since spoken out to encourage voters in the Greater Houston area to support Republican judges, and she put the Democratic Party on blast for "intentionally allowing crime to increase," despite being a Democrat herself. She's in a better position than anyone to know, because they tried to pay her off to do just that. It's shocking to see a politician do the right thing for

---

23   "Houston Prosecutor Kim Ogg Unloads on Bail Reform, Supported Legislative Move to Tighten Down on Release on Free Personal Bonds," American Bail Coalition, October 5, 2021. https://ambailcoalition.org/houston-prosecutor-kim-ogg-unloads-on-bail-reform-supported-legislative-move-to-tighten-down-on-release-on-free-personal-bonds

24   Andrew Schneider, "Kim Ogg, Attacking Sean Teare for Accepting Donations from George Soros, Took Donations from Soros in 2016," *Houston Public Media*, March 1, 2024. https://www.houstonpublicmedia.org/articles/news/politics/election-2024/2024/03/01/479391/kim-ogg-attacking-sean-teare-for-accepting-donations-from-george-soros-took-donations-from-soros-in-2016

a change, but Ogg was different from other Soros DAs in that she didn't ever echo the fanatical rhetoric you usually hear from them. She just gave the policies a try, discovered they didn't work, and realized she'd been fooled at the expense of her community.

Her replacement is already off to a bumpy start.

There were early signs after Teare's victory that he wasn't going to be the most competent man for the role; namely, that his law license had been suspended the day before he was sworn in, because he didn't pay a required fee to the State Bar of Texas. He was in office for nearly a week without a license before it was retroactively reinstated.[25]

Only weeks into his tenure, Teare was already going on an apology tour after a campus rape suspect who elbowed a cop in the head was back on the streets less than twenty-four hours after the attack. He blamed a "broken system" for the ordeal, which is true—just not for the reason he thinks.[26]

MARY MORIARTY, THE QUEEN OF CRAZY

Alex sure knows how to pick them.

Mary Moriarty was previously chief public defender in Hennepin County, Minnesota—a position from which she was suspended and ousted from in 2019 by the Board of Public Defenders in 2019. Then she ran for Hennepin County DA in 2022 with Alex's backing and was sworn in 2023. Nonetheless, as chief prosecutor she still played the role of public defender.

---

25 Clare Amari, "Harris County DA Sean Teare's Law License Reinstated After Brief Administrative Suspension," *Houston Landing,* January 6, 2025. https://houstonlanding.org/harris-county-da-sean-teares-law-license-reinstated-after-brief-administrative-suspension

26 "Harris County DA Blames Broken System for Mistakes That Led to Release of UH Sexual Assault Suspect," KHOU-11, February 14, 2025. https://www.khou.com/article/news/crime/rape-suspect-released-university-of-houston-parking-garage/285-d4244fa2-2dad-4edb-a4f6-e94ecf7a0cb3

Months into her term, she gave an assist to two teens charged as adults with murder (before she took office) for the slaying of a woman in her apartment after they invaded her home. Moriarty entered a plea that would result in the duo being confined for two years and released on their twenty-first birthdays, just in time for them to be able to legally purchase a drink to celebrate getting away with murder. So egregious was the move that Governor Tim Walz intervened to have the state's Attorney General Keith Ellison take over the case.[27]

You read that right; her judgment is so bad that Tim Walz and the George Soros-funded Minnesota AG Keith Ellison are the good guys in this situation. Though, to be fair, the bar here is so low that it's set at: "opposes setting murderers free." Don't forget that both egged on the 2020 riots and excused the carnage during that moment of national racial psychosis.

Another case where a crime was committed before Moriarty was in office involved two teenagers who confessed to murdering a man sitting in his car during a carjacking attempt in 2019. One of the teens was sentenced to twenty-two years in an adult court, and the Minnesota Supreme Court ruled in November 2022 that the other, Husayn Braveheart, should be certified for trial as an adult. Yet after Moriarty took office, she entered into a plea agreement where Braveheart would serve just one year of confinement and five years of probation, arguing that he had "changed" during his four years of pre-trial custody. That was false, and in their reasoning for why he should be charged as an adult, the Minnesota Supreme Court had even cited Braveheart's failure to "participate in programing and other therapy," or complete a single treatment program. A psychologist's report cited

---

27   David Zimmer, "Mary Moriarty's Consistently Poor Judgment," Center of the American Experiment, August 11, 2023. https://www.americanexperiment.org/mary-moriartys-consistently-poor-judgement

in that ruling said Braveheart "is at high risk for future violence, including serious violence"—and for good reason. When he participated in a "Bar None" rehab program in custody, he fled and committed another felony.[28]

None of that mattered to Moriarty.

Braveheart was sentenced to time served in December 2023, setting him free, and by September 2024 he was charged once again, this time with fleeing police.[29]

Among Moriarty's other worst hits include dropping charges her first week in office against a thirty-five-year-old man accused of raping a teen girl;[30] refusing to charge a teen accused of causing a crash that killed a teen girl, and who, days later, was charged for a violent stabbing;[31] and petitioning for the release of a man convicted of first-degree murder in 1995, which was successful.[32]

If this is who Moriarty sees are worth of "second chances," who is it that she does prosecute?

As with the case with Diana Becton, the incompetent George Soros DA who wouldn't prosecute vandals unless they defaced a Black Lives Matter mural, Moriarty is much more sympathetic to prosecuting those who haven't done anything wrong, so long as they're from a group the left has disdain for, such as the police.

---

28   Ibid.

29   "Husayn Braveheart Charged with Fleeing Police in Eagan," FOX 9, September 14, 2024. https://www.fox9.com/news/husayn-braveheart-charged-fleeing-police-eagan

30   Olivia Land, "Fury as Minneapolis' 'Woke' DA Mary Moriarty Allows Accused Rapists and Killers to Stay Free—Too Much Even for Soros-backed AG," *New York Post*, October 3, 2023. https://nypost.com/2023/10/03/minneapolis-woke-da-draws-criticism-from-families-soros-ally

31   Alexa Cimino, "Feral Teen Freed by America's 'Wokest Prosecutor' Commits Another 'Horrific Act' After Killing Girl in Crash," *The Daily Mail*, March 4, 2025. https://www.dailymail.co.uk/news/article-14460089/feral-teen-freed-Americas-wokest-prosecutor-commits-horrific-act-killing-girl-crash.html

32   Casey Marble, "Man Serving Life Sentence to Be Released After Hennepin County Judge Uses New Sentence Adjustment Process," 5ABC KSTP, March 3, 2025. https://kstp.com/kstp-news/local-news/man-serving-life-sentence-to-be-released-after-hennepin-county-judge-uses-new-sentence-adjustment-process

Moriarty charged trooper Ryan Londregan with second-degree unintentional murder, first-degree assault, and second-degree manslaughter for fatally shooting Ricky Cobb II during a traffic stop. During that traffic stop, it was discovered that Cobb was wanted for violating a no contact order, leading to Cobb trying to speed off while one officer was partially inside the car. Londregan fired twice as Cobb took off, killing him.

Moriarty dismissed the analysis from a use-of-force expert, who found that Londregan acted reasonably, and as a result the officer faced allegations of misconduct from the Minnesota Police and Peace Officers Association.

After a lengthy saga, Moriarty ended up dismissing the charges, but only because Walz was again going to intervene to remove her from the prosecution.[33]

As has been made evident, the law under Moriarty is whatever she wants to be to serve her political interests, especially when it comes to politics.

After a Minnesota state employee for their Department of Human Services was allegedly caught committing $20,000+ worth of vandalism to Tesla vehicles in April, Moriarty refused to file charges, and the suspect was instead entered into a "diversion program." This breaks the rules of her own office, which states that diversion programs are for property crimes of $5,000 or less.[34]

The vandalism came amid a left-wing campaign against Elon Musk and his influence within the White House.

---

33   Andy Mannix, Rochelle Olson, and Liz Sawyer, "Gov. Walz Planned to Remove Moriarty from Trooper Prosecution, Fueling Speculation Over Dismissal," *The Minnesota Star Tribune*, June 3, 2024. https://www.startribune.com/walz-said-he-planned-to-remove-moriarty-from-state-trooper-murder-prosecution/600370692

34   Germania Rodriguez Poleo. "America's Wokest DA Breaks Her Own Rules To Let Tim Walz Worker Who Keyed Six Teslas Off The Hook," *Daily Mail*, April 24, 2025. https://www.dailymail.co.uk/news/article-14644541/americas-wokest-da-scandal-tim-walz-teslas-mary-moriarty.html

She tried to hedge the narrative to get ahead of accusations of political bias and argued that if people see this as politically motivated it's only because they are choosing to. "We try to make decisions without really looking at the political consequences. Can we always predict how a story will be portrayed in the media or what people will say? No," she "explained."[35]

It's as if she was mocking us all to our faces; a mere *two days* prior Moriarty's office charged a nineteen-year-old woman with no criminal record with first-degree felony property damage after she allegedly keyed her coworker's car at a White Castle, with damages estimated at $7,000.

When asked by a reporter how she could balance that charging decision with the decision to not charge the Tesla vandal, Moriarty sidestepped the question and nonsensically said her office's main goal is to hold "the person accountable for keying the car, get restitution to the people affected, and avoid felony convictions when possible, because it can waylay someone's life."[36]

It was a complicated way to avoid saying the obvious; that had the nineteen-year-old decided to vandalize Teslas for political purposes instead of her co-workers' car, she wouldn't have been charged. As was the case with the aforementioned Diana Becton selectively enforcing laws against vandalism only when it offended her political sensibilities, the tyranny of the woke DA also comes in the form of unequal enforcement of the law.

After the Trump administration began cracking down on the tentacles of DEI wherever they exist, Moriarty officially brought DEI to plea deals to the table (though she was already doing that in practice, and this just made it official).

---

35   Ibid.
36   Jeff Day. "In Diverting Tesla Vandalism Charges, Mary Moriarty Again Finds Herself At The Center Of A Firestorm," *The Minnesota Star Tribune*, April 23, 2025. https://www.startribune.com/in-declining-tesla-vandalism-charges-mary-moriarty-again-finds-herself-at-the-center-of-a-firestorm/601337388

She issued a directive reading that:

While racial identity and age are not appropriate grounds for departures [from the Minnesota Sentencing Guidelines], proposed resolutions should consider the person charged as a whole person, including their racial identity and age. While these factors should not be controlling, they should be part of the overall analysis. Prosecutors should be identifying and addressing racial disparities at decision points, as appropriate.[37]

A spokesperson for Moriarty's office defended the directive on the basis that a defendant's race matters because of "unconscious biases" leading to "racial disparities." If there is any racial bias in our legal system nowadays, thanks to their own actions it isn't in the direction that the left believes it to be.

BRIAN SCHWALB TARGETS THE RIGHT'S NETWORKS WHILE DEFENDING SOROS'S

Schwalb won the 2022 DC Attorney General election and took office in January 2023 with Alex's backing.

His first year in office, he began investigating the political funding networks of Leonard Leo, a conservative activist who has created many influential conservative legal groups, all of which are registered in other states.

In an attempt to avoid the obvious perception of political targeting, Schwalb also opened a show investigation into Arabella Advisors, which the Soros network often funnels money through.

It wasn't until he faced allegations of politically targeting opponents from many, including the *Wall Street Journal* edito-

---

37   Matthew Xiao. "Prosecutors in Minnesota's Largest County Must Now Consider 'Racial Identity' in Plea Deals," *The Washington Free Beacon*, April 28, 2025. https://freebeacon.com/latest-news/far-left-prosecutor-mandates-that-attorneys-consider-racial-identity-in-plea-deals

rial board, that he opened the Arabella Advisors investigation. In other words, it's one he only opened due to the optics of only investigating a conservative network.

The investigation into Leo came after a complaint from the left-wing group Campaign for Accountability, which alleged he profited from consulting fees through his network. Critics of the investigation pointed out that Arabella's fee structure is similar.[38]

Campaign for Accountability, which kicked off the investigation into Leo, itself started as a project in the Arabella Advisors network.

Before winning the AG spot, Schwalb worked for a law firm that has performed work for companies in Arabella's sphere. To the surprise of no one, the investigation into Arabella Advisors would close in April 2024 with no charges filed, as was always going to be the case.[39] As of writing, the Leo investigation preceding it goes on.

While tough on political opponents, Schwalb is weak on actual criminals. When it comes to young criminals specifically (which is most criminals), he has taken a "let kids be kids" approach, which means: "let kids be criminals."

In June 2023, his office dropped charges against an eleven-year-old boy accused of assault and robberies—only for the child to be arrested again immediately for armed robbery. In another case, a fifteen-year-old carjacker's charges were dropped, enraging even the teen's own foster parents. According to police data, 88 percent of carjacking arrests in early 2024 involved the minors that Schwalb refuses to hold accountable.

38   Joe Schoffstall, "DC Prosecutors Probe Liberal Dark Money Network After Backlash for Investigating Conservative Orgs," Fox News, October 5, 2023. https://www.foxnews.com/politics/dc-prosecutors-probe-liberal-dark-money-network-backlash-investigating-conservative-orgs

39   Joseph Simonson, "DC Attorney General Will Not Bring Charges Against Left-Wing Dark Money Group," Washington Free Beacon, April 9, 2024. https://freebeacon.com/democrats/dc-attorney-general-will-not-bring-charges-against-left-wing-dark-money-group

Overall, in 2023, violent crime rose 39 percent and motor vehicle theft surged 82 percent in DC. In the face of this, Schwalb kept doubling down on the same failed policies that caused it in the first place.

Schwalb has also opposed legislation that would've increased penalties and detention for criminals, specifically when it comes to juveniles. He publicly opposed Mayor Muriel Bowser's so-called "tough on crime" bill, which ultimately just undid some of the weak-on-crime policies she herself implemented during the George Floyd-era racial hysteria.

In response to skyrocketing crime, Schwalb summarized his whole backward philosophy in a single sentence: "We cannot prosecute and arrest our way out of it."[40]

In reality, it's the only solution.

OTHER DISHONORABLE MENTIONS

In November 2023, Anthony Parisi became the first Democrat elected in Dutchess County, New York, in forty years.[41]

While serving as assistant DA, he aligned himself with the anti-law enforcement Working Families Party (WFP). The WFP is a minor left-wing party with representation only in the Philadelphia City Council, but it has influence in New York politics in boosting candidates running as Democrats. WFP supports defunding police. Parisi also appeared on the WFP ballot line (meaning one could vote for him as either a Democrat or WFP, and both would count toward him). To appear on the WFP line, Parisi had to

40   Aubrie Spady and Cameron Cawthorne, "DC AG Infuriates Residents After Saying City 'Cannot Prosecute and Arrest' Out of Crime Crisis: 'Madness,'" Fox News, February 1, 2024. https://www.foxnews.com/politics/dc-ag-residents-city-cannot-prosecute-arrest-crime-crisis-madness

41   Emily Saul, "Anthony Parisi Becomes First Democrat Elected to Dutchess County DA in Decades," Law.com, November 8, 2023. https://www.law.com/newyorklawjournal/2023/11/08/anthony-parisi-becomes-first-democrat-elected-to-dutchess-county-da-in-decades

fill out a pledge that included committing to no rollbacks of bail reforms and refusing donations from law enforcement organizations.[42] (A more detailed examination of the WFP's "transformative" agenda is in the final chapter of this book.)

Then there are your standard social justice warriors. Chris Liberati-Conant won Columbia County, New York, DA in November 2023. Among his priorities before taking office has included complaining about New York's Mental Hygiene Law, which concerns the administration of mental health services and substance use treatment. His beef? That the name term belittles the mentally ill. In a nearly 2,400-word paper with fifty-seven citations, Liberati-Conant links the term "mental hygiene," a synonym for "mental health," to eugenics and sterilization movements.[43]

Bear in mind, this is the sanest Alex DA thus far.

Liberati-Conant supports Alex's position on reproductive rights more than on crime, as when he was an Assistant Attorney General, he protected New York's 2019 Reproductive Health Act, guaranteeing abortion rights across the state.[44] So this pick seems to have more to do with abortion laws than crime.

As for Alex's anti-Trump agenda, New Mexico AG Raúl Torrez has given him an assist in his battles against the president. In February 2025, Torrez boarded the left's "I didn't vote for Elon Musk" bandwagon. He joined attorneys from thirteen other states in filing a lawsuit challenging the "unlawful delegation of executive power to Elon Musk," claiming that his Department of Government Efficiency (DOGE) is illegal and seeking a restrain-

42   "New York State Young Republicans: Parisi Unfit to Serve as Dutchess County District Attorney," NYSYR, November 2, 2023. https://nysyr.com/2023/11/02/new-york-state-young-republicans-parisi-unfit-to-serve-as-dutchess-county-executive

43   Chris Liberati-Conant, "It's Time to Take 'Hygiene' out of the Mental Hygiene Law," NYSBA, December 9, 2022. https://nysba.org/its-time-to-take-hygiene-out-of-the-mental-hygiene-law

44   "About Chris Liberati-Conant." https://www.chris4da.com/about

ing order to ban DOGE from exercising any governmental authority. The restraining order request was so absurd that the infamously anti-Trump judge Tanya Sue Chutkan, who would've presided over Trump's January 6 trial had he not been reelected, rejected it days later.[45]

Steve Mulroy was sworn in August 2022 and was the first Democrat to hold the Shelby County, Tennessee DA position in decades. He campaigned on bail reform, "restorative justice" (not punishing criminals), and expanding juvenile court jurisdiction to age twenty-five, to help grown men be treated like kids, among other policies.

"We need to move to a system where...the presumption is in favor of pretrial release," he said of bail.[46]

Memphis, not known for being safe in the first place, reached its highest number of homicides on record during Mulroy's first full year in office, up 42 percent from the year prior.[47] Undeterred, in 2024 Mulroy announced he'd pursue a "diversion" program for felons charged with illegal possessions of a firearm—but dropped it amid threats from Tennessee's House speaker and attorney general to have him removed from office.[48]

In January 2025, the Tennessee Senate has passed a resolution to form a joint committee that would consider removing Mulroy from office, and by March Tennessee Republicans were looking to have the Supreme Court remove him from office.

45　Julie Goldberg, "Judge Rejects NM Bid for DOGE Restraining Order," *Source NM*, February 18, 2025. https://sourcenm.com/briefs/judge-rejects-nm-bid-for-doge-restraining-order

46　Lisa Bennatan and Matt Leach, "Memphis' District Attorney Will Push Bail Reform Despite Critics Blaming It for Crime Increases," Fox News, September 25, 2022. https://www.foxnews.com/politics/memphis-district-attorney-push-bail-reform-despite-critics-blaming-crime-increases

47　Tavarious Haywood, "Memphis Has Broken Homicide Record, New Numbers Show," *K8 News*, November 20, 2023. https://www.kait8.com/2023/11/21/memphis-has-broken-homicide-record-new-numbers-show

48　Lucas Finton, "Shelby County DA Drops Plans for Diversion Program After Threats to Remove Him from Office," *Memphis Commercial Appeal*, June 17, 2024. https://www.aol.com/shelby-county-da-drops-plans-190503185.html

CRIME DAMAGE CONTROL

In one attempt at damage control following growing awareness of his father (and now his) degradation of law and order in America, in 2023 Alex shared an article on his social media by writer Mike Males titled, "Where Are Murder Rates Actually Higher? Not in Progressive Cities."

The factual basis of the article aside (of which there is none), it shows that Alex is on the record being ideologically committed to his father's policies, as if the evidence presented before this wasn't enough.

The article hardly lives up to the title and begins by arguing that red states are more violent than blue states. As Alex is clearly aware due to his father's funding of progressive DAs, crime is a highly localized issue.

As one writer put it: "I hate to use the term brilliance with Soros, but one of the brilliant things he realized is that when you want to get policy reform done with law and order and in this case, degrading it, going through a DA is so efficient because you don't have to go through a state legislature or go through a mayor to get something done."[49]

Within red states, crime is overwhelmingly concentrated in blue cities, so comparing crime at the state level makes no sense. The crime in "violent" red states like Missouri is in St. Louis, and it's a common trend whether it's Tennessee (with Memphis responsible) being criticized, or Louisiana (thanks to New Orleans and Baton Rouge), among others.

The rest of Males's analysis is a handful of cherrypicked statistics to distract us away from the fact that the overwhelming majority of carnage in this country is in blue cities. For example,

---

49   Me on *Fox & Friends First*, January 24, 2023. Watch here: https://www.foxnews.com/media/george-soros-funded-das-represent-20-americans-40m-funneled-races-report-finds

he claims that among white people specifically, the murder rate is rising faster in rural red areas than urban blue ones. He doesn't provide any actual figures, just a rate of change.

Because rural red areas have lower homicide rates to begin with, an increase will be larger as a percentage increase compared to a blue area that's already more violent. To review basic math: if a safe city goes from having a murder rate of one per 100,000 residents to two per 100,000, its murder rate increased 100 percent. If a murder rate in a dangerous city rises from twenty per 100,000 to thirty per 100,000, it increased 50 percent.

That's one of the reasons he singles out white people for this kind of criticism. Of any major ethnic group in America (composing over 10 percent of the population), whites have the lowest homicide rates, so any increase in the rate will appear larger proportionally.[50] But this allows Males to attempt damage control while portraying the only ethnic group that has voted majority Republican in every presidential election in the twenty-first century as the "real culprit" for the disaster that progressive policies caused.

Similarly torturing the statistics, Males claims that there are ninety rural red counties that have higher murder rates than cities like New York City, San Francisco, Seattle, and Jersey City. But again, he's cherry-picking rural red counties that have low populations, and thus even a single homicide could, on paper, give them a murder rate as astronomical as it is misleading. If a small town of 1,000 goes fifty years without a murder, and then one year has one that resulted from a domestic dispute, the town will have a murder rate of "100 per 100,000" that year, putting it on par with Chicago, Caracas, or parts of Mexico that has cartels going to war with one another. But for good reason, no one in the small towns will suddenly feel nervous about going out at

---

50   "FBI Crime Data Explorer." https://cde.ucr.cjis.gov/LATEST/webapp/#/pages/home

night or makes changes to their behavior. These "violent rural red counties" will once again be the safest within a year—but the same can't be said about Detroit, Chicago, St. Louis, and others.

This whole exercise brings to mind the time the *Washington Post* tried to debunk the claim from conservative pundits that the twenty major cities with the most violent crime are all run by Democrats by arguing that "only" nineteen out of twenty actually were (the exception was Springfield, Missouri, where mayoral elections are nonpartisan).[51] You can feel the desperation.

The Capital Research Center's Parker Thayer[52] dug into Males's background and found that he's a senior researcher for the Center on Juvenile and Criminal Justice, which is Soros-funded.[53] You don't have to be a conspiracy theorist to see that the poorly argued piece was commissioned specifically to defend Soros policies.

ALEX SCORES BIG ON THE WISCONSIN SUPREME COURT

Alex Soros has contributed heavily to flipping Wisconsin's Supreme Court liberal.

Alex had his initial success in getting Democrat Janet Protasiewicz elected to the Wisconsin Supreme Court in the then-most-expensive Supreme Court race in history, with $51 million being spent.[54] He funded her campaign to the tune of $2.8 million, and Soros-linked groups like A Better Wisconsin

---

51   Philip Bump, "Trump keeps claiming that the most dangerous cities in America are all run by Democrats. They aren't," *Washington Post*, June 25, 2020. https://www.washingtonpost.com/politics/2020/06/25/trump-keeps-claiming-that-most-dangerous-cities-america-are-all-run-by-democrats-they-arent

52   twitter.com/ParkerThayer/status/1728901733315936676

53   Michele Byrnes, Daniel Macallair, and Andrea D. Shorter, *Aftercare as Afterthought: Reentry and the California Youth Authority* (San Francisco: Center on Juvenile & Criminal Justice, August 2002); Open Society Foundations. https://www.opensocietyfoundations.org/publications/aftercare-afterthought-reentry-and-california-youth-authority

54   "Wisconsin Supreme Court Race Cost Record $51 Million," Wisconsin Democracy Campaign, July 18, 2023. https://www.wisdc.org/news/press-releases/139-press-release-2023/7390-wisconsin-supreme-court-race-cost-record-51m

Together Political Fund spent $6.2 million, amid other spending.[55] She outraised her opponent by over $10 million,[56] flipping the Wisconsin Supreme Court liberal for the first time in fifteen years in 2023, and winning her race by eleven points.

In 2025, in the first major election following Donald Trump's 2024 victory, Democrat Susan Crawford faced off against former Wisconsin Attorney General Brad Schiumel. This race set a new record for "most expensive judicial race in US history" by an astronomical margin, with spending exceeding $90 million, according to a tally by the Brennan Center for Justice. Groups connected to Elon Musk spent $17 million, much more than Alex's $2 million, but more was spent on Crawford overall.[57]

In addition to aspects of the Trump agenda, the state's legislative maps were at stake.

Protasiewicz has accused Wisconsin's legislative maps of being gerrymandered in favor of Republicans, while an email from days ago inviting people to a Crawford campaign event advertised her winning as an opportunity to "put two more House seats in play for 2026."[58]

The stakes were high, as this came at a time the GOP had a zero-seat advantage in the House of Representatives. Republicans

55   Joseph Simonson and Andrew Kerr," How Millions from George Soros Fueled Democrats' Court Victory in Wisconsin," *Washington Free Beacon*, April 7, 2023. https://freebeacon.com/democrats/how-millions-from-george-soros-fueled-democrats-court-victory-in-wisconsin

56   "WI's Protasiewicz Outraises Opponent by $10.2m as Soros, Pritzker Donations Roll In," Fox News, March 28, 2023. https://www.foxnews.com/politics/wis-protasiewicz-outraises-opponent-10-2m-soros-pritzker-donations-roll

57   Michael Waldman, "The Most Expensive Judicial Election Ever," Brennan Center for Justice, April 2, 2025. https://www.brennancenter.org/our-work/analysis-opinion/most-expensive-judicial-election-ever

58   Alison Dirr and Daniel Bice, "Hakeem Jeffries Says a Crawford Victory Could Lead to Congressional Maps Better for Democrats," *Milwaukee Journal Sentinel*, March 25, 2025. https://www.jsonline.com/story/news/politics/elections/2025/03/25/hakeem-jeffries-says-susan-crawford-could-give-democrats-better-maps/82645251007

currently hold six of the eight seats Wisconsin is given in the House.

If 2024 was a battle of the billionaires between Musk and Alex (among other factors), it was Musk who came out on top. But in Wisconsin, Alex got his first act of revenge, and Susan Crawford easily fended off her Republican opponent, former Wisconsin AG Brad Schimel, 55–45 percent. It didn't expand the liberal majority on the Wisconsin Supreme Court, but did maintain it, and with it increased the likelihood that Republicans' representation in the US House shrinks by about a percent.

SOROS ON DRUGS

George Soros has done more than any individual to shape the narrative on drugs in America in favor of legalization of some drugs, and so-called decriminalization of others. In 2017, David Callahan, the editor and founder of *Inside Philanthropy*, wrote that "no philanthropist has done more than Soros to soften America's drug laws."[59]

As early as 1994 he was pushing the narrative that the "war on drugs" caused more harm to society than drugs itself. While it's questionable if America ever even fought a true "war on drugs," what we're to believe is that arresting people for drug possession, public use, or trafficking is worse than fentanyl or heroin.[60]

It's not just legalization of marijuana, but all drugs, that Soros wants.[61] He might frame it in terms of "decriminalization," but that "decriminalization" would be enforced in a way they were be de facto legalized.

To advance his goal, George gave $15 million to establish and support pro-drug organizations, including the Drug Policy

---

59   Rachel Ehrenfeld, *The Soros Agenda* (Washington, DC: Republic Book Publishers, 2023), p. 38.
60   Ibid., page 48.
61   Ibid., page 39.

Foundation, Lindesmith Center, and Drug Strategies.[62] Alex Soros is on the board of the Drug Policy Alliance, which formed as a merger of the first two groups listed.

I imagine there's a variety of opinion on the matter among readers, and I don't propose a solution to America's drug problem here, but rather aim to show that the George and Alex's approaches doesn't work. If there is a working "decriminalization" model out there, it's not theirs.

The only aside I'll take is to criticize a common cliché that I myself had uttered in my teenage years, that "nobody should be in jail for marijuana possession." It's something I still believe—but it is used as a talking point to paint a misleading picture that has itself has become a gateway drug to argue for reducing penalties for possession of other drugs. The good news is practically nobody goes to jail or prison for simple possession—and sensationalist think tanks and activist groups calculating tens of thousands of "marijuana prisoners" never mention if the person jailed had other drugs on them, or had drugs on them while committing a violent crime, or committed other crimes worthy of jail time. Most "man spends decades in jail for marijuana" stories involve drug trafficking, which I still don't believe justifies such a long sentence for marijuana specifically. My point is that those are circumstances that should be easy to avoid finding oneself in.

When Joe Biden pardoned everyone for federal marijuana possession charges, it resulted in zero people being released from jail. That doesn't mean someone can't find a one-off case with a Google search, but it was never a widespread phenomenon.[63]

A main benefit of criminalizing possession is to reduce their use in public. Criminalization of possession doesn't pose a prob-

---

62   Ibid., page 38.
63   Zeke Miller, "Biden Pardons Thousands Convicted of Marijuana Charges on Federal Lands and in Washington," Associated Press, December 22, 2023. https://apnews.com/article/biden-marijuana-pardons-clemency-02abde991a05ff7dfa29bfc3c74e9d64

lem to someone getting high in the confines of their own home. Even in the case of marijuana, it wouldn't be a stretch to assume that most people who want it legal would also be fine with there being heavy fines for smoking in public. Anyone that's ever breathed in a major city knows what I'm talking about.

Alex has again mimicked the philosophy of his father and is pushing full steam ahead.

In a 2021 op-ed, Alex blasted the war on drugs for causing a surge in police budgets and incarceration, noting over 1.6 million arrests each year for drug possession, or as he puts it, "for the simple act of possessing drugs for their personal use."[64]

And of course, he turns to now-cliched argument that the drug war is racist, in that a disproportionate share of those arrested are nonwhite, fueling "institutional and structural racism."

The "disproportionate impacts" canard is a favorite of the left and is among the laziest arguments to make. Nothing impacts any demographics equally, so one can always argue that anything "disproportionately impacts" a certain group 100 percent of the time.

Not even sugar was safe from this argument. So powerful is this sort of illogic that the NAACP took money from Coca-Cola to call a 2009 proposed federal excise tax on sugary drinks "racist." They'd later join the fight against NYC Mayor Michael Bloomberg's soda ban. The NAACP and Hispanic Federation would eventually file an amicus brief arguing that soda taxes are racist against black and Hispanics. The "logic" behind such a claim is outright laughable the more you think about it: if a group disproportionately consumes sugar, they would be "disproportionately impacted" by a tax on sugar. But think about the flip-

---

64   Alex Soros, "Nixon's War on Drugs Has Failed for Half a Century. It's Time to End It: Alexander Soros," *International Drug Policy Consortium*, June 21, 2021. https://idpc.net/news/2021/06/nixon-s-war-on-drugs-has-failed-for-half-a-century-it-s-time-to-end-it-alexander-soros

side; they're also "disproportionately impacted" by the negative health impacts of sugar, which is exactly what the tax sought to reduce in the first place.[65] Why is the tax racist, but not the bad consequences the tax aims to prevent them from experiencing? The same can be observed from policing: if increased policing were to lead to increased police brutality (a rare event), why not also credit it to leading to increased safety (a common event)?

Alex does at least attempt to hold numbers constant, and points to a popular claim from the American Civil Liberties Union that "Black people are almost four times as likely as white people to be arrested on marijuana charges, despite similar rates of consumption." So common has this statistic become in drug war discourse that even Rand Paul cited it to argue that the drug war has disproportionately affected "men and women of color."[66]

While the statistic is supposed to make us conjure up images in our mind of racist cops pulling black men off the street while allowing whites to go free, it's not hard to think off the top of one's head of other reasons for the disparity. If whites disproportionately live in rural and suburban areas where it's extremely easy to smoke pot without being seen (or smelled), while blacks tend to live in population-dense areas where secret use is difficult, which group do you think is going to rack up more arrests? It's also the case that more black criminal offenders are arrested overall every year for actual crimes. Isn't it a guarantee that some percent of them will have marijuana on them and catch a charge for that? Furthermore, usage rates are self-reported. It's absurd to treat racism as the null hypothesis for any disparity, but most left-wing arguments today are dependent on just that.

---

65   Hannah Cox, "Did the NAACP Take Coca-Cola Money to Call Sugar Taxes Racist?" *BASEDPolitics*, January 3, 2023. https://www.based-politics.com/p/did-the-naacp-take-coca-cola-money-to-call-sugar-taxes-racist

66   Rand Paul, "Give Kids a Second Chance After Drug Crime," *USA Today*, July 11, 2014. https://www.usatoday.com/story/opinion/2014/07/11/voting-rights-drugs-minorities-column/12404979

Alex also blames Mexico's war on drugs and cartels for killing over 150,000 people at the time of writing. There is some truth to this, as the killings of top drug lords have caused power vacuums within their respective cartels, and caused them to splinter, which has led to violence too gruesome to even describe. Cartels also began targeting military police and others.

Drug war violence in Mexico is often used to argue for America legalizing drugs, though few say outright that're trying to stem violence in Mexico by opening the world's first Cocaine Depot.

Alex's solution for the consequences of drug use in the United States is advocacy for so-called "harm reduction" strategies.

During a discussion titled "Rehab: Shaping a more effective response to drug trafficking worldwide" with the Paris Peace Forum, Alex emphasized that harm reduction, exemplified by efforts like those of President Ruth Dreifuss in Switzerland, has led to significant public health benefits, including a claimed 80 percent drop in new drug use, a 50 percent reduction in overdoses, and a 65 percent decrease in AIDS transmission.[67] The possession of narcotics and marijuana was still illegal (narcotics with jail time) in Switzerland during Dreifuss's tenure, so it's hardly the kind of "decriminalization" that Alex and his father have pursued, nor does it in any way resemble the "San Francisco" model of open-air drug markets and the normalization of third-world living conditions. Police in Switzerland still continued enforcing drug laws, including against drug dealing and trafficking.[68]

Alex argues that the war on drugs parallels a war on open society, where both are about "controlling" and "marginalizing"

---

67   "Rehab: Shaping A More Effective Response to Drug Trafficking Worldwide," Paris Peace Forum, February 19, 2019. https://www.youtube.com/watch?v=KUDyAXD13nI

68   Ruth Dreifuss, "The Secret to Fighting U.S. Heroin Epidemic," CNN, April 19, 2016. https://www.cnn.com/2016/04/19/opinions/preventing-heroin-overdose-u-n-drugs-dreifuss/index.html

certain populations. This again is the "disproportionate harm" argument, excluding the obvious fact that it's because the "victim groups" disproportionately use drugs, or are more likely to use them in public.

Harm reduction would be the most rational strategy in a world where there is a fixed number of drug users that can never change—in which case the only possible way to reduce death would be "harm reduction" measures. Fortunately, that is not the world we live in. In fact, we're fortunate enough to live in a world where we can make at least public drug abuse impossible. It's simply due to a lack of willpower from liberal "leaders" that major cities haven't.

The simplest way to illustrate the absurdity of "harm reduction" is to imagine if we approached drunk driving—which has been greatly reduced over the decades by public awareness campaigns, increased fines and enforcement, and social stigma—in the same way that "harm reduction" does to drugs. Is there a single person on the planet that believes the government distributing lower-potency alcohol, encouraging people to sympathize with drunk drivers, and reducing their fines would have been a better approach?

The best-case scenario for drug "harm reduction" is when it is about harm to drug users themselves—but the majority of the damage from drugs isn't to the user, it's to society at large. One must wonder if the liberals and libertarians arguing that people should "be able to put whatever they want in their bodies because it only hurts them" are listening to themselves. We're supposed to believe that a drug user is only harming themselves—and not their families? Try explaining to a child raised by drug addicts that drug use was only harming their parents the entire time. Or try explaining to someone who can't walk down the needle-laden streets of Kensington, Philadelphia, or San Francisco's

Tenderloin district—which are among the closest things you'll see to a post-apocalyptic America—that no one else is being harmed.

What about the physical and property crimes committed by junkies looking to fund their next high, the reduction in economic activity they cause, the cost of imprisoning those who commit crimes, or even the cost to the taxpayer to fund these "harm reduction programs" themselves? The list could go on for the entire length of the book.

To go back to the alcohol example: the greatest victim of an alcoholic driving drunk isn't the drunk driver. The addicts aren't the victims here.

My opinions aside, harm reduction programs have exacerbated harm everywhere they've been tried.

San Francisco's Tenderloin district has been the face of open drug use in America, enabled by a progressive local government that caters to drug addicts and criminals before its residents. In January 2022, the Tenderloin Center—a $22 million "safe services site" that addicts could use to get high under supervision—was created. It had the goal of reducing overdoses and addicts getting robbed. The project was initially supposed to cost $10 million. In its first four months in operation, it referred eighteen of the 23,000 addicts it welcomed for treatment—a whopping 0.08 percent.[69]

The Tenderloin Center closed in December 2022. Defenders claim it reversed 333 overdoses, but some percentage of those would've been reversed regardless. It's also the case that since these centers encourage drug use, many of the "reversed overdoses" are overdoses that would've never occurred in the first place without the safe site's incentives.

---

69   Hope Sloop, "San Francisco Shuts Down $22m Open-air Drugs Market After It Referred Less Than 1% for Treatment—or Just 18 Addicts Out of 23,000 It Welcomed in Its First Four Months," *Daily Mail,* December 6, 2022. https://www. dailymail.co.uk/news/article-11509001/Tenderloin-Center-shuts-22-million-open-air-drug-market.html

San Francisco had 623 fatal overdose deaths in 2021, and 635 in 2022,[70] roughly the same amount. The only argument the "harm reduction" crowd can make is one impossible to prove— that without their program it would've gone up by even more. While the most drastic consequence of drug use, overdoses aren't the only health consequence of drug use, either. Even if these types of programs reduced overdoses to zero, all other consequences of drug use to the user's health remain in effect. No one would be fine with a loved one doing heroin, even if they could be given a 100 percent guarantee that they'd never overdose.

British Columbia, Canada, implemented a "safer supply" in 2020, allowing addicts to receive pharmaceutical-grade opioids for free. In 2023, British Columbia reported the highest drug-death toll on record.[71] Total overdoses (most of which were not fatal) increased from 24,116 in 2019 to 27,067 in 2020. It then increased further to 35,585 in 2021 and hit a record of 42,172 in 2023.[72]

Alex is not stupid, and he, just like his father, is aware of all of this.

As is the case with the woke DAs they fund, destruction is the point.

In 1998, the OSF (then the Open Society Institute) opened its first US field office in Baltimore with $20 million in funding. Arguing in defense of so-called "harm reduction" policies, Alex highlighted his father's work in Baltimore when they partnered with the Casey Foundation. "We partnered with them in Baltimore, where we had a standalone project particularly dealing

70   "Unintentional Drug Overdose Death Rate by Race or Ethnicity," SF.gov. https://www.sf.gov/data--unintentional-drug-overdose-death-rate-race-or-ethnicity

71   "B.C. Sets Grim Record With 2,511 Toxic Drug Deaths In 2023," CBC, January 24, 2024. https://www.cbc.ca/news/canada/british-columbia/b-c-sets-grim-record-with-2-511-toxic-drug-deaths-in-2023-1.7093528

72   "Overdose & Drug Poisoning Data." *BC Emergency Health Services.* http://www.bcehs.ca/about/accountability/data/overdose-drug-poisoning-data

with drug addiction when Baltimore was the most drug-addicted city in the country."[73]

Then-OSI president Aryeh Neier explained that "We chose Baltimore mainly because we thought it epitomized the urban problems we wanted to address. The city suffered from economic problems that reflected a substantial decline in population caused largely by 'white flight' from the city; a high level of drug addiction; a severe crime problem; and a public education system plagued by student and teacher absenteeism and by suspensions and expulsions from the schools."[74]

"White flight" is a term deployed by leftists to describe whites leaving an area as it becomes more violent, giving the implication that not wanting to be a crime victim is racist. Of course, if a large number of white people move into an area it's called "gentrification," and blamed for pricing out minorities from certain real estate markets, which is also called racist. Everything with the left is a "heads I win, tails you lose" game.

The actual impact of George's efforts in Baltimore largely went under the radar, with only some apparent initial successes ever drawing attention. But recently the Baltimore-based investigative reporter Patrick Hauf decided to read the score, and it's devastating:

> Though the fatal drug overdose rate in Baltimore was cut in half from 2000 to 2011, it steadily increased by more than 500 percent from 2011 to 2022, according to data from the Centers for Disease Control and Prevention.

---

73   Tom Olohan, "Alex Soros PUSHES Radical Drug Agenda in Interview with WashPost's Capehar," *NewsBusters,* September 26, 2023. https://www.newsbusters.org/blogs/business/tom-olohan/2023/09/26/alex-soros-pushes-radical-drug-agenda-interview-washposts

74   Patrick Hauf, "How George Soros Used Baltimore as a 'Testing Ground' for Liberal Policies," ABC7, January 16, 2025. https://wjla.com/news/local/how-george-soros-used-baltimore-as-a-testing-ground-for-liberal-policies-spotlight-on-maryland-open-society-institute-medal-of-freedom

The persistent increase in drug overdoses coincided with murder rates in Baltimore, which increased by 80 percent from 2011 to 2020. The overall violent crime rate steadily decreased by 45 percent from 2000 to 2014 but spiked by 51 percent leading up to 2017.

That's just a city—what about a whole state?

The OSF marked 2020 as a special year for "winning decriminalization worldwide," leading with America. "Open Society grantee the Drug Policy Alliance and its partners sought and won a ballot initiative making Oregon the first US state to decriminalize personal possession of all drugs and to use tax revenue from legal cannabis sales to fund treatment, recovery, and harm reduction services."[75]

On November 3, 2020, Oregon had four statewide ballot measures, the most notable of which was Ballot Measure 110, the "Drug Decriminalization and Addiction Treatment Initiative." Passing with nearly 60 percent of the vote, the ballot measure decriminalized hard drug use, with the promise that the state would invest in a fund for treatment, housing, and recovery services.

Individuals convicted for possession of hard drugs would face only a $100 maximum fine and then be invited to call a phone number to undergo a "drug evaluation," which would negate the fine. Any investment in treatment options was for voluntary treatment, which few addicts pursue. Proponents also promoted it on "racial justice" grounds, enthusing that it would reduce drug arrests of blacks by 94 percent.[76]

---

75   "Three Decades of Drug Policy Reform Work," Open Society Foundations, November 16, 2021. https://www.opensocietyfoundations.org/voices/three-decades-of-drug-policy-reform-work

76   "Measure Reduces Black Arrests by 94%," *Porland Observer*, October 22, 2020. https://web.archive.org/web/20230609094808/http://portlandobserver.com/news/2020/oct/22/measure-reduces-black-arrests-94

It was the pinnacle of George' efforts for decades, and Alex publicly celebrated the move, too, sharing a X/Twitter post on November 4, 2020, from the Drug Policy Alliance, reading: "Oregon made history tonight by becoming the first state to decriminalize drug possession! Drug Policy Action led this campaign with Vote Yes on 110 to make this visionary initiative a reality! This victory is truly transformative."

Alex was involved somehow.

Reminiscent of disproportionate Soros spending on DA races, the Drug Policy Alliance's political arm spent $5 million backing Measure 110, while the opposition to it brought in only $167,000.[77]

Oregon-based journalist Jeff Eagar exposed how the measure was immediately a failure after its decriminalization provisions took effect on February 1, 2021.

> It fell to the Oregon Health Authority (OHA) to try to implement Ballot Measure 110. From the beginning, there were problems. Addicts weren't calling the toll-free addiction hotline number on the citations that replaced possible arrest under the new law. OHA struggled to disperse grants funded by a tsunami of marijuana tax revenue the law redirected to drug treatment. Fentanyl and a new, more potent and deadly form of methamphetamine hit Oregon streets around the same time they were decriminalized. Oregonians quickly soured on decriminalization as the streets of Portland and other cities filled with homeless campers, many of whom were addicted to the hard drugs Measure 110 decriminalized.[78]

---

77   Jeff Eager, "Soros: Measure 110's Indispensable Man," *Oregon Roundup*, November 29, 2023. https://oregonroundup.substack.com/p/soros-measure-110s-indispensable

78   Jeff Eager, "The Failure of Oregon's Hard-Drug Decriminalization," *National Review*, February 7, 2022. https://www.nationalreview.com/2022/02/the-failure-of-oregons-hard-drug-decriminalization

In the first half of 2021 (of which the law was in effect for five months), there were 291 deaths from meth overdoses, compared to 391 in the entirety of 2020. For fentanyl, there were 237 deaths, compared to 230 in all of 2020.

Nine months into the experiment, a mere eight people cited under the law requested drug treatment after undergoing an assessment.

Deaths didn't stop increasing through 2022 and 2023. In the twelve months ending September 2023, overdose deaths grew 42 percent compared to only 2 percent nationwide over the same time period.[79]

In 2024, Oregon's Democrat-controlled House passed House Bill 4002, effectively repealing Measure 110, in a 51–7 vote. The Democrat-controlled Senate passed it 21–8, and Democrat Governor Tina Token signed the bill on April 1.

Alex and George's biggest "win" on drugs quickly became its biggest failure.

On the issue of law and order, George walked so Alex could run.

---

79   Keith Humphreys and Rob Bovett, "Why Oregon's Drug Decriminalization Failed," *The Atlantic*, March 17, 2024. https://www.theatlantic.com/ideas/archive/2024/03/oregon-drug-decriminalization-failed/677678

Chapter 4

Albania—Inside Alex's Second Home

Albania is among the many post-communist states that George Soros tried to infiltrate following the fall of the Soviet Union, though Albania wasn't part of the Soviet Union.

For over four decades, ending in 1985, Albania was run by communist strongman Enver Hoxha, a ruthless dictator. After rising to power in the wake of World War II, Hoxha's Stalinist regime banned religion, murdered intellectuals, banned international tourism, terrorized the public with secret police, and closed them off from the rest of the world, turning the nation into what many historians have called the "North Korea of Europe." [1]

The artifacts of the paranoid communist regime are visible to anyone visiting the country; Hoxha's unwavering fear about being invaded by then-Yugoslavia led him to order the construction of up to 750,000 bunkers scattered throughout the country. As overused as the word "literally" has become, they're literally impossible to miss by anyone visiting the country.

By the time of his death in 1985, Albania was the third-poorest nation—not in Europe, but in the entire world. The communist regime would finally begin to unravel under his successor, Ramiz Alia, as communism began to fall in the rest of Europe.

---

[1]   "Enver Hoxha: The Lunatic Who Took Over the Asylum," *openDemocracy*, March 15, 2016. https://www.opendemocracy.net/en/can-europe-make-it/enver-hoxha-lunatic-who-took-over-asylum

ENTER: GEORGE SOROS

Albania's first elections, post-communism, were held in 1991. George Soros began spending heavily in 1992, when the nation's second elections were held, and Sali Berisha of the center-right Albanian Democratic Party took power. Berisha was president from 1992–1997 and prime minister from 2005–2013. The Socialist Party was in control during the intermission between Berisha's presidency and prime ministership, and has controlled Albania's government since 2013.

The collapse of communism in 1990 provided Berisha with a platform to lead. He co-founded his Democratic Party of Albania, the first significant opposition group to exist in the country, and became its chairman. Clad in a white coat—an homage to his medical roots as a cardiologist—he rallied students and workers during mass protests in Tirana, demanding democracy.

A second opposition party, the Republican Party of Albania, also sprung up, with its name an ode to the GOP. Albania is one of the most pro-American countries in the world today, and to this day the Republican Party of Albania's platform is modeled on the GOP's (when applicable). The Democratic Party of Albania's name has no relation to US politics, and they're currently in a coalition with the Republicans against the ruling Socialist Party.

One challenge stood greatest when building Albania's economy from scratch: that due to decades of communist repression, no one had been exposed to free-market economics or even basic economics at all. While not educated in or knowledgeable about economics himself, Berisha had been inspired by Reaganism and found that Reaganomics made sense to him personally, so he began modeling tax policy off that, and sought advice from the Heritage Foundation.[2]

---

2   Conversation with Sali Berisha, March 22, 2022.

George Soros had a drastically different vision for the country.

The Soros family's engagement with Albania dates to the early 1990s, when George Soros founded the Open Society Foundation for Albania. The initial focus was on supporting Albania's transition from communism, funding projects in education, health, and civil society.

In the 1990s, the elder Soros spent over $57 million building 275 schools across the country and the nation's first internet antenna in 1997.[3] George made sure to get his propaganda apparatus planted there, too, and educated ninety student journalists through a four-month training program to help them spread leftist propaganda on radio, TV, and text journalism.

Having to build what was almost the poorest country on Earth from scratch, Berisha initially didn't have any complaints about Soros's money, and he was willing to take any financial support the nation could get. But it quickly became apparent to him what George's real goal was as the billionaire tried to exercise influence over him; and it also became clear what George was infecting Albanian society with: a different flavor of the leftist ideology they had just escaped from.

"He came and I welcomed him. He started to help civil society, and I appreciated it. Members of civil society in Albania had no chance of doing any projects [because of how poor the country was], so I appreciated all of these," Berisha explained. But, of course, there was an ulterior motive. "Then I saw, after a few years, that the organizations he created were Marxist-Leninist cells. They were all left-wing extremist." [4]

---

3   "The Open Society Foundations in Albania," Open Society Foundations, March 25, 2021. https://www.opensocietyfoundations.org/newsroom/open-society-foundations-albania

4   "The Man Behind the Curtain, influenca e Soros ne politiken e huaj, promovohet librit Matt Palumbo," *Sali Berisha* YouTube channel, March 25, 2022. https://www.youtube.com/watch?v=rwZ-a2MqAFY&

Berisha then referenced a parable about dictator Enver Hoxha. "We have associations, the dictator said, but he controlled those associations from beginning to end. Now Soros has given us back the same parable. All associations were under the control of the Socialist Party...[and] we went back to monism. It was all propaganda machines of the Socialist Party, and all disinformation machines against the Democratic Party."[5]

TENSIONS ARISE

In 1993, the Albanian government declared non grata two employees of the Soros Foundation, Fron Nahzi and Fred Abraham, whom the Berisha government says were proven, through audio and visual recordings, to be collaborators with Yugoslav intelligence. After this decision, George Soros reportedly came the next day and took them away on a special plane.[6]

"After a few years, it became crystal clear that George Soros had not established a network of NGOs in Albania as the voice of a free society, but rather a network of NGOs as the voice of the party that had ruled the country for forty-five years," Berisha said.[7]

Abraham denies being part of Yugoslav intelligence, or that he was flown out of the country; but he did write a book on Albania based on his twenty years there, titled *Modern Albania*, which gives a comprehensive history of the country during the period when he was there. One thing that stands out is his admission that he, in his capacity as someone part of the OSF Albania, was working to thwart Berisha from early on.

Among the first people he acquainted himself with in Albania were ex-members of the Democratic Party who formed the

---

5   Ibid.
6   Conversation with Sali Berisha, March 5, 2025.
7   Ibid.

Democratic Alliance, which would be part of the Socialist Party's coalition following the 1997 and 2001 elections. "They gathered every night at the home of the Soros Foundation director. We watched as Albania's new opposition got drunk on bad wine...cursing Berisha." Nahzi also sided with the Democratic Alliance's leaders.[8]

Abrams was upset that people at the OSF didn't do more to stop Berisha's agenda, admitting in the process that the OSF's employees there opposed him: "In private they disliked Berisha, but they lacked the courage to take a stand."[9]

Abrams published a student newspaper called *Reporteri*, which the University of Tirana shut down four days after its first issue (Abrams claimed this was at Berisha's orders). "The president cared little about the student newspaper, but he was furious with our funder, the Soros Foundation, and in particular its director in Tirana. That man, Fron Nahzi, had begun challenging Berisha's democratic credentials, and he had the budget to give his challenge weight."[10]

In February 1993, Nahzi held a media seminar with foreign journalists, leading to the first piece critical of Berisha in the international press. Nahzi explained that "Between me and Sali Berisha was a deep hatred."[11]

Soros sided with Nahzi, stating that he didn't do anything wrong, but ended up dismissing him out of fears of Berisha shutting down his whole organization.[12]

Regardless, the situation ended Soros's attempts to influence Berisha.

---

8   Fred C. Abrahams, *Modern Albania: From Dictatorship to Democracy in Europe* (New York: NYU Press (reprint), March 1, 2016), p. 126.
9   Ibid., p. 128.
10   Ibid., p. 130.
11   Ibid., p. 131.
12   Ibid., pp. 131–132.

George would go on to complain about Berisha in an interview with the *New Yorker* in early 1995. In conflict with Berisha's narrative, he said that to try to accommodate Berisha, he fired a director in charge of his foundation in Tirana for challenging some of Berisha's policies—while also expressing "disappointment" in Berisha for expressing "totalitarian tendencies."[13] So, Soros is trying to portray himself as so accommodating that he fired someone for challenging Berisha, while simultaneously complaining about Berisha's policies. He can't have it both ways.

"Berisha was not what he was cracked up to be, and partly my man didn't build the foundation right," Soros said. In other words, Berisha couldn't be bought.

George hadn't spoken much on Berisha since, but did send Hillary Clinton an email in 2011 after the opposition (Rama's Socialist Party) called for protests against the Berisha-controlled government. The protests amassed tens of thousands and eventually turned violent, leading to three deaths and general destruction of property. George criticized "rhetoric being used by both sides," but singled out Berisha over National Guard members firing on demonstrators attempting to violently storm the prime minister's office[14] in what some described as a coup attempt.

The OSF budgeted $2 million for Albania in 2020 and $93 million (the most recent year they offer data for) for the entirety of Europe.[15] That that may seem small in relative terms: Albania is a nation of only 2.8 million (in 2020), while Europe's population (minus Albania) is 743 million, meaning Albania has only 0.4 percent the population of the rest of Europe. Over the years,

---

13   Connie Bruck, "The World According to George Soros. *The New Yorker*, January 15, 1995. https://www.newyorker.com/magazine/1995/01/23/the-world-according-to-soros

14   https://wikileaks.org/clinton-emails/emailid/28972

15   "The Open Society Foundations in: Albania." Open Society Foundations, 2017. https://www.opensocietyfoundations.org/uploads/465f70b4-830e-4c0b-ab47-9ca3c0ad4152/factsheet-osf-albania-eng-20170515.pdf

OSF invested significantly, with reports suggesting over $131 million between 1992 and 2020.[16]

George never forgot about the initial rejection of his influence, and it would create a decades-long rivalry climaxing with him completely transforming Albania's legal system and eventually getting revenge. And with that, Alex would be given the perfect environment from which to exert influence over the country he's visited more than any other.

The rest of this chapter has been the most fun for me to write in the book—it chronicles a decades-long rivalry that escalated into the Open Society Foundation uprooting a nation's legal system, using that corrupted system to arrest a chief critic, and using their influence in the Biden White House to target their opposition, Alex then used his newfound influence to partner with the man credited with turning Albania into a narco-state. The account shows how Alex, Rama, and the Biden administration intersect through their relationship with the FBI agent who kicked off the Trump-Russia investigation. There also have been allegations that Alex Soros's support for Rama could be linked to Albania's issues with organized crime and drug trafficking, with some sources suggesting that his work there might extend to protecting or even enabling these activities.[17]

Even before taking the helm of OSF, Alex Soros has intensified the OSF's involvement in Albanian affairs, with his proven involvement dating back to at least 2019, but potentially as early as 2013.

---

16 Ibid.
17 John R. Schindler, "Why Does Tim Walz's Billionaire Buddy Alex Soros Love Albania's Narco-state?" *Washington Examiner*, September 26, 2024. https://www.washingtonexaminer.com/opinion/3166794/why-tim-walz-buddy-alex-soros-love-albania-narco-state

GEORGE AND ALEX REMAKE ALBANIA'S JUDICIAL SYSTEM
The role that George Soros had in remaking Albania's judicial system from scratch makes his role in corrupting America's justice system at the local level look like amateur hour.

As is the case in America, Soros "reform" left Albania far worse off, far more corrupt, and far more dysfunctional politically than before. But it's not like it mattered to George and Alex, because their efforts had tremendous benefits for them, helping their allies in the ruling Socialist Party (which, as of writing, has remained in power since 2013) consolidate power, and helping the Socialist Party persecute their, and the Soros's, enemies.

The Socialist Party is the successor to Enver Hoxha's communist Party of Labor, and the Socialist Party's official newspaper *Zëri i Popullit* is the same as the Party of Labor's. It was originally edited by Hoxha himself.

The Socialist Party is led by Prime Minister Edi Rama, who is the true leader of Albania, as the position gives more power than the presidency. Rama has long been an ally to George, and he and Alex are now "best friends," according to their regular photos together shared on Alex's social media accounts.

Albania has historically been the nation most affected by administrative corruption in the region, with 57 percent of citizens being asked for bribes occasionally, and 47 percent taking part in corrupt transactions. In collaboration with USAID, the OSF has contributed $60 million between 2000–2015 to Albania's justice sector, and they allocated the funds.[18] Albanian parliament approved constitutional reform in July 2016 that was designed and then initiated by the OSF Albania. The OSF had

---

18   Grégor Puppinck. "Influence of the OSF: Albania's Case," European Centre for Law & Justice, October 5, 2023. https://eclj.org/geopolitics/un/influence-of-the-open-society-foundation-the-typical-case-of-albania

previously drafted a strategy paper in 2013 that outlined how to reform Albania's Constitution.[19]

This would only have the effect of worsening corruption in an already corruption prone nation.

This document was titled "Open Society Foundation Albania (OSFA) 2014–2017 Strategy Plan." Drafting of the document began in the summer of 2013, after Rama and his Socialist Party won in the June elections, with his coalition taking nearly 60 percent of the seats (83 out of 140).[20]

At the time, Ilir Meta's Socialist Party for Integration (which held sixteen seats)[21] was Rama's main coalition partner, but he eventually would leave the coalition. Meta would later rebrand it into a more left-of-center party called the Freedom Party, which aligned itself with Berisha against Rama.

The OSF strategy document calls Albanian constitutional reform one of the foundation's "big ideas," and outlines four main objectives. They include (on paper only): strengthening checks and balances, strengthening the role of the president, reducing political influence in the appointment judges of the Constitutional and Supreme Court, and increasing the independence of public institutions, including the general prosecutor's office, statistical office, and people's advocate.[22]

The OSF expected it to take at least two years to assess parts of the constitution they wanted revised, and to present their pro-

---

19   "Constitutional Reform—Conceived, Planned and Carried Out by Soros Foundation," *Exit News*, August 22, 2016. https://exit.al/en/constitutional-reform-conceived-planned-and-carried-out-by-soros

20   "Open Society Foundation Albania (OSFA) 2014-2017 Strategy Plan," Scribd. https://www.scribd.com/document/326653998/Ja-Dokumenti-i-Strategjise-se-Fondacionit-Soros-Albania-2014-2017-qe-tregon-se-kush-po-e-ben-Reformen-ne-Drejtesi-dhe-Reformen-Zgjedhore

21   Rama's Socialist Party had sixty-five seats, while Meta had sixteen, and other coalition parties had two. Seventy-one are needed for a majority.

22   "Constitutional Reform—Conceived, Planned and Carried Out by Soros Foundation."

posals. The document also confirmed that they intimately discussed their reform ideas with Rama.

Constitutional changes in Albania require a two-thirds vote (ninety-four votes), which they were nine seats short of. The OSF organized a wide-reaching campaign that included using international pressure against politicians, influencing public opinion campaigns, as well as launching media campaigns, citizen petitions, and more. US Ambassador Donald Lu carried out a campaign of intimidation and threatened members of the Democratic Party.

Luan Omari, the nephew of Enver Hoxha, was chosen by OSF as the "brain of judicial reform,"[23] and he became a member of the Group of High-Level Experts (GHLE), which served as the intellectual backbone of justice reform.

In the end, that worked, constitutional reform was passed— and the worst was yet to come.

SOLIDIFYING SOCIALIST POWER

The goal of Rama and the Soros family was never what was advertised, but instead was to solidify control of state institutions by their allies in the Socialist Party.

In 2019, the Albanian government was to appoint three judges for the European Court of Human Rights. They chose Sokol Berberi, Marjana Semini, and Darian Pavli, of which Berberi and Pavli were once OSF employees. Semini was the national chair of the commission that picked the three for the shortlist, and he was also the brother of socialist minister Eglantina Gjermeni, who is an advisor to Edi Rama.[24]

Berberi is the brother-in-law of Rama's interior minister. He ended up being appointed as an "ad hoc" (substitute) judge at the

---

23 Phone call with Sali Berisha, February 4, 2024.
24 Ibid.

ECHR. None of them were subjected to standard anti-corruption vetting procedures.[25]

Pavli, who graduated from the George Soros-founded Central European University, ended up being the one elected to the ECHR. Pavli also worked for the Soros-funded Human Rights Watch—and the OSF itself from 2003–2017. Pavli is Rama's cousin and has no experience as a judge. It was never proven that he has the fifteen years of experience as a judge, law professor, or lawyer to be eligible for appointment to the ECHR, as Albanian law requires.[26]

REFORM AFTERMATH

A review of judicial reform efforts in July 2021, exactly five years after their enactment, shows how they didn't live up to the rosy language that the OSF and socialists used to promote them.[27] As every critic expected, the justice system became less free—just like what happened with Soros' meddling in the US legal system that was going on at the same time.

To summarize:[28]

- The OSF and Socialist Party's attempts to capture Albania's Constitutional Court and High Inspectorate of Justice left the public without them for nearly four years.

- Appeals Courts and Courts of First Instance only have a quarter of the judges they need, and the Supreme Court just half. As a result, it's estimated

---

25   Ibid.
26   Ibid.
27   "The Role of Open Society Foundation in Putting the Justice System Under the Control of the Albanian Socialist Party Through the Judicial Reform," International Institute for Middle East and Balkan Studies, October 22, 2021. https://www.ifimes.org/en/researches/the-role-of-open-society-foundation-in-putting-the-justice-system-under-the-control-of-the-albanian-socialist-party-through-the-judicial-reform/4949
28   Ibid.

it would take two decades to clear the backlog of over 100,000 legal cases, 36,000 of which are awaiting consideration by the Supreme Court.

- Only 420 of 830 judges have undergone a vetting process, and 200 of those have failed and left the justice system.

- The High Judicial Council outsourced the administration of Supreme Court case files to the East-West Management Institute, which is run by Delina Fico, PM Rama's former wife, and former chair of the OSFA board. Fico is currently married to Bledi Çuçi, who is PM Rama's Minister of Foreign Affairs.

- Reforms put NGO networks under the purview of the Socialist Party, stripping them of independence.

- The government, post-reform, controls all governing bodies and the administration process of court files.

- The price of public works with state budget money in Albania costs between six to eight times more than public works performed in "similar terrains" with the financing of European Banks. Secret procurement increased fifteen-fold since 2013.

Ilir Meta voiced his concern to Alex about the absence of a Constitutional Court in a meeting in 2019. Meta was the president of Albania at the time. A photo of the meeting is the second-earliest of Alex in Albania (the earliest being when he was photographed with Rama earlier that year). A spokesman for Meta said Alex requested the meeting, proving he had an active role in judicial reform, though we don't know the exact start year. [29]

---

29   "Meta Sqaron Takimin Me Djalin E Sorosit: Tema E Të Ashtuquajturit 'Mini-shengen' Nuk Ka Ekzistuar Në Bisedë." *Telegrafi*, 2019 (exact date not specified). https://telegrafi.com/en/meta-sqaron-takimin-djalin-e-sorosit/

Meta said the three topics he focused on in the meeting were state capture by PM Rama, the erosion of media freedom and freedom of speech, and how to revitalize society against the violations of human rights and democratic values so-called reform had enabled. The meeting came after Meta had made public accusations about the OSF's "capture" of Rama, and because multiple members of the OSF had requested meetings with him as a result, to "clarify their position"—the disastrous consequences of which could already be seen.[30]

More directly, Meta has accused the Soros family of attempting to "capture the state" and even of "total state capture."[31] Meta largely reiterated the same points to me when I had the opportunity to speak with him.[32]

Relevant to how Alex's friend Edi Rama turned Albania into a narco state, it's now the case that 90 percent of cases go in the government's favor or in the favor of drug-linked gangs. It's a stark contrast to the 65–70 percent of the time cases against the government were in the favor of individuals or business.

Saimir Tahiri, Rama's Minister of Interior from 2013–2017, resigned over drug trafficking, and the socialist parliament tried to block his arrest.[33] His successor, Fatmir Xhafaj, resigned over allegations of his involvement in drug trafficking.[34] Rama's younger brother, who worked for OSF from 1993–1997, was also investigated for drug trafficking, and even admitted to driving in a car with a trafficker convicted of cocaine distribution.

30   Ibid.

31   Gjergj Erebara, "Albanian President Claims Country Avoided 'Soros Destabilization Plot," *Balkan Insight*, July 2, 2019. https://balkaninsight.com/2019/07/02/albania-president-claims-country-avoided-soros-plot-of-destabilization

32   Conversation with Ilir Meta, March 23, 2022.

33   Gjergj Erebara, "Albania Ex-Minister Quits Parliament to Fight Smuggling Claims," *Balkan Insight*, May 3, 2018. https://balkaninsight.com/2018/05/03/albania-beleaguered-former-minister-resigns-as-mp-05-03-2018

34   Gjergj Erebara, "Albania's Interior Minister Quits, PM Names New Nominee," *Balkan Insight*, October 27, 2018. https://balkaninsight.com/2018/10/27/albania-minister-of-interiors-fatmir-xhafaj-resigns-10-27-2018

In another parallel to the Soros infection of the US criminal justice system, the prosecution of people linked to criminal gangs and drug cartels came to a screeching halt. Those serving life sentences before 2013 are now free. [35]

"Despite" the Soros-backed "anti-corruption" system, Albania ranks second in the world for bribes.[36]

Born out of Albania's new constitution was the creation of the Special Structure Against Corruption and Organized Crime (SPAK), which had widely been panned as being a tool weaponized against the critics of Rama and the Socialist Party. There are some examples to the contrary, but they're outliers. SPAK was set up according to a draft from the Open Society Foundation in Tirana.[37]

Two years after the creation of SPAK, no senior official had been convicted of corruption, as corruption increased by an estimated 300 percent.[38]

In 2020, 63 defendants were sent to SPAK for corruption charges—in comparison to the special unit for corruption indicting 383 in 2009, of which 346 were found guilty. Over the 2005–2007 period, the Serious Crimes Prosecution and the Court sentenced 1,050 members of criminal groups—and hundreds of other officials for corruption.[39] When SPAK later investigated Edi Rama's brother, they miraculously found no evidence implicating him.[40]

The public has spoken, and they think it's a disaster: 63 percent of citizens don't trust the vetting process, and only 32

---

35   "The Role of Open Society Foundation…," International Institute for Middle East and Balkan Studies.
36   Ibid.
37   Ibid.
38   Ibid.
39   Ibid.
40   "SPAK clears PM's brother, Olsi Rama of Xibraka case allegations," *Albanian Times*, January 10, 2025. https://albaniantimes.al/spak-clears-olsi-rama-xibraka-case

percent think reform has been implemented correctly.[41] Most
believe corruption in the justice system has instead increased—
because it has.

THE (SOROS) EMPIRE STRIKES BACK

With justice reform completed, and a White House the Soros
family could control, Soros finally had the opportunity for the
revenge he had waited decades for.

In May 2021, Secretary of State Antony Blinken announced
sanctions against Berisha, alleging "significant corruption" while
he was prime minister (2005–2013), and banned him, his wife,
and his children from entering the United States. Berisha hadn't
been investigated or charged with corruption, and no specific
evidence was detailed in the announcement, which is atypical for
these kinds of public designations.

Nine days later, Biden's ambassador to Albania, Yuri Kim,
met with officials at SPAK, and posted to her social media that
SPAK was "committed to delivering justice and ensuring no one
is above the law.... Whether for corruption, organized crime,
or elections, the time of impunity is coming to an end." SPAK
didn't charge Berisha—but Kim's comments heavily implied their
involvement in the sanctions. Kim later lobbied Leader of the
Opposition Lulzim Basha to expel Berisha from the Democratic
Party of Albania.[42] Berisha was expelled, but would later take
control of the party again.

This would lead to a fractured Democratic Party with pro-Ber-
isha and pro-Basha factions, and eventually Basha would found

---

41   "The Role of Open Society Foundation...," International Institute for Middle East
     and Balkan Studies.
42   Tiana Lowe Doescher, "Albania Lawfare? How Biden Aided Soros's Favorite Narco-
     state," *Washington Examiner,* January 31, 2025. https://www.washingtonexaminer.
     com/premium/3297339/tirana-lawfare-biden-blinken-soros-albania

his own splinter party called Euroatlantic Democrats (taking four seats away from the Democrats). Then another party splintered off, which opposed both factions (and which also took away four seats), called Djathtas 1912 (in Albanian, *djathtas* means "right," as in direction). If the goal was to weaken opposition to the Socialist Party, Kim did just that.

In July, ahead of the 2021 local elections, Kim publicly questioned members of Berisha's "Freedom House" coalition how they could participate in a campaign sponsored by him, stating that it would be "a historic irony, but also a tragedy for this country, not just the party, if the party were to eat grass for the sake of one man's personal interest."[43] She was invoking a quote from Enver Hoxha, who once vowed that Albanians would rather eat grass than cooperate with capitalists; "The Albanian people eat grass and do not extend their hand to the enemy."[44]

The fracturing of the Democratic Party did end up crushing them in the 2025 parliamentary elections, working in the favor of the Socialist Party and increasing their share of seats in Parliament from seventy-four to eighty-three (out of 140). The Socialist Party's vote share only increased by 4.6 percentage points compared to the past election, while the turmoil caused the Democrats to shed 13.6 points, with all Democrat Party splinter parties except one (which only secured 2 seats) failing to meet the vote threshold to earn a single seat. The Democratic Party went from holding sixty-three seats to forty-two (fifty if you include other parties that ran in their coalition.

It was a major reversal from the prior parliamentary elections in 2021, which took place a month before the Berisha sanctions,

---

43   "Statement by Ambassador Yuri Kim," U.S. Embassy in Tirana, July 30, 2021. https://al.usembassy.gov/statement-by-ambassador-yuri-kim-2

44   "Nga 'bari', 'flirtet' me qeverinë te fushatat kundër opozitës, pse do mbahet mend Yuri Kim," *Politoko*, January 1, 2024. https://politiko.al/e-tjera/nga-bari-flirtet-me-qeverine-te-fushatat-kunder-opozites-pse-do-mbahet-m-i499045

the Democrats picked up sixteen seats (for fifty-nine total) while the Socialist Pary gained zero, and the next biggest party, the Socialist Party for Integration, lost fifteen.

Kim was Antony Blinken's chief of staff from 2015–2017, when Blinken was deputy secretary of state. "He is one of the most intelligent and strategic-minded people I have ever encountered in public service. And we who know him look forward to seeing him return to the State Department and, as a friend, I could not have been happier," she said.[45]

Blinken said in a statement that during his second stint in leadership, Berisha "was involved in corrupt acts, such as misappropriation of public funds and interfering with public processes, including using his power for his own benefit and to enrich his political allies and his family members."[46]

No details or supporting evidence was provided. Berisha has insisted there is "zero evidence" behind the corruption allegations, asserting the US ban was based on "misinformation" from outlets backed by Soros. It's interesting that the allegations are specific to Berisha's later term as prime minister, as if someone involved in such corrupt acts simply forgot to be corrupt the first time around.

During a session of parliament on January 31, 2019, Rama foreshadowed the sanctions to come in the event of a Trump loss. He addressed Berisha:

---

45   "Ambasadorja Yuri Kim, për marrëdhënien e afërt me Sekretarin e Shtetit amerikan: Blinken nuk është nga ata që favorizon në bazë të lidhjeve personale," *TiranaPost,* January 29, 2021. https://tiranapost.al/lajme-nga-bota/ambasadorja-yuri-kim-per-marredhenien-e-afert-me-sekretarin-e-sht

46   Antony J. Blinken, "Public Designation of Albanian Sali Berisha Due to Involvement in Significant Corruption," press statement, US Department of State, May 19, 2021. https://2021-2025.state.gov/public-designation-of-albanian-sali-berisha-due-to-involvement-in-significant-corruption

Sali, can you cross the ocean? Come on, answer. I gave you a direct answer, answer me directly. If I were the one you describe, you can be sure that I would not cross the ocean and not communicate with the White House at the request of the White House.[47]

The comment didn't make any sense at the time, but it would be clear what he was talking about a mere two years later.

In an open letter, Berisha asked Blinken for any documentation of his corruption, and said he'd immediately withdraw from politics if he provided it.[48] He also challenged the Biden administration in general to produce any evidence of corruption, stating:

It is my deep conviction that this declaration against me has been based entirely on misinformation that Mr. Secretary of State Antony Blinken has gotten from a corrupted lobby process involving Edi Rama and George Soros, who are close friends. They have no evidence. None at all. If they announced one bit, I will be most thankful. But they have no concrete proof based on fact, not manipulation or slander.

...

I have been an outspoken critic of George Soros and his close friend [Prime Minister] Edi Rama, and because of this, the State Department has made this allegation against me and blocked me. There is no other reason. There could be no other reason.

---

47   "'Non grata' nga SHBA/ "E kapërcen dot oqeanin?," si përgjigjej Berisha në debat me Ramën gjatë seancës së 2019-ës." *Politiko*, May 19, 2021. https://politiko.al/e-tjera/non-grata-nga-shba-e-kapercen-dot-oqeanin-si-pergjigjej-berisha-ne-debat-i436282

48   Sali Berisha, Sokol Mengjesi, and Genc Gjokutaj. *Transnational Corruption and Cancel Culture—The Case Against Albanian Ex-PM Sali Berisha: From U.S. and British Non Grata to Illegal Court Prosecution* (Politiko Books, 2024), p. 60.

Berisha would later file a lawsuit over the non grata designation.

Then-former Special Presidential Envoy for Serbia and Kosovo Peace Negotiations Ric Grenell also said he saw no evidence for Blinken's claims.[49]

If we were working under the assumption that Blinken's allegations were true, the sanctions seemingly came out of the blue. New York Republican Representative Lee Zeldin immediately flagged the move as abnormal and penned a letter to the State Department's Bureau of Legislative Affairs to request a detailed explanation of the process that the State Department followed.

Rep. Zeldin referred to the Soros connection when questioning Blinken during a House Foreign Affairs Committee meeting in June 2021 about the drastic sanctions that came "seemingly out of nowhere." "What specific information can you share with the committee at this time to justify this dramatic move?" asked Zeldin.[50]

In response to the questioning, Blinken denied having any communication with Soros, but said he couldn't speak for anyone else at the State Department. When pressed on the evidence for corruption, Blinken said that all proper protocols were followed, while providing no substantive evidence of corruption whatsoever.

Evidently, Blinken can't speak on behalf of anyone else at the State Department when it comes to their connections to Soros—or even his own father. Antony's father Donald Blinken and his wife Vera funded the Vera and Donald Blinken Open Society Archives at Central European University, which houses

---

49   Ibid., p. 69.
50   "Rep. Zeldin Questions Sec. Blinken on Sudden Sanctioning of Former Albanian President," press release, US House, July 7, 2021. https://web.archive.org/web/20210707065930/https://zeldin.house.gov/media-center/press-releases/rep-zeldin-questions-sec-blinken-sudden-sanctioning-former-albanian

a digital collection of Hungarian historical documents. In one Soros Foundations Network report from 2002, Donald Blinken is listed on the Board of Trustees for CEU, third after Soros (the chair) and Aryeh Neier, implying he's high in the pecking order.[51] Donald Blinken was US ambassador to Hungary from 1994 to 1998, right as Soros was setting up shop. He and his wife had close ties to the socialist government.

The State Department deflected in their initial (and only) response to Zeldin, basically arguing "we investigated ourselves and we did everything right," writing: "[The State] Department can confirm it followed established procedures to determine he was involved in significant corruption at the time he was a public official"; but again, no evidence was provided.

In August 2021, Zeldin replied, inquiring about how it is that sanctions were coming now, despite Berisha leaving office as prime minister in 2013, during the Obama-Biden administration. Zeldin requested a written response and meeting with the appropriate State Department official to discuss and review, in-depth, any new intel for the alleged corruption, and the process the department used "that led to these sanctions eight years and two US presidential administrations later."[52]

In November, five months after his original request, Zeldin requested for the third (and last) time additional information about Berisha's sanctions, noting that it was "unacceptable and suspicious that the Department of State has not sufficiently fulfilled this request for additional information in a timely manner and has instead chosen to slow-walk a Congressional request for transparency."

51   "Building Open Societies: 2002 Report," Soros Foundations Network, 2003. https://www.opensocietyfoundations.org/uploads/569ceb5a-5a08-472e-ac5f-00b0c0595cf2/a_complete_report_0.pdf

52   Matt Palumbo, "Questions Remain Over Secretary of State Antony Blinken's Alleged Ties to George Soros," *Bongino*, November 16, 2021. https://bongino.com/questions-remain-over-secretary-of-state-anthony-blinkens-ties-to-george-soros

FOIA requests also went unanswered.

All attempts to obtain the evidence through FOIA requests during the Biden administration failed, as they went rejected or completely ignored.

STATE DEPARTMENT IGNORES ALL BERISHA-SOROS RELATED FOIA REQUESTS			
Date Request Received and Request ID	Requester	Request	Status
June 9, 2021 F-2021-07181	Sorkadh Mustafa	evidence that led to former president Sali Berisha to be declared persona non grata (Date Range for Record Search: From 1/1/2000 To 6/8/2021)	Closed June 16, 2021 (No documents provided)
August 5, 2021 F-2021-08973	Petet, Lucas	non-confidential records concerning the banning from the US on May 19, 2021, of Sali Berisha, former Prime Minister and President of Albania under Section 7031(c) (Date Range for Record Search: From 5/3/2021 To 5/28/2021)	Never answered
October 7, 2021 F-2022-00199	Sorkadh Mustafa	information on the specific acts of "significant corruption" involving former Prime minister of Albania Sali Berisha, designated non-grata	Never answered
February 7, 2024 F-2024-05898	William Marshall (Judicial Watch)	All records which formed the basis of the State Department's decision in 2021 to sanction and/or declare persona non grata former Albanian President Sali Berisha, his wife and his children.	Never answered

Date Request Received and Request ID	Requester	Request	Status
		Such records shall include, but not be limited to, reports, memoranda, directives, State Department email communications, and/or diplomatic notes. emails sent to and from Secretary of State Antony Blinken referencing "Soros," "Rama" and/or "Berisha." Date Range for Record Search: From: 1/20/2021 to 2/7/2024	

I submitted my own FOIA request, but was told I wouldn't get a response until after this book is published.

Yuri Kim was equally evasive. When asked why these sanctions came after Berisha hadn't been in power for eight years, she vaguely claimed that the decision was based on a "multi-year process." She also dismissed criticism of the decision as conspiracy theories. "The days of conspiracies have to belong to the past. Now, it's about facts," she told Voice of America, while providing none.[53]

She's also refused to answer any questions about her role in the sanctions, and said she "had no idea" what a reporter was talking about when asked about Berisha suing Blinken over the sanctions.[54]

With Kim's help, SPAK would deliver a one-two punch in 2023.

In the final days in her position as Biden's ambassador to Albania, Kim met the head of SPAK, Altin Dumani, which was followed by

53 "Transcript off Interview of U.S. Ambassador Yuri Kim with Armand Mero, Voice of America," US Embassy Tirana, September 16, 2021. https://al.usembassy.gov/transcript-of-interview-of-u-s-ambassador-yuri-kim-with-armand-mero-voice-of-america

54 "Yuri Kim s'merret më me Berishën por pyetjes së gazetarit a ishte peshku i parë i madh i jep sqarim," *TiranaPost*, May 21, 2021. https://tiranapost.al/politike/yuri-kim-smerret-me-me-berishen-por-pyetjes-se-gazetarit-a-ishte-peshku-i498140

Berisha being put on house arrest for 256 days before being charged with a crime. The two remaining opposition leaders (Ilir Meta and Fatmir Mediu) would also be arrested by the end of 2024.[55]

It's likely Alex was pulling the strings there—Nard Ndoka of the extra-parliamentary, center-right Christian Democratic Party alleged in February 2025 that Alex Soros has connections to twelve individuals running the show: "Alex Soros had 12 characters who controlled the justice system and SPAK."[56]

And how could he not, when it was the OSF that single-handedly created Albania's justice system in its current form? If anything, twelve cronies is an understatement.

ALEX'S BEST FRIEND: PRIME MINISTER EDI RAMA

Alex loves to post to his socials photos of himself and the politicians he's influencing, and Edi Rama is the man he shares buddy photos with more than any other.

Their relationship is more than just political. During one visit, Alex referred to Rama as his "brother," and similar language has appeared on other posts.

Alex Soros' first photo with Edi Rama was posted to his social media in the wake of Albanian justice reform on September 22, 2017—where he's joined with George as well. The caption on the photo, "Always a pleasure to meet with Albanian Prime Minister Edi Rama," indicates that it wasn't their first meeting. [57]

When I asked Berisha what Alex is up to during his constant visits, he told me that "nobody knows" for sure, when he's visiting "every two or three weeks"[58] (which implies they're more

---

55   Tiana Lowe Doescher, "Albania Lawfare? How Biden Aided Soros's Favorite Narco-state," *Washington Examiner*.

56   "Ndoka: Alex Soros ka pasur 12 personazhe që kontrollonin SPAK dhe drejtësinë." *Politiko*, February 18, 2025. https://politiko.al/english/ditari-i-opozites/ndoka-alex-soros-ka-pasur-12-personazhe-qe-kontrollonin-spak-d-i525769

57   https://www.instagram.com/p/BZXA-n_lG9c

58   Phone call with Sali Berisha, February 4, 2025

common than his social-media posts suggest). But with visits that frequent, it's clear he's not just there for fun. Alex reportedly has stayed previously at Enver Hoxha's personal home when visiting,[59] which, if the reports are true, would require intervention on Rama's part because it's not open to the public.

In addition to their interests in Albania, Alex and Rama have a shared opposition to Donald Trump.

Edi Rama has been criticizing Trump since before he was the Republican nominee, first blasting him in April 2016 over his "Muslim ban" comments (Albania is majority Muslim—Rama is Catholic).[60]

The same month he told CNN, "God forbid [Trump get elected]! I believe he would hurt the USA and the democratic world too, since he will be forced to do some of the things he is promising. And this would be very harmful."[61]

After Trump's 2025 win he, like all other world leaders, suddenly moderated his position. "In 2016, I didn't have all my hair white. I was younger and he wasn't president, he was a candidate. Then he became president. I was able to see him in action up close, and of course I changed my mind." If he really did change his mind about Trump during his 2016–2020 presidency, it's a bit odd Rama didn't bother to say anything about it until after he won again.[62] It came after Rama hailed Biden's "spectacular victory" in 2020, indicating his comments were just to avoid conflict.

---

59 Paula Froelich, "Alex Soros, Jared Kushner Reportedly Obsessed with Albania," NewsNation, November 14, 2024. https://www.newsnationnow.com/entertainment-news/alex-soros-jared-kushner-albania

60 "Albanian PM: Trump Nomination Would Harm America," CNN, March 13, 2016: https://edition.cnn.com/videos/business/2016/04/13/albanian-prime-minister-edi-rama-intv-qmb.cnn

61 "Rama shfaqet i penduar për deklaratat ndaj Trump në 2016-ën: Atëherë isha më i ri, kam ndryshuar mendim," Hashtag.al, February 26, 2025. https://www.hashtag.al/en/index.php/2025/02/26/rama-shfaqet-i-penduar-per-deklaratat-ndaj-trump-ne-2016-en-atehere-isha-me-i-ri-kam-ndryshuar-mendim

62 Talha Ozturk, "Balkan Country Leaders Hail Biden's U.S. Election Victory," Anadulo Agency (AA), August 11, 2020. https://www.aa.com.tr/en/europe/balkan-country-leaders-hail-bidens-us-election-victory/2036683

In addition to constant meetings in Albania, Alex and Rama have been spotted together at the Paris Peace Form,[63] the UN General Assembly,[64] Clinton Forum,[65] Southeast Europe Summit, World Economic Forum,[66] and more.

Alex didn't start regularly posting photos with Rama until 2022, though the two must have been acquainted since at least when he and his father were working on judicial reform with him. The earliest photo of the two dates to mid-2019.[67]

While 2021 was light on public visits, the first and only one that took place in Albania itself coincided with Rama about to start his third term as prime minister, marking his second government without any coalition partners. Rama announced the composition of his new cabinet and finalized all preparations for the new session of parliament in late August, when Alex was visiting.

Alex Soros and Edi Rama Pictures 2021		
Date Posted	Meeting Location	Notes
July 26[68]		Not long after Berisha non-grata declaration
September 2[69]	Tirana, Albania	Picture taken the week prior

63   https://www.facebook.com/Alexandersorospublic/posts/708454417309076
64   "Pas Veliajt edhe Edi dhe Linda Rama me Alex Soros," *CNA*, September 29, 2024.   https://www.cna.al/english/politike/pas-veliajt-edhe-edi-dhe-linda-rama-me-alex-soros-i409957
65   https://www.instagram.com/alexsoros/p/CuSONpmOrjl
66   "*Hashtag.al*, January 23, 2025. https://www.hashtag.al/en/index.php/2025/01/23/aleks-soros-poston-foto-me-ramen-ne-forumin-e-davos-it-shqiperia-eshte-e-para/
67   https://x.com/AlexanderSoros/status/1166780035371536387
68   https://www.instagram.com/p/CRy3UH6LPGs
69   Eduart Halili, "Alex Soros Praises PM Rama as Inspiring World Leader," *Albanian Daily News*, September 3, 2021. https://albaniandailynews.com/news/alex-soros-praises-pm-rama-as-inspiring-world-leader

Date Posted	Meeting Location	Notes
September 26[70]	New York City	Rama introducing Alex to the president of Senegal
November 5[71]	Serbia	Also met Serbia's president and deputy PM for North Macedonia. Not posted to Alex's social media
November 13[72]	Paris	Paris Peace Forum. Captioned "brothers at the Élysée!"

Rama's third government, holding 74 of 140 seats, was given a vote of confidence by the Kuvendi (Albanian parliament) on September 10, 2021, making his third term official. His cabinet was sworn in on September 18.

Alex Soros and Edi Rama Pictures 2022		
Date Posted	Meeting Location	Notes
February 25[73]	Germany	Munich Security Conference. Photo taken a week prior
March 22[74]	Albania	Celebrating Tirana being awarded "European Youth Capital"
August 25[75]	Austria	European Forum Alpbach

70   https://twitter.com/AlexanderSoros/status/1442178403541651458
71   "Rama, Vuçiç dhe Dimitrov takohen me Aleksandër Soros në Serbi," *Politiko*, November 5, 2021. https://politiko.al/ditari-i-maxhorances/rama-vucic-dhe-dimitrov-takohen-me-aleksander-soros-ne-serb-i447122
72   https://www.instagram.com/p/CWN0HTtMgUA
73   https://www.facebook.com/photo/?fbid=523206949167158
74   https://www.facebook.com/photo/?fbid=539950050826181
75   https://twitter.com/AlexanderSoros/status/1562823762247962624

Date Posted	Meeting Location	Notes
September 23[76]	Unclear	Rama pictured with a copy of George Soros's book *In Defense of Open Society*
November 11 and 12[77]	Paris Peace Forum	Captioned "brothers in Paris!"

Sometimes Alex brings a friend.

In July 2023 Alex, Rama, and Bill Clinton met with Pope Francis in a private meeting at the Casa Santa Marta papal residence. Alex was part of Clinton's delegation. Clinton received a public-gratitude medal from Rama for his support for Albania and intervention in the Kosovo War (admittedly, this is deserved). Francis presented Clinton with a statue of a woman holding a dove, which he said was "a work for peace."[78] (Contrary to the Church's stance, the OSF and its aligned groups have tried to legalize abortion in Ireland, Poland, and Mexico.)

Clinton accepted the Great Star of Gratitude for Public Achievements from Rama, the highest honor given by Albanian PMs to foreigners.[79]

Alex and Rama also are often pictured with Serbia's president and North Macedonia's prime minister. They were also pictured twice with North Macedonia's president at the time (lots more on him and the Soros network's impact there in the final chapter of this book, in the portion on USAID).

---

76   https://twitter.com/AlexanderSoros/status/1573339543730024449
77   https://twitter.com/AlexanderSoros/status/1591428882535964672
78   Kevin J. Jones, "Pope Francis Hosts Bill Clinton and Foundation Head Alex Soros," *National Catholic Register*, July 5, 2023. https://www.ncregister.com/cna/pope-francis-hosts-bill-clinton-and-foundation-head-alex-soros
79   Ibid.

Alex Soros and Edi Rama Pictures 2023		
Date Posted	Meeting Location	Notes
February 17[80]	Germany	Munich Security Conference. Captioned "Brothers in sneakers!"
May 21[81]	Albania	Refers to Rama as his "brother from another"
May 31[82]	Macedonia	Pictured with North Macedonia's PM while waiting for Rama
June 1[83]	Slovakia	
July 4[84]	Albania	Joined by Bill Clinton
July 7[85]	Serbia	Joined by President of Serbia
September 3[86]	Albania	Congratulates Rama on a successful tourist season
September 21[87]	New York City, New York	With North Macedonia's prime minister to discuss Open Balkan Initiative
November 10[88]	France	Paris Peace Forum

Alex's May 2023 visit came a week after the Socialist Party dominated in local elections, winning fifty-three of sixty-one

80   https://twitter.com/AlexanderSoros/status/1626653576155041815
81   https://twitter.com/AlexanderSoros/status/1660319521293434883
82   https://twitter.com/AlexanderSoros/status/1663990658959302656
83   https://www.facebook.com/photo/?fbid=836409497846900
84   https://www.facebook.com/photo/?fbid=855228439298339
85   Kristi Ceta. "Rama-Vucic at Dinner Meeting in Belgrade, Alex Soros Joins Them," *Albanian Daily* News, July 8, 2023. https://albaniandailynews.com/news/rama-vucic-at-dinner-meeting-in-belgrade-alex-soros-joins-them
86   https://www.facebook.com/photo.php?fbid=886815919472924
87   https://www.facebook.com/photo/?fbid=896544688500047
88   https://www.facebook.com/photo/?fbid=923624452458737

municipalities—with historically low voter turnout. Rama had benefited heavily from the Democratic Party being fractured between pro- and anti-Berisha factions and couldn't compete as a unified party. Additionally, due to internal party disputes, Berisha's candidates weren't allowed to run as members of the Democratic Party.

Alex Soros and Edi Rama Pictures 2024		
Date Posted	**Meeting Location**	**Notes**
January 24[89]	North Macedonia	Western Balkans Meets EU Conference
February 17–19[90]	Germany	Munich Security Conference
March 2[91]	Albania	South-East Europe Summit. Alex pictured shaking hands with Volodymyr Zelenskyy (in footnote)
March 5[92]	Albania	
May 18[93]	Montenegro	EU-West Balkans Summit
July 7[94]	Albania	Week after Edi Rama's birthday
August 29[95]	Albania	Refers to Rama as his "brother in Tirana"
September 28[96]	Alex's Home	For the United Nations Assembly in NYC

89   https://www.facebook.com/photo/?fbid=965327234955125
90   https://www.facebook.com/photo/?fbid=981120213375827
91   https://www.facebook.com/photo/?fbid=988231515998030
92   https://www.facebook.com/photo.php?fbid=989769079177607
93   https://www.facebook.com/photo/?fbid=1033774748110373
94   https://www.facebook.com/photo.php?fbid=1063937805094067
95   https://www.facebook.com/photo/?fbid=1097090255112155
96   https://www.facebook.com/photo/?fbid=1117330529754794

Alex and Rama's meetup on March 2, 2024, was roughly two weeks before Antony Blinken's visit to Tirana, where he praised Rama for reasons that will make much more sense in the next section (The McGonigal Connection).

In 2025, the two even joked about it after it was incorrectly reported that Rama had removed all photos with Alex from his Instagram account (he had never posted any in the first place). Days later, Alex posted a photo of them both in Munich, captioned "Back by popular demand!"[97]

Alex Soros and Edi Rama Pictures 2025 (As of July 1)		
Date Posted	Meeting Location	Notes
January 23[98]	World Economic Forum (Davos, Switzerland)	Two days after Rama and Zelenskyy concluded Bilateral Security Agreement
February 17[99]	Munich Security Conference	Captioned "back by popular demand!"
July 14	The Hamptons	Alex's Wedding

The Albanian publication *Pamphleti* noted in a May 2025 report that while there hadn't been many recent social media posts about meetings between the two, Rama had been keeping his meetings with Alex secret and avoiding posting photos with him (presumably asking Alex to do the same). One likely reason for this is to

97   https://www.instagram.com/p/DGLQdNKt7iK
98   https://www.facebook.com/photo/?fbid=1197681685053011&set=pcb.119768
1715053008
99   https://www.facebook.com/photo/?fbid=1214648176689695&set=pb.10004433
5724180.-2207520000

avoid any press involving Alex ahead of the May 11 parliamentary elections, because their relationship is a common line of attack from his opposition. There was no sudden schism—Rama said he was proud to be friends with Alex during a speech at the Hay Festival in Wales that May, just over a week after the election.[100] And the next month, Rama would be seen at Alex's wedding to Huma.

Humorously, Rama has dismissed reports on his ties to the Soroses as fake news. "I had Alex Soros as a friend, his father as well. And I am proud of that friendship. Tales and stories that connect unrelated things do not impress me."[101] Apparently, we're supposed to believe Alex is just there to talk sports?

During another occasion, when asked by a female journalist about his relationship with Alex, he ignored the question and pushed her before walking away, in a widely condemned incident.[102]

Does that seem like the behavior of a man with nothing to hide?

ALEX'S OTHER "BROTHER"—THE MAYOR OF TIRANA

The now-former mayor of Tirana, the capital city of Albania, was Erion Veliaj, a member of the Socialist Party and close friend of Alex Soros.

Like dozens of American politicians, Veliaj is among those pictured on Alex's social media accounts. Just a casual Google search for "Erion Veliaj Alex Soros" brings up plenty of results.

---

100 Rama i rikthehet dashurisë për Aleksin: Krenar që jam mik me dhëndrin e Trump dhe djalin e Soros," Pamfleti, May 24, 2025. https://pamfleti.net/politike/rama-i-rikthehet-dashurise-per-aleksin-krenar-qe-jam-mik-me-dhendrin-e--i281814

101 "Rama i përgjigjet akuzave për lidhjet me Sorosin: E kam mik, lërini historitë me amerikanë se s'jemi kërthiza e botës." Telegrafi, February 18, 2025. https://telegrafi.com/en/rama-pergjigjet-akuzave-per-lidhjet-sorosin-e-kam-mik-lerini-historite-amerikane-se-sjemi-kerthiza-e-botes

102 Fjori Sinoruka, "Albanian PM's 'Intimidation' of Woman Journalist Condemned," Balkan Insight, March 19, 2024. https://balkaninsight.com/2024/03/19/albanian-pms-intimidation-of-woman-journalist-condemned

In a photo from September 2023, Alex posted a photo of the two at Air Albania Stadium.[103] In another photo of the two from February 2024, Veliaj was the one to post the photo of the two, with a caption referring to Alex as his "brother," just like Rama.[104]

Veliaj has since been arrested in February on nine charges of corruption and money-laundering and is being held in jail. His wife is also under investigation, and it's already been discovered that she made purchases of luxury items totaling nearly 900,000 Euros.[105] For context, the maximum salary for the mayor of Tirana is about 3,000 Euros.[106]

Albania's Special Prosecution Office against Corruption and Organized Crime (SPAK) says the two made over one million Euros in a corrupt scheme over four years. SPAK alleges that money was laundered through nonprofit organizations that his wife, Ajola Xoxa, controlled from businessmen who were suspected of obtaining construction permits by making corrupt payments to the nonprofits. She's charged with corruption, money laundering, and concealment of assets.[107]

This is one of the rare cases of SPAK investigating one of their own.

Alex wasn't in on the action himself, but could he be coming to their rescue? Alex is close to PM Rama, the most powerful man in the country, after all.

---

103   https://www.facebook.com/Alexandersorospublic/photos/good-to-be-back-in-albania-and-check-out-one-of-tiranas-new-great-additions-air-/886302729524243/

104   "Veliaj krah për krah me Alex Soros/ E quan sërish vëlla," *CNA*, February 28, 2024.   https://www.cna.al/politike/veliaj-krah-per-krah-me-aleksander-soros-kenaqesi-te-takoj-vellain-tim-i391289

105   "NJOFTIM PËR SHTYP." *SPAK*, February 20, 2025. https://spak.gov.al/njoftim-per-shtyp-date-10-02-2025

106   "Paga mbi 3 mijë euro edhe për kryetarët e bashkive," *CNA*, September 21, 2024.   https://www.cna.al/ekonomi/paga-mbi-3-mije-euro-edhe-per-kryetaret-e-bashkive-i409037

107   Elira Kadriu, "The Charges That Led to Erion Veliaj's Arrest," *Citizens*. https://citizens.al/en/2025/02/10/akuzat-qe-sollen-arrestimin-e-erion-veliajt

In other words, Alex has sway there. So much so that he's been accused of using Albania as a political laboratory, with Rama and Veliaj as the "laboratory technicians."[108]

While unconfirmed, Albanian media is speculating that wiretaps implicating Veliaj make mentions of Alex as someone that could bail out him and his wife. In an interception published by the Albanian publication *CNA*, on February 19, Veliaj appears to ask his wife to meet with Alex, and that he'll fix things:

"19.02.2025": At 18:15, Erion Veliaj talks about Ajola's call to the American Embassy, where he tells her that she doesn't have to go and that it's a different administration. He tells her that when Aleksi comes, things will be fixed and you don't need to answer to parties that are not your country," the intercepts obtained by CNA say.[109]

According to the Albanian network *Syri*:

Member of the Democratic Party, Gent Strazimiri, in an interview commented on the recent wiretaps of Erion Veliaj, emphasizing that they confirm the accusations that the opposition has been raising since 2016.

According to him, the transcripts clearly show that Veliaj, implying his influence on Albanian justice. Strazimir stated that in Albania the law does not put you in prison, but Alex makes the decisions.

He added that the justice system in the country has turned into a corrupt and politically oriented instrument. "This is not American justice, but Alex Soros' justice," he said.

---

108   "Shqipëria, laborator politik i Soros: Eksperiment që duhet ndalur me çdo kusht më 11 maj," *Politiko*, February 17, 2025. https://politiko.al/opinews/shqiperia-laborator-politik-i-soros-eksperiment-qe-duhet-ndalur-me-cdo-k-i525659

109   "Përgjimet, Xoxën e thërrasin amerikanët/ Veliaj: Mos shko, kur të vijë Aleksi...," *CNA*, April 8, 2025. https://www.cna.al/denoncim/pergjimet-xoxen-e-therrasin-amerikanet-veliaj-mos-shko-kur-te-vije-alek-i426710

According to him, this situation should alarm all constitutional institutions and Albanian politics as a whole.[110]

The transcripts being referenced in the blockquote above include references "Aleksi," which is Albanian for Alex. In an intercepted phone call from Veliaj to his wife just over a week after he was arrested in February, he tells her that "when Aleksi comes, things will be fixed." He also advises her to avoid the US Embassy, with it being implied that it's because Donald Trump is in charge now.[111]

Genc Pollo, the former deputy prime minister of Albania and former minister of education, believes that this is a reference to Alex Soros, too:

> Interesting judicial wiretaps: Tirana mayor Veliaj, in pretrial detention for grand corruption & money laundering, tells his wife to avoid US Embassy "since there is a new administration there" and "things will be alright when Alex (Soros) comes"[112]

Alex hasn't made any public appearances yet in Albania this year (this is likely to change by the time this book is published). He did meet with Rama twice, but this was at the World Economic Forum and the Munich Security Conference.

If Valiaj and his wife do mysteriously get off, we all know why.

---

110   "'Rri e qetë, do ta rregullojë…'/ Strazimiri: Në Shqipëri arrestohesh dhe lirohesh vetëm nëse do Alexi, SPAK vegël e Sorosit," *Syri*, April 6, 2025. https://www.syri.net/politike/777300/rri-e-qete-do-ta-rregulloje-strazimiri-ne-shqiperi-arrestohesh-dhe-lirohesh-vetem-nese-do-alexi-spak-vegel-e-sorosit

111   "'Kur të vijë Aleksi do të rregullohen gjërat,' përgjimet nxjerrin zbuluar çiftin, Xoxën e thërrasin amerikanët-Veliaj: Mos shko…," *Alfapress*, April 4, 2025. https://www.alfapress.al/politike/kur-te-vije-aleksi-do-te-rregullohen-gjerat-pergjimet-nxjerrin-zbuluar--i153053

112   https://x.com/GencPollo/status/1908943235881324640

Veliaj has also proven that Rama is no stranger to getting his rivals, either personally or on behalf of a friend, sanctioned by the US.

As the journalist, former National Security Agency analyst and counterintelligence officer John Schindler explained:

> It is reported that Rama's allies, such as the mayor of Tirana, Erion Veliaj, have paid Charles McGonigal about 8 million euros to declare non-grata from Washington a political rival, Ylli Ndroqi [the designation was announced in 2022]. A frequent critic of the Rama government, Ndroqi had his media empire seized by the ruling Socialists in 2020 amid allegations of drug trafficking and money laundering—the same things the Rama government is widely alleged to be involved in.[113]

Much, much more on McGonigal to come.

THE MCGONIGAL CONNECTION

The story of the now-disgraced FBI agent Charles McGonigal is a complicated one, to the point where I thought it would be necessary to put a flowchart together (on the next two pages) to better help the reader keep track of the many connections between all the players.

Most American conservatives first learned about him when he was indicted in January 2023. McGonigal was an FBI special agent in charge of counterintelligence at the FBI's New York

---

113   Ibid.

City field office, and he played a "pivotal role" in launching the Trump-Russia probe into Trump's nonexistent Russian ties.[114]

There were two indictments that ultimately resulted in him being sentenced to a total of seventy-eight months in prison.

Ironically, one of his two indictments related to doing work with Russian oligarch Oleg Deripaska, with charges including violating and conspiring to violate the International Emergency Economic Powers Act (IEEPA), money laundering, and conspiracy. He also tried to have Deripaska's sanctions lifted. Conservative commentators blasted the hypocrisy of McGonigal investigating Trump over nonexistent Russia ties, while having his own Russian ties—which further tarnished the FBI's reputation.

Alex's "brother" PM Rama is at the center of the other indictment, which was unsealed the same day and didn't receive quite as much attention, because it didn't relate as much to US politics. In it, McGonigal was accused of selling access to Rama and other top Albanian officials for hundreds of thousands of dollars while working for the FBI.[115]

Of McGonigal's total sentence, twenty-eight months of it was Albania-related.

The number of characters and connections in this section may be hard to keep track of, so I included a web illustrating them on the following page that can be referenced when reading.

---

114 Ari Blaff, "FBI Official Who Helped Launch Trump-Russia Probe Sentenced to Four Years in Prison for Work with Russian Oligarch," *National Review*, December 15, 2023. https://www.nationalreview.com/news/fbi-official-who-helped-launch-trump-russia-probe-sentenced-to-four-years-in-prison-for-work-with-russian-oligarch

115 "Retired FBI Executive Charged with Concealing $225,000 in Cash Received from an Outside Source," US Attorney's Office—District of Columbia, January 23, 2023. https://www.justice.gov/usao-dc/pr/retired-fbi-executive-charged-concealing-225000-cash-received-outside-source

A diagram connecting:

- **Biden Admin** — Sanctioned Berisha
- **Hunter Biden**
- **"The Dinner"** — Meeting of McGonigal, Rama, and Hunter Biden Associates
- **Dorian Ducka** — Rama Advisor
- **Agron Nezaj** — Gave McGonigal $225k for Lobbying
- **Patrick Ho** — "Spy Chief of China"
- **Sali Berisha** — Rama's Opposition
- **Charles McGonigal** — Lobbied Edi Rama Played "pivotal role" in Trump-Russia Investigation
- **Spygate** — Manufactured Russia Scandal to Attack Trump
- **Edi Rama** — Socialist Albanian PM
- **Mark Rossini** — McGonigal's "Right Hand Man," Pushed anti-Berisha propaganda
- **Alex Soros** — Best Friend of Rama
- **Clinton Family** — Collaborated with Soros family for decades

McGonigal was also accused of lobbying Rama on behalf of Albanian-American businessman Agraj Neza, who reportedly paid him $225,000 to arrange meetings with Rama and his advisor, Dorian Ducka.[116] Neza reportedly was seeking contracts with the Albanian government. Neza had previously admitted in 2019 of making an illegal $80,000 contribution to Barack Obama's 2012 campaign on Rama's behalf, because Rama wanted a photo op with Obama to help his own campaign for prime minister.[117]

The lobbying would go both ways, with Rama himself using McGonigal to his benefit.

Rama had fed McGonigal information about an American lobbyist who worked for one of his political rivals, and McGonigal then used this information to pressure the FBI to open an investigation into the lobbyist.[118] This proved Rama was more than comfortable using whatever influence he could muster at America's institutions to target his political opponents.

McGonigal and Rama met in 2017 on one of at least four occasions, this one followed by McGonigal asking a federal prosecutor to investigate a lobbyist named Nicholas Muzin, who worked for Rama's opposition, the Democratic Party. McGonigal obtained information about Muzin and gave it to his FBI colleagues, who then opened an investigation into him in February 2018. Neza and Ducka were FBI sources for the investigation.[119]

Some in the opposition allege that Berisha's travel ban was already in effect prior to Secretary of State Blinken, thanks to actions from McGonigal at the behest of Rama. They interpret Rama's taunts in 2019 about whether Berisha could enter the

---

116   Ibid.
117   Ibid.
118   Chuck Ross, "George Soros's Son Spent July 4th with European Leader Linked to FBI Bribery Case," *Washington Free Beacon*, July 7, 2023. https://freebeacon.com/democrats/george-soross-son-spent-july-4th-with-european-leader-linked-to-fbi-bribery-case
119   Ibid.

United States as referencing an unannounced travel ban, rather than a prophecy of a future travel ban and sanctions. This isn't my opinion on the matter, because I don't understand the point of Blinken later announcing a travel ban—though it could be speculated that McGonigal laid the groundwork for the later ban, and this is what Yuri Kim was referencing when talking about a "multi-year process."

In a move that many in the Albanian press believe was to distract attention away from the McGonigal scandal, the day before McGonigal's sentencing on February 15, 2024, Blinken visited Tirana and held a joint press conference with Rama. When news of the McGonigal scandal broke, it escalated to protests calling for Rama's removal.

Blinken referenced the "judicial reform" efforts Alex and Rama had pushed to praise them. "Justice reform has not been easy, perfect, or quick, but it is showing real results, and you heard the prime minister describe them. Today I met with key judges and prosecutors who are helping lead the reform effort."[120] The two didn't talk about many real issues, and the presser appeared to happen out of nowhere.

The timing suggested a connection between Blinken, Rama, and McGonigal. The meeting wasn't announced by the State Department or embassy, but instead by a journalist close to the Socialist Party. The timing of the visit could just be a coincidence; but as one Albanian publication put it, "history has shown that whenever dignitaries of such a high level arrive in Tirana, something else is hidden." [121]

---

120   John Schindler, "Biden Cozies Up Closer to Europe's Only Narco State," *Washington Examiner*, February 20, 2024. https://www.washingtonexaminer.com/restoring-america/2863517/biden-cozies-up-closer-to-europes-only-narco-state

121   "Çfarë fshihet pas vizitës së Blinken në Tiranë, në ditën e gjyqit të McGonigal për dosjen shqiptare?," *Pamfleti*, February 7, 2024. https://pamfleti.net/politike/fare-fshihet-pas-vizites-se-blinken-ne-tirane-ne-diten-e-gjyqit-te-mcgo-i211810

Consider the precedent. When Secretary of State Hillary Clinton descended on Tirana on November 1, 2012, in what was billed as a "pro-government visit," it was agreed during her visit that Albania would receive three hundred Iranian Mujahideen. Similarly, when Secretary of State John Kerry visited in 2016, the purpose of the visit was a secret, but then it also turned out to be about the Mujahideen, of which 155 were later given sanctuary in Albania. If Blinken was there for his stated reason, it would be the exception to the rule.

Albanian media saw it as off, too, and they differed in their speculations for its reason—ranging from it being a diplomatic gesture to downplay US-Albanian tensions over the McGonigal scandal (since it exposed Rama's corrupt circle[122]), to it being a distraction to hide Rama from scrutiny in the press.

Curiously, Blinken praised the ruling Socialist Party, making no mention of the opposition, including Rama's rival whom he had sanctioned.

THE HUNTER BIDEN CONNECTION

The McGonigal rabbit hole goes deep, connecting him not just to Rama but also to the Hunter Biden saga that the media were desperate to censor ahead of the 2020 presidential election.

A single piece of evidence, which no one would've ever thought would be significant at the time, ties it all together.

In 2013, a photograph was taken during a dinner in Tirana. It links together an associate from the Chinese energy giant that infamously did work with Hunter Biden (CEFC), the associates of McGonigal, China's ambassador, and power players linked to Rama.

122　"Blinken zbarkon në Tiranë ditën e gjyqit të McGonigal, mister vizita blic, politika në ankth nga frika e një "non-grate" tjetër." *SOT*, February 7, 2024. https://sot.com.al/politike/blinken-zbarkon-ne-tirane-diten-e-gjyqit-te-mcgonigal-mister-vizita-bli-i641407

The men pictured include then-Speaker of Parliament Ilir Meta (whose party was still in coalition with Rama's at the time), Patrick Ho, Dorian Ducka, Agron Neza, Mark Rossini, and Ye Hao. Each requires a proper introduction.

Patrick Ho, a man closely tied to Hunter Biden, was convicted in US federal court of bribing top officials in Chad and Uganda in pursuit of oil deals for CEFC. He was sentenced to three years in prison in March 2019 and then expelled from the United States. Hunter has referred to Ho as the "f---ing spy chief of China,"[123] and there was a $1 million wire to Hunter in March 2018 that had the memo line: "Dr Patrick Ho Chi Ping Representation." The first person that Ho called after being arrested by the FBI was Joe Biden's brother James, but the call was intended for Hunter.[124]

CEFC was one of Hunter's most lucrative clients,[125] and it's his work related to CEFC that the infamous "10 percent for the big guy" email, allegedly referencing Joe Biden, is in connection to.[126]

Dorian Ducka is listed as "Person B" in the indictment of McGonigal. Ducka has been Rama's advisor of investments since 2016 and was deputy minister of energy and industry of Albania from 2013–2015. Ducka also worked for CEFC and was photographed with the chairman of CEFC in May 2017, as was reported

123   Chuck Ross, "Hunter Biden's Chinese Client Appealed to CCP for Help in Legal Case, Court Records Show," *Washington Free Beacon*, May 30, 2024. https://freebeacon.com/biden-administration/hunter-bidens-chinese-client-appealed-to-ccp-for-help-in-legal-case-court-records-show/

124   Michael Isikoff and Zach Dorfman, "New Hunter Biden Revelations Raise Counterintelligence Questions," *Yahoo! News*, April 11, 2022. https://news.yahoo.com/new-hunter-biden-revelations-raise-counter-intelligence-questions-090046438.html

125   Emma-Jo Morris and Gabrielle Fonrouge, "Emails Reveal How Hunter Biden Tried to Cash in Big on Behalf of Family with Chinese Firm," *New York Post*, January 20, 2023. https://nypost.com/2020/10/15/emails-reveal-how-hunter-biden-tried-to-cash-in-big-with-chinese-firm

126   Olivia Land, "Joe Biden Named in 2017 Email to Hunter Seeking Chinese Gas Deal," *New York Post*, January 20, 2023. https://nypost.com/2023/01/20/joe-biden-named-in-2017-email-discussing-hunters-china-deal

in China state media.[127] Internal court documents, obtained by *Business Insider* when McGonigal was initially under scrutiny from a grand jury, revealed that he was asked to preserve all materials and communications with a number of people that included Neza and Ducka.[128]

One of Hunter Biden's emails from his "laptop from hell" reveals that Ducka once sent him a "follow" request on Twitter in January 2019. Also of note, Yuri Kim follows Ducka on social media.

Adding further proof that Ducka and Hunter worked together, one of Hunter's own emails has the header "Dorian," where he and another business associate discuss "taking care" of him, because he was a "real help."[129]

Another man pictured is the aforementioned "Person A" in the McGonigal indictment, Agron Neza, from whom McGonigal received the $225,000 wire that he was indicted over.

A significant McGonigal-tied individual pictured is his right-hand man, Mark Rossini. Rossini is a disgraced ex-FBI agent who left the bureau in 2008 amid scandal, and then faced separate bribery charges from an August 2022 federal indictment in Puerto Rico. In 2019, Rossini appeared in an Albanian propaganda film about alleged Russian involvement in the country, where he tried to link protests from the opposition, including Sali Berisha, as

---

127   "Berisha e quan 'shërbëtori i Ramës', shikoni si Dorian Duçka lobonte mes familjes Rothschild dhe gjigantit kinez për marrëveshje," *Shqiptarja*, January 27, 2023. https://shqiptarja.com/lajm/fotolajm-berisha-e-quan-sherbetori-i-rames-shikoni-si-dorian-ducka-lobonte-mes-familjes-rothschild-dhe-gjigandit-kinez-per-marreveshje

128   Mattathias Schwartz, "Exclusive: Former Top FBI Official Involved in Trump-Russia Investigation Under Scrutiny by Federal Prosecutors for His Own Ties to Russia," *Business Insider*, September 15, 2022. https://www.businessinsider.com/exclusive-fbi-charles-mcgonigal-trump-russia-grand-jury-oleg-deripaska-2022-9

129   "Report on the Biden Laptop," *Marco Polo*, October 19, 2022. https://bidenlaptopemails.com/biden-emails/email.php?id=20190114-045150_53986

being Russian influenced.[130] This proves that McGonigal's right hand man was pushing anti-Berisha narratives at the same time Rama was publicly mocking him about his ability to travel.

McGonigal, Rossini, Neza, and a man named Shefqet Dizdari were all partners in a firm called Lawoffice & Investigation,[131] which was founded in 2007 and closed in 2019.[132]

A potential direct connection between Hunter and McGonigal exists, which was discovered from evidence on Hunter's laptop, and the laptop of Pamela McGonigal (his wife). Retrieved emails show that both received at least twenty-nine emails related to the Next Level Lacrosse program and other lacrosse activities between October 7, 2014, and May 7, 2015. Two of Hunter's daughters (that he acknowledges) are known to have played on a varsity lacrosse team at the Sidwell Friends private school, but it's unconfirmed if McGonigal's kids did. When Pamela was asked if her kids played with Hunter's, she angrily berated reporters while denying a connection.[133]

Also at the table is the Chinese ambassador in Albania, Ye Hao. Edi Rama launched a Confucius Institute at the University of Tirana in the months following the meeting. The Confucius Institutes present themselves as a Chinese cultural institution but are actually Communist Party funded and directed propaganda.

130 "Russian Money," Part Two—Exclusive Interview with Former FBI Agent, Mark Rossini—Inside Story," *Top Channel Albania*, 2019. https://www.youtube.com/watch?v=GDNx7kF2HKQ

131 Josh Kovensky, "Albanian Firm Ties Indicted Former FBI Official to Yet Another Disgraced Former Agent," *Talking Points Memo*, January 27, 2023. https://talkingpointsmemo.com/muckraker/albanian-firm-ties-indicted-former-fbi-official-to-yet-another-disgraced-former-agent

132 "Lawoffice & Investigation: Informacioni ëShtë I Përditësuar Sipas Të Dhënave Të Qkb/rregjistër Biznesi Deri Në," *Open Corporates Albania*, January 24, 2023. https://opencorporates.al/sq/nipt/K81310029E

133 Steven Vago and Bruce Golding, "Emails About Lacrosse-playing Kids Link Hunter Biden, Wife of Ex-FBI Agent Charles McGonigal," *New York Post*, January 26, 2023. https://nypost.com/2023/01/25/kids-link-hunter-biden-wife-of-fbi-agent-charles-mcgonigal-tied-to-oligarch

At the opening of the Institute, Hao praised it as a milestone in relations between China and Albania.[134]

The intricate web of connections unveiled by the dinner photograph ties together a cast of controversial figures across political, criminal, and international spheres. From the disgraced FBI counterintelligence chief McGonigal to Hunter Biden and his lucrative dealings with the Chinese energy conglomerate CEFC, the threads of influence and corruption stretch far and wide.

The presence of key players like Patrick Ho, convicted of bribery and linked to Hunter, alongside Rama's advisor Dorian Ducka and Agron Neza, both named in McGonigal's indictment, illustrates a nexus of power and illicit financial dealings. Add to this Mark Rossini's propaganda efforts in Albania to take down Berisha, which aligns with the goals of Rama and Alex, and the picture emerges of a shadowy network operating at the intersection of politics and personal gain.

It's a big club, and you ain't in it.

A month before McGonigal pleaded guilty in September 2023 John Schindler predicted that if McGonigal were to plead guilty, it would bury the rest of the case, leaving the full extent of his dealings with Rama unknown.[135]

As you can imagine by the tangled web weaved so far, there was plenty to bury.

As Schindler explained, McGonigal faced allegations of using his FBI cred to "shake down" wealthy businessmen in collaboration with Rama. "McGonigal is believed to have extorted wealthy Albanians in a sort of protection racket, where the bureau chief promised to protect the oligarchs from US sanctions in exchange

134 "Albania launches Tirana Confucius Institute," *China.org*, November 19, 2013. http://www.china.org.cn/arts/2013-11/19/content30640572.htm

135 John Schindler. "The FBI's Balkan Scandal Keeps Spreading," *Washington Examiner*, February 16, 2023. https://www.washingtonexaminer.com/opinion/2578397/the-fbis-balkan-scandal-keeps-spreading

for large bribes. McGonigal's withdrawal from this was about $32 million (which was apparently split with his partners). I [Schindler] also reported that McGonigal shook down Shefqet Kastrati, Albania's top oil magnate, for 12 million euros in 2017." Representatives for Kastrati denied the allegations.[136]

While still just allegations, this makes far more sense than someone with McGonigal's status and reputation throwing it all away for "only" $225k. Profiting from corruption via Rama is also an explanation for why Alex is so interested in such a minor country—though this is just speculation. No one I spoke to in the opposition provided me with any examples of corruption Alex could potentially be involved in.

WASHINGTON INTERVENES TO PROTECT RAMA

The Biden administration's relationship with Rama were significant enough that they took action to squash reporting on McGonigal and Rama on at least one known occasion.

The *Washington Examiner*'s John Schindler was contacted by the Germany magazine *Bild*, the highest circulation newspaper in Europe, to answer questions about Albania and Rama. Schindler recalled that *Bild* asked him about Dorian Ducka, to which he replied that he was a "high-level consigliere to PM Rama" and "involved in the McGonigal scandal in an unflattering way"— hardly nonpublic information.

The article was set to go public ahead of the 2023 local elections in Albania, but that never happened, as Schindler explained:

> The Bild reporter informed me, with surprise and dismay, that top editors had killed the story (which included comments from others besides myself, such as top

---

136   Ibid.

German security experts). *When I asked why, the reporter informed me that Bild leadership explained that "Washington stands by Rama," and therefore, the report cannot run.* [Emphasis mine].

In other words, Germany's highest-circulation newspaper, which enjoys a reputation for muckraking journalism, won't publish negative reports about Rama and his friends lest they offend Tirana—and, more important, Washington.[137]

The Socialist Party went on to win 53 out of 61 Mayoral positions in those elections, and a majority of council seats in nearly 90% of municipalities.

THE SHOW GOES ON

The indictment of McGonigal was specific to his time as an FBI agent, but his presence in Albania stretches years beyond that. In fact, he likely spent more time involved there after leaving the FBI in 2018 than he spent there in his capacity as an FBI agent. He wasn't charged for any potential criminality after leaving the FBI, and as argued previously, what he was charged with represented only a fraction of his activities in Albania.

In Albania in September 2021, McGonigal met with the socialist Mayor of Tropojë, Rexhë Byberi, where Byberi gave him the title of "Honorary Citizen." Three photos of the event were posted to Byberi's Facebook account and have since been deleted.

This was four months after Berisha was sanctioned.

---

137   John Schindler. "German Newspaper Cancels Corruption Report on Biden's Albanian Buddy," *Washington Examiner*, May 13, 2023. https://www.washingtonexaminer.com/opinion/beltway-confidential/2769035/german-newspaper-cancels-corruption-report-on-bidens-albanian-buddy

Byberi, the Mayor of a town with a population just above 14,000, has himself been embroiled in many scandals that include granting illegal construction permits in protected areas, violating procurement laws, authorizing work on private property without consent, and breaking his house arrest in 2024 to sign an inflated municipal budget that allocated 74% of funds to just 381 employees.[138]

The photos have been reported on in Albanian media before they were deleted by Byberi, and Albanian journalist Armela Ferko shared copies of all three of the now-deleted photos from the event with me (as the articles didn't contain all of them for whatever reason).[139] The photos and accompanying text on the now-deleted Facebook post confirmed that McGonigal was joined by Agron Neza at the event.[140]

Another man McGonigal was photographed with there was Socialist MP Damian Gjiknuri, who the opposition has accused of financing parties with Hunter Biden, and as being one of the people who organized McGonigal's "official" activities in Albania.[141]

---

138 "Rexh Byberi theu arrestin shtëpiak dhe shkoi në zyrë", akuzat e PD: Skandal në Bashkinë e Tropojës, shpenzimet më të larta se buxheti vjetor," *BalkanWeb,* January 25, 2025. https://www.balkanweb.com/rexh-byberi-theu-arrestin-shtepiak-dhe-shkoi-ne-zyre-akuzat-e-pd-skandal-ne-bashkine-e-tropojes-shpenzimet-me-te-larta-se-buxheti-vjetor

139 WhatsApp chat with Armela Ferko, April 18, 2025.

140 "Pas korruptimit, zyrtari i FBI u dekorua nga bashkia Tropojë, e shoqëronte "sponsori" person A," *Insajderi,* January 23, 2023. https://insajderi.org/pas-korruptimit-zyrtari-i-fbi-u-dekorua-nga-bashkia-tropoje-e-shoqeronte-sponsori-person-a

141 "Berisha: Gjiknuri dhe Balla, njerëzit që organizuan veprimtaritë "zyrtare" të McGonigal në Shqipëri," *Telegrafi,* February 2023. https://telegrafi.com/berisha-gjiknuri-dhe-balla-njerezit-qe-organizuan-veprimtarite-zyrtare-te-mcgonigal-ne-shqiperi

CONCLUSION

The saga of Albania under the shadow of the Soros family and Edi Rama reads like a geopolitical thriller, but the stakes are real, the players are powerful, and the consequences have reshaped a nation.

What began as George Soros's claimed post-communist mission to plant the seeds of a so-called "open society" in a battered Albania has, over decades, morphed into state capture. From the seeds he planted through faux-philanthropy in the 1990s, to the wholesale remaking of Albania's judicial system, George has planted his flag for everyone to see (though he'd rather you didn't).

With a nation's judiciary already remade in his image, which has resulted in the Socialist Party's continued dominance, the keys have been handed over to Alex Soros.

Albania today stands as a paradox: a pro-American nation where US aid and Soros millions have fueled a system that, critics argue, mocks the very values it claims to uphold. The bunkers of Enver Hoxha's paranoia still dot the landscape; but the new fortifications are less concrete and more insidious, built of corrupted institutions, silenced opposition, and a judiciary that bends to the will of Rama and his benefactors.

For Alex Soros, Albania may indeed be a second home, a proving ground where his father's vision has been realized—not as a beacon of freedom, but as a cautionary tale of unchecked influence. For Albanians, the question remains: how long can a nation endure as a pawn in this high-stakes game before its people demand the reckoning that justice, so far, has failed to deliver?

ADDENDUM: Q&A WITH GENC POLLO: MEMBER OF ALBANIAN PARLIAMENT (1996–2019), MINISTER OF EDUCATION AND SCIENCE (2005–2008), DEPUTY PRIME MINISTER (2008–2009) AND MINISTER OF TELECOMMUNICATIONS AND IT (2009–2013).

Question: When you were in office, what kind of projects did George Soros propose and implement? My understanding is that they were generally useful projects at first, but that he wanted something in return for them.

Answer: When I was Minister of Education (2005–2008), the Open Society Foundation had a professional unit on education. They commented on reforms and policies I adopted in a generally professional and constructive way. I did find it mostly helpful.

During the previous socialist government (1997–2005) the Foundation had dedicated a very large sum to education which was disbursed by themselves to teachers, officials etc. It rivaled the government budget. Officials in the ministry alluded that the OSF was the de facto ministry, which was interesting given the Soros ambiguous stance on state sovereignty. The program ended as I assumed office in 2005.

Follow Up: Did Soros continuously fund education in Albania for the past three decades, or did it start again when the socialists took power in 1997? I didn't know if Berisha put an end to it as president, or as prime minister (2005–2013) allowed Soros to operate this program at all. I'm trying to make sure I have my timeline right. I was under the impression that Berisha and Soros never worked together after their relationship soured in the

'90s, so I wanted to clarify whether there was some level of cooperation between them over a decade later.

Answer: The Soros engagement started again on a big scale after 1997 with the Socialist government; their Education Cooperation ended just before our government assumed office in 2005. No cooperation with Soros started with the [second] Berisha government. But the local OSF continued to finance projects and activities in Albania that were unrelated to the government; they had a good cooperation with Rama while he was Culture Minister and mayor of Tirana (2000–2011).

Question: Are there any rumors about what Alex Soros and Rama are discussing in their meetings?

Answer: I wonder if Rama offers him money and deals like he reportedly does with others.

But certainly, they would talk about expanding their influence. Alex Soros was so much involved in the failed Kosovo/Serbia land swap deal and in the Open Balkans project with Rama and Serbia's President Vučić. Both projects were problematic and both failed.

(*Note*: the Kosovo/Serbia land swap deal was a proposed plan to redraw the Kosovo/Serbia border on ethnic lines. Kosovo is 95 percent Albanian, with the remaining population being Serbian, and living in northern Kosovo, bordering Serbia.

Pollo also pointed me to an article by Marc Crawford, a former chairman of the American Chamber of Commerce in Albania, who said "While Americans tend to view the Balkans as a muddy pond, full of potential friends, if the economic and political sticks and carrots can be harmonized, the Balkans governments view the Americans as a big brother with chinks in its armor. The chinks in the armor being politically exposed individuals or their circle of influencers, which can be influenced by cash, sex, substances, finder's fees or sweetheart deals. The game is to find the cocktail of incentives to achieve one's objectives.... The Prime Minister of Albania [Rama], for example, has long had ties to Democratic donors, such as the Soros family.")

Question: When was it that Berisha and the Democrats soured on George Soros? I saw that George Soros criticized Berisha in a *New Yorker* article in 1995.

Answer: In the early 1990s the OSF, which was established to promote democracy, had an initial good cooperation with the Democratic Party but soon shifted support to opponents of the Democratic Party, who were mostly close to the Socialist Party (ex-Communist). I think this is a general pattern as Soros supported ex-Communist elsewhere in Eastern Europe.

Question: Are there any current events (legislation, proposed initiatives, etc.) in Albanian politics linked to Alex?

Answer: I can't say for sure but certain legislation proposed by the Rama government is very much in line with what Soros supports: for instance, the law on cannabis cultivation (adopted) and family and gender (LGBT+) legislation pieces (not yet adopted).

(*Note*: Alex's agenda on drugs is coming to Albania but appears to be in its infancy. The Democrats have submitted a draft law to try to enshrine that the country only recognizes two genders as part of a "de-Sorosization campaign.")

Question: If there's anything else you think an American audience should know about Alex and George's influence, you can add it here.

Answer: I have followed the US situation with crime spiraling out of control also because of activist, "soft on crime" prosecutors and judges who Soros helped elect or appoint. I gladly see the Trump administration pushing back. The US should strike down any overseas Soros subsidy (in the form of USAID funding etc.) or support and keep them at safe distance from the State Department and its embassies abroad. For the good of the US, Albania and the rest of the world.

Chapter 5

Alex and The Ukraine

Ukraine isn't just another pin on Alex's global map; it's the proving ground where his vision clashes with a world in chaos. With George's first meddling being in post-Soviet upheaval, Alex sees a war-torn nation as both opportunity and obligation: a chance to funnel OSF billions into reconstruction while locking in progressive ideals amid the rubble. His frequent Kyiv visits and Zelenskyy ties signal more than supposed philanthropy; they're a bid to outmaneuver Russia's orbit and cement Soros influence in a geopolitical hot zone.

All eyes have been on Ukraine since Russia's full-scale invasion in February 2022, and Joe Biden sending them hundreds of billions of US tax dollars. But the Soros influence has gone largely unnoticed.

SETTING THE STAGE
George Soros has had his flag planted there for over three decades. In a nation plagued by corruption, George saw opportunity, and he has used Ukraine to further his quest to spread his vision of a so-called "open society," and to attack his political opponents in the United States.

As in Albania, George has invested not only decades of his time, but also hundreds of millions of dollars. *The Man Behind the Curtain* had a lengthy chapter on George's web in Ukraine. To provide background on how he first entrenched himself there,

I have provided a highly condensed version in the following pages to show what Alex has inherited—before I dive into how he's entangling himself with the Ukrainian elite and using his Albanian connections to do so.

Among the nations in Europe that stand out for obscene levels of corruption, Ukraine couldn't be more obvious about it—and it's not-so-coincidentally the nation that George holds the most influence in. The Russian-language Ukrainian newspaper *Vesti* publishes a list of the most influential one hundred people in the country at the end of every year, and in 2019 it picked George as second to only President Volodymyr Zelenskyy. The prime minister took third place after Soros.

As part of his strategy of trying to influence nations while the USSR was heading towards failure, George began inserting his tentacles in Ukraine in 1989, two years before the evil empire fell.[1]

The most notable organization George started was the International Renaissance Foundation in April 1990, in Kyiv. The IRF is a subsidiary of the OSF and thus inherited by Alex. George's influence would only grow in 1991 onwards when the country became fully independent.[2]

The IRF became the biggest international donor to Ukraine by 1994, with an annual budget of $12 million, which it claims was for "projects that ranged from retraining tens of thousands of decommissioned soldiers to the creation of a contemporary arts center in Kyiv," named the Soros Center for Contemporary

---

1   Michael R. Caputo, *The Ukraine Hoax: How Decades of Corruption in the Former Soviet Republic Led to Trump's Phony Impeachment* (New York: Bombardier Books, 2020), p. 41.

2   Orysia Lutsevych, "How to Finish a Revolution: Civil Society and Democracy in Georgia, Moldova, and Ukraine," Chatham House, January 2013. https://www.chathamhouse.org/sites/default/files/public/Research/Russia%20and%20Eurasia/0113bp_lutsevych.pdf

Arts. The most recent data from the OSF shows an 2023 annual budget for Ukraine of roughly $19 million.[3]

George (and now Alex) have spent a whopping $230 million (in non-inflation-adjusted dollars) in Ukraine since 1991.[4] George bought politicians left and right—he financed Mikheil Saakashvili, the president of Georgia (2004–2013), who became governor of Ukraine's Odessa region (2015–2016), and Svitlana Zalishchuk, a former member of Ukrainian parliament. He's also given money to Mustafa Nayyem, an MP who was appointed VP of Ukroboronprom, a state association of the nation's major defense conglomerates[5]—the "Ukrainian military complex," as it could be called.

The IRF played a large role in aiding the 2010-2014 Maidan protests, which resulted in the removal of President Viktor Yanukovych. Many of the main directors of the Maidan protests were tied to Soros-sponsored programs.[6] The IRF played a role in aiding the protests, with the OSF's website admitting they "ensured that legal aid was made available throughout the crisis to civic activists, protesters, and journalists; supplied victims of violence with medical care; enabled civil society solidarity and organization; supported channels like Hromadske TV in independent, live reporting about events on the Maidan; and documented cases of torture, beatings, and police and courts abuse."[7]

3   "The Open Society Foundations in Ukraine," Open Society Foundations, February 14, 2025. https://www.opensocietyfoundations.org/newsroom/the-open-society-foundations-in-ukraine

4   Ibid.

5   "George Soros Named Second-Most Influential Person in Ukraine," *ReMix,* December 20, 2019. https://rmx.news/article/article/soros-secondmost-influential-person-in-ukraine

6   Caputo, *The Ukraine Hoax,* page 38

7   "Understanding Ukraine's Euromaidan Protests," Open Society Foundations, May 2019. https://www.opensocietyfoundations.org/explainers/understanding-ukraines-euromaidan-protests

Following the ouster of Yanukovych, George's preferred candidate Petro Poroshenko would win 54.7 percent of the votes, take office in June 2014, and then praise George and the IRF months later.[8]

Early the following year, the two met numerous times to discuss the possibility of joining the EU, and George had announced his intent to invest $1 billion into Ukraine.[9] The next year, the two discussed opportunities for increasing "economic assistance" and implementing "judicial reform."[10]

Later that year, Poroshenko awarded George the Order of Liberty, one of Ukraine's highest awards, practically admitting his meddling. Only eighty-two people have ever been awarded it (as of this writing), and George was the thirty-second recipient.

Upon giving him the award, Poroshenko said of George: "Your intense activities during recent years have extremely promoted the democratic change that we now have happening in Ukraine." He praised Soros's role in the country and the IRF's contributions to the establishment of a new Eurocentric Ukraine over the preceding twenty-five years.[11] The presidential decree commended Soros for working toward "the strengthening of the international authority of the Ukrainian state" and the "implementation of socio-economic reforms." Or, in other words: "Thank you for making me president."

---

8   "Petro Poroshenko thanks George Soros for supporting Ukraine," International Renaissance Foundation, August 23, 2014. https://www.irf.ua/en/petro_poroshenko_expressed_gratitude_to_george_soros_for_the_support_to_ukraine

9   "US Billionaire George Soros Ready to Invest $1 Billion in Ukrainian Economy," *Tass*, March 30, 2015. https://tass.com/economy/785780

10   "Petro Poroshenko had a meeting with George Soros," Consulate General of Ukraine in Chicago, January 13, 2015. https://chicago.mfa.gov.ua/en/news/31457-petro-poroshenko-proviv-zustrich-z-dzhordzhem-sorosom

11   "Ukrainian President Gives High State Award to Soros," Radio Free Europe, November 13, 2015. https://www.rferl.org/a/ukrainian-president-gives-high-state-award-to-george-soros/27362587.html

The quid pro quo continued with George later joining Ukraine's National Investment Council, an advisory body under the president of Ukraine[12] (and thus now chaired by Volodymyr Zelenskyy). It's unclear if George is still a member; if he isn't, his departure was never reported.

As always, the money didn't come without the price of influence, and this time his foreign influence was more evident in America than in Ukraine. George used Ukraine as a hub to create a handful of organizations that would later be weaponized against his political enemies in America, including Donald Trump—peaking with the first of two failed attempts to remove Trump from office through impeachment.

It was in 2014 that George's IRF and its grantees were active supporters in the creation of the Anti-Corruption Acter Centre (AntAC) of Ukraine, an NGO as powerful as its name is ironic.[13] AntAC was co-founded by Daria Kaleniuk, an American-educated lawyer who serves as its executive director.

Her name would become relevant to an American audience when an anonymous CIA analyst filed a complaint on August 19, 2019, centered on a phone call between Trump and Zelenskyy, where Trump allegedly requested investigations into Joe and Hunter Biden's activities in Ukraine, or else a $400 million military aid package to Ukraine would be blocked. Zelenskyy publicly denied that Trump threatened to withhold aid at least twice, comments that largely went ignored.[14]

---

12   "Lozhkin invites Soros to join Ukraine Investment Council," *UA Position: Focus on Ukraine,* August 30, 2016. https://uaposition.com/latest-news/lozhkin-invites-soros-join-ukraine-investment-council

13   "Declaring Anti-Corruption Action Stories," AntAC, March 31, 2018. https://antac.org.ua/en/news/declaring-anti-corruption-action-stories

14   Mark Moore, "Ukraine's Zelenskyy Again Denies Quid Pro Quo During Trump Phone Call," *New York Post,* December 2, 2019. https://nypost.com/2019/12/02/ukraines-zelensky-again-denies-quid-pro-quo-during-trump-phone-call

The CIA whistleblower has widely been suspected to be Eric Ciaramella, who joined the agency during Obama's second term and focused on Ukraine policy. He was acquainted with Kaleniuk, and thus AntAC, as White House logs say that Kaleniuk visited the White House on December 9, 2015, and met with him.[15] This was months after an investigation into Hunter Biden's alleged corruption was quickly shut down with the help of AntAC—and Joe Biden himself.

In February 2015, Viktor Shokin was appointed prosecutor general of Ukraine and was soon unjustly scrutinized for investigating the energy company Burisma.

Burisma was made famous by Hunter Biden's involvement in the company. He was appointed to the company's board of directors in 2014 at a reported salary of up to $83,333 per month, all with no relevant experience.[16] This, like Hunter's art sales, was among his many actions that led to allegations of him selling access to the White House. Like clockwork, AntAC was quick to intervene to protect Hunter, as exposing him as a conduit to potential involvement by Joe would damage the Biden White House and cause problems for Democrats as a whole.

AntAC tweeted on December 25, 2015 that "One of the major goals of #AntAC for 2016 is to force #Shokin to resign."[17] A supposed an "anti-corruption" organization was aghast that someone would look to investigate corruption, further calling into question their real purpose.

Shokin attempted to begin a probe into Burisma that "included interrogations and other crime-investigation procedures into all

15   "Judicial Watch Sues CIA and DOJ for Communications of Eric Ciaramella," *Judicial Watch,* December 26, 2019. https://www.judicialwatch.org/judicial-watch-sues-cia-and-doj-communications-of-eric-ciaramella

16   Dan Bongino, *Follow the Money: The Shocking Deep State Connections of the Anti-Trump Cabal* (New York: Post Hill Press, 2020), p. 138.

17   https://twitter.com/ANTACua/status/680314247923036160

members of the executive board, including Hunter Biden." This never materialized because Joe Biden (then VP) threatened to withhold a $1 billion loan to Ukraine unless Skokin was removed as prosecutor general. Biden even bragged about it on video to the Council on Foreign Relations in 2018, stating that when he attended a meeting with Ukraine's president and prime minister, he said, "'I'm leaving in six hours. If the prosecutor is not fired, you're not getting the money.' Well, son of a bitch. He got fired. And they put in place someone who was solid at the time."[18] And he had an assist from the Soros network.

Burisma's operations, and thus the reputation of the Biden family, then continued unscathed. One could hardly miss the irony in Biden doing exactly what Trump got impeached for.

AntAC had a direct connection to the alleged whistleblower who sparked the first Trump impeachment on a premise immediately debunked by Zelenskyy, and it had protected the Obama White House from a major scandal when Biden was vice president. AntAC wasn't the only Soros-backed group playing offense against Trump during the Ukraine impeachment. To bolster the case, the whistleblower's complaint made multiple references to a report titled "Meet the Florida Duo Helping Giuliani Investigate for Trump in Ukraine," published by an international NGO, Organized Crime and Corruption Reporting Project (OCCRP).[19] George is one of OCCRP's top donors, and they've published articles and reports defending him against his critics and targeting his opponents.[20]

18   Bongino, *Follow the Money*, p. 14.
19   Aubrey Belford and Veronika Melkozerova, "Meet the Florida Duo Helping Giuliani Investigate for Trump in Ukraine," OCCRP, July 22, 2019. https://www.occrp.org/en/investigations/meet-the-florida-duo-helping-giuliani-dig-dirt-for-trump-in-ukraine
20   Tom Ozimek, "Whistleblower's Complaint against Trump Cites George Soros-Funded NGO," *The Epoch Times*, September 27, 2019. https://www.theepochtimes.com/whistleblowers-complaint-against-trump-cites-george-soros-funded-ngo_3098685.html

Within the whistleblower complaint, an OCCRP report is cited relating to claims about Rudy Giuliani's efforts to investigate Joe Biden.[21] In the bizarre world of the whistleblower, we're to believe that investigating Biden for alleged crimes is a crime itself, but that anything Biden may have allegedly done is not. That's why they're able to allege that Trump committed a quid quo pro while mentioning *Biden's* alleged quid pro quo, while experiencing no cognitive dissonance.

The OCCRP report is referenced in the fourth, ninth, tenth, and eleventh footnotes in the complaint, and it claims that Giuliani was key in pushing Ukrainian officials to probe the Bidens in 2019.[22] Given what we know now about Hunter Biden's business dealings in the post-laptop-from-hell era, it would seem like a group called the "Organized Crime and Corruption Reporting Project" missed out on a major story—but as was the case with AntAC's sudden disinterest in investigating corruption, that was the point the whole time.

Through his web, George was able to use Ukraine to protect Joe Biden as VP, and then get Trump impeached for trying to launch the same sort of investigation George had blocked earlier. It's a key point of influence for the Soros web—and it's one Alex is looking to keep.

ALEX TAKES OVER GEORGE'S UKRAINE LEGACY

Alex assumed role of OSF chairman two months before Russia launched a full-scale invasion of Ukraine in February 2022.

The OSF pledged $25 million to create the Ukraine Democracy Fund in support of Ukraine against Russia.[23] The fund sought to

---

21   "Meet the Florida Duo Helping Giuliani Investigate for Trump in Ukraine," OCCRP.
22   "Whistleblower's Complaint against Trump Cites George Soros-Funded NGO," *The Epoch Times*.
23   "Open Society Launches Fund for a Free and Democratic Ukraine," Open Society Foundations, March 3, 2022. https://www.opensocietyfoundations.org/newsroom/open-society-launches-fund-for-a-free-and-democratic-ukraine

raise $100 million dollars during and after the war to advance three goals.

The first was to fund "independent Ukrainian organizations" that fight corruption, defend the rights of citizens, and defend independent media. According to the foundation, this is "vital" to the "country's democratic development." The second was to provide resources for journalists, artists, scholars, and advocacy groups with which to document war crimes. And the third was to fund humanitarian aid, "[bolster] public health work," assist refugees, and fund reconstruction.

Even when it's aid amidst a war, the OSF's first priorities are funding supposedly "independent organizations" to fight corruption. We all know how George's "anti-corruption" organizations ended up being used, and Alex learned from his father.

Similarly, "independent media" is an oxymoronic term when coming from the Soros family. What media that they've had a hand in has ever been "independent"? Perhaps it could be independent from state influence, but it won't be independent from Soros influence.

Even claims of aid to hire journalists, artists, and scholars to "document war crimes" have to be viewed through skeptical lenses. They may start in that function, but they end up becoming ideological foot soldiers for the left once the war is over.

On the OSF's list of priorities, humanitarian aid and assisting refugees comes last after political goals. As always, the OSF's true interests come first.

Alex, then deputy chair of the OSF, remarked, "We have one simple message: we will never abandon Ukraine. As Putin tries to wipe the country off the map, we will do all we can for the people of Ukraine. We urge others to step forward and join us."[24]

---

24   Ibid.

Since the war escalated, Alex has become a cheerleader for war, which he's played an active role in, trying both to shape policy in America to the benefit of Ukraine, and to aid his desire for a role in a post-war Ukraine. In some cases, this "cheerleading" has been almost literal, such as when he celebrated Biden giving Ukraine the green light to use US-made long-range missiles to strike deep within Russian territory.[25]

Less than a week before it was announced he'd be taking over the OSF entirely in June 2023, Alex spoke at the European Council on Foreign Relations (ECFR) in defense of US involvement in Ukraine. [26] There he argued that the notion that the United States cannot engage on multiple global fronts is flawed, citing historical precedent where America successfully mobilized resources in multiple theaters. He dismissed the idea that America is on the brink of war with China, and highlighted that most American legislators are not eager to send troops into a potential conflict over Taiwan. Thus, he argued, we can afford to divert more resources to Ukraine, even as the tab kept increasing to the tune of tens of billions of dollars.

Alex expressed confidence in the Biden administration's commitment to maintaining transatlantic unity and continuing support for Ukraine, emphasizing that the Democratic Party remains largely unified on the issue. He noted that a range of the party's lawmakers, from Alexandria Ocasio-Cortez to Joe Manchin, have broadly supported military aid to Ukraine. However, he acknowledged that funding Ukraine's post-war reconstruction, such as rebuilding schools, may be harder to justify to American voters.

Reflecting on past efforts to build consensus on foreign policy, Alex credited initiatives like ECFR for helping shape the party's approach to transatlantic relations. He warned that Trump, if

25   https://x.com/AlexanderSoros/status/1858245904651743341
26   "Foreign Policy of a Polarized America: US Presidential Elections | ECFR Annual Council Meeting 2023." https://www.youtube.com/watch?v=Iml9fRow8nA

re-elected, would likely abandon Ukraine and prioritize domestic conflicts over international ones (the horror!).[27]

Confirming what was already evident, ECFR's Mark Leonard said that Ukraine is among Alex's top interests (only Albania appears higher), and that he was in "daily contact" with the OSF's branch in Ukraine to coordinate how to talk to different governments about their policy towards Ukraine.[28]

He wasn't exaggerating. Alex is more visibly involved with Ukraine's political elites in just the past few years than his father ever was.

ALEX MEETS UKRAINIAN POWER

Alex has had at least four meetings with Andriy Yermak, Zelenskyy's "right-hand man" that he appointed to be Head of the Office of the President of Ukraine. In addition to being Zelenskyy's chief of staff, he's also part of the Headquarters of the Supreme Commander-in-Chief, the armed forces of Ukraine's higher command and control body.

According to the *Kyiv Post*, Yermak is the second most influential person in Ukraine,[29] and no one in the country is closer to Zelenskyy than he is.

Like Alex's friend Edi Rama, Yermak is plagued by corruption allegations. Just a month after he became chief of staff, video surfaced showing his brother discussing appointments to government jobs, suggesting he could use his position to get people those

---

27   Ibid.

28   Kurt Zindulka, "Democrat Mega-donor Alex Soros Declares 'We Must Not Abandon Ukraine,'" *Breitbart*, February 18, 2024. https://www.breitbart.com/europe/2024/02/18/democrat-mega-donor-alex-soros-declares-we-must-not-abandon-ukraine

29   Oleksiy Sorokin, "Andriy Yermak Becomes Second Most Influential Person in Ukraine," *Kyiv Post*, February 14, 2020. https://archive.kyivpost.com/ukraine-politics/andriy-yermak-becomes-second-most-influential-person-in-ukraine.html

cushy jobs.[30] An investigation into Yermak's brother was later dropped[31] by the National Anti-Corruption Bureau of Ukraine, which the OSF were active in creating.[32]

The corruption whiff around Yermak? Alex doesn't care; it's a feature, not a bug. A greased wheel for a machine that thrives on chaos.

During Trump's first term, Yermak was contacted by Giuliani, who urged him to open an investigation into Hunter's role at Burisma. Yermak refused to cooperate and personally advised Zelenskyy to not get involved.[33]

Alex and Yermak met in Kyiv on November 7, 2023,[34] December 9, 2023,[35] May 13, 2024,[36] and August 27, 2024.[37] The two were also pictured together at Davos in January 2025.[38]

---

30   Stephen Grey and Dan Peleschuk, "Corruption Accusations Continue to Plague Top Zelenskiy Aides," Reuters, September 19, 2023. https://web.archive.org/web/20231118105200/https://www.reuters.com/world/europe/graft-accusations-dog-top-zelenskiy-aides-2023-09-19

31   Oleg Sukhov, "Case Against Brother of Zelenskyy's Chief of Staff Closed, Says Anti-corruption Agency," The Kyiv Independent, March 14, 2025. https://kyivindependent.com/nabu-says-it-closed-corruption-case-against-brother-of-Zelenskyys-chief-of-staff

32   "The Open Society Foundations in Ukraine." https://www.opensocietyfoundations.org/newsroom/the-open-society-foundations-in-ukraine

33   David Averre, "US Sits Down in Saudi Arabia for Crucial Ukraine Peace Talks with Zelenskyy's Friend Who Is 'Hated by Trump Because of His Link to Hunter Biden'... Hours After Huge Drone Attack on Moscow," Daily Mail, March 11, 2025.https://www.dailymail.co.uk/news/article-14485319/Zelenskyys-close-friend-HATED-Trumps-team-involvement-Hunter-Biden-corruption-probe-sent-crucial-peace-talks-risking-US-fury-Ukraine.html

34   "Andriy Yermak Discussed with American Businessman Alexander Soros the Restoration of Infrastructure and Investments in the Ukrainian Economy," Official Website of the President of Ukraine, November 7, 2023. https://www.president.gov.ua/en/news/andrij-yermak-obgovoriv-z-amerikanskim-biznesmenom-oleksandr-86817

35   "Andriy Yermak met with Alexander Soros," Official Website of the President of Ukraine, December 9, 2023. https://www.president.gov.ua/en/news/andrij-yermak-proviv-zustrich-z-oleksandrom-sorosom-87617

36   "Ukrainian Peace Formula and Ukraine's Priorities in International Politics: Andriy Yermak met with Alexander Soros," Official Website of the President of Ukraine, May 13, 2024. https://www.president.gov.ua/en/news/ukrayinska-formula-miru-ta-prioriteti-nashoyi-derzhavi-v-miz-90857

37   "Andriy Yermak Met with Alexander Soros," Official Website of the President of Ukraine, August 27, 2024. https://www.president.gov.ua/en/news/andrij-yermak-zustrivsya-z-oleksandrom-sorosom-92865

38   https://www.facebook.com/photo/?fbid=1201715851316261&set=pb.100044335724180.-2207520000

According to the Ukrainian government, at these meetings, the two discussed Ukraine's Peace Formula, redeveloping the nation's infrastructure and economy (which the Soros nexus will undoubtedly stand to profit from), amid other issues pertaining to the war. Yermak expressed gratitude to Alex for all the prior meddling; "Your family does a lot for Ukraine: important projects to protect our people, strengthen democracy, for the success of the Ukrainian state."[39]

On social media, Alex touts a close relationship with Yermak. There, they publicly exchange birthday wishes[40] and compliments[41] like old friends.

Also, during the May visit, he met with Yulia Svyrydenko, Ukraine's first deputy prime minister and minister of economy, to discuss, according to her, economics and "eurointegration efforts,"[42] and met Energy Minister German Galushchenko. During the August visit, Alex also met with Katarina Mathernova, EU ambassador to Ukraine, with whom he reportedly discussed continued EU support for Ukraine and further integration of the Ukraine into the EU.[43]

While the Munich Security Conference on Germany was going on, Alex met with Ukrainian Foreign Affairs Minister Dmytro Kuleba and posted about their meeting on February 18, 2024. "We must not abandon Ukraine," he wrote accompanying the photo. As this was going on, Republicans were pushing back on the Biden Administration's "endless aid for Ukraine" policy—specifically his push for an additional $60 billion in aid.[44]

---

39   "Andriy Yermak met with Alexander Soros," December 9, 2023.
40   https://x.com/AlexanderSoros/status/1859664889771590103
41   https://x.com/AndriyYermak/status/1850457852357263641
42   https://x.com/Svyrydenko_Y/status/1789961311050154484
43   "Alexander Soros Visits Kyiv for the Fourth Time in a Year," International Renaissance Foundation, August 28, 2024. https://www.irf.ua/en/aleksandr-soros-vchetverte-za-rik-vidvidav-kyyiv
44   JD Rucker, "The Real Reason Alex Soros Is Demanding More Money for Globalist Incubator Ukraine," *The Liberty Daily*, February 18, 2024. https://thelibertydaily.com/real-reason-alex-soros-is-demanding-more-money

He'd also meet in November 2023 with Denys Shmyhal, the prime minister of Ukraine and Zelenskyy cabinet member, who expressed gratitude for the Soros family's support for their country since 1990. In addition to reconstruction and economics, Alex was also there to discuss the "social sphere"—implementing a progressive social agenda in a post-war Ukraine.

During this visit, Alex also met with members of the Verkhovna Rada (Ukrainian parliament), including its first deputy chairman and deputy chairman, as well as the heads of its factions and committees.[45] Alex thanked Yermak for "welcoming me so warmly back"[46] to talk investments in the Ukrainian economy.[47]

During one meeting, Alex expressed his commitment to the country, saying, "Ukraine is the place where my father, George Soros, spent a lot of time and where he directed many of his efforts to build the Open Society. I came to express my solidarity. Our support for Ukraine remains steadfast. It doesn't matter what happens on the battlefield. It doesn't matter what happens in the US. We will continue to support Ukraine and the International Renaissance Foundation, which works here."

And that's just the tip of the iceberg in terms of whom he was meeting with. No one gets to Zelenskyy without going through Yermak, and for Alex that was a walk in the park.

ZELENSKYY WELCOMES ALEX

On December 9, 2023, Alex was invited by Ukrainian President Volodymyr Zelenskyy and his wife Olena Zelenska to speak at the first meeting of the International Coalition of Countries for

45   "Alexander Soros Held Meetings in the Office of the President, the Cabinet of Ministers and the Verkhovna Rada," International Renaissance Foundation, November 7, 2023. https://www.irf.ua/en/aleksander-soros-zustrivsya-z-kerivnycz tvom-derzhavy-ta-uryadu
46   https://x.com/AlexanderSoros/status/1721956432067616931
47   https://x.com/AndriyYermak/status/1721866900118847835

the Return of Ukrainian Children. At the coalition meeting, Soros announced that OSF would partner with the Ukrainian first lady's foundation, The Olena Zelenska Foundation, and donated one million dollars to its projects.[48]

Alex wrote in a tweet, "Thank you President @ZelenskyyyUa for inviting me back to #Ukraine to speak at the first meeting of the 'International Coalition of Countries for the Return of Ukrainian Children.' Honored to partner with you on this important initiative to bring back the Ukrainian children—as many as 700,000—stolen by Russia."

Kids "stolen by Russia" make a tear-jerking headline, but the real play is deeper: embedding Soros influence in the social fabric.

It's an amusing juxtaposition to comments Zeleneskyy made in 2020 when he tried to downplay Soros influence over Ukraine to the point of pretending to not even know who George Soros was. "I am not familiar with a person named Soros. I have never met him. The question of the influence of Mr. Soros on Ukraine—I do not feel it. I think this is all an exaggeration."[49]

Weeks after Zelenskyy was elected in 2019, the Ukraine Crisis Media Center (USMC) issued a statement of "red lines" he was not to cross—as if he wasn't the real president. The UCMC's funding came from the Soros family's International Renaissance Foundation, the Embassy of the United States—Kyiv, USAID, NATO, and other quasi-CIA groups that have the vague, professed purpose of "promoting democracy."

The core demand was to "protect the values that Ukrainians fought for during the Revolution of Dignity"—a reference to the

---

48   Greg Wehner, "Soros Heir Pledges $1 Million to Ukrainian First Lady's Charity During Weekend Meeting with Zelenskyy," Fox News, December 10, 2023. https://www.foxnews.com/world/soros-heir-pledges-million-ukrainian-first-ladys-charity-during-weekend-meeting-zelenskyy

49   "Zelensky: Power is an Opportunity. I Have the Chance to Help," Interfax-Ukraine, February 11, 2020, https://en.interfax.com.ua/news/interview/640646.html

2014 Soros-backed "Maidan Uprising." [50] In 2014, George Soros wrote an article calling for the "spirit of the Maidan" to be preserved.[51] They were upset that Zelenskyy had appointed members of Yanukovych's government (who lost to the Soros-backed Poroshenko). Zelenskyy has acted consistently like this.

UCMC warned that any crossing of these red lines would lead to "political instability" and a "deterioration of international warnings"—reading more like a threat than a caution. Among the red lines included Zelenskyy holding a referendum on the negotiations to be used with Russia on the principles for a peaceful settlement; negotiating with Russia without any members of their "Western partners"; initiating any actions that may contribute to the reduction or lifting of sanctions against Russia; and implementing policies against the International Monetary Fund.

Other red lines included any policies that would accommodate the nearly fifth of the country that's Russian—such as preventing him from restoring Russian TV channels; disallowing him from reviewing Poroshenko's language law that prohibits anyone from state positions if their knowledge of Ukrainian is insufficient; or supporting the Russian Orthodox Church (which Zelenskyy later banned, earning him a condemnation from the Pope).

But it had weight—and it was a reminder of who was really in charge. Zelenskyy may have been democratically elected, but he didn't do it alone if this group can have so much power in what he is and isn't allowed to do.

Alex wasn't just an activist—he used his connections in his favorite country to visit, Albania, to come to the aid of his father's favorite.

50   "Joint Statement by Civil Society Representatives on the First Political Steps of the President of Ukraine Volodymyr Zelenskyy," Ukraine Crisis Media Center, May 23, 2019. https://uacrisis.org/en/71966-joint-appeal-of-civil-society-representatives

51   George Soros, "Keep the Spirit of the Maidan Alive," Open Society Foundations, April 7, 2014. https://www.opensocietyfoundations.org/voices/keep-spirit-maidan-alive

Albania had been providing humanitarian assistance to Ukraine since the beginning of the war—despite Ukraine's economy nearing $180 billion and Albania's being $23 billion. Albania (which isn't part of the EU but wants to join) also backed Ukraine joining the EU, as it has done in the past.

During the Ukraine Summit in Tirana at the end of February 2024, PM Rama was seen standing with Albania's Interior Minister Taulant Bella—but instead of where the foreign minister and defense minister should've been, stood Alex Soros.[52] The symbolism was clear.

At the same event, Alex was pictured shaking hands with Zelenskyy.[53]

ALEX'S ALBANIAN CONNECTIONS RESURFACE

Albanian media reported in March 2024 that Albania had secured a contract for the mass production of munitions for warfare purposes in Ukraine, and that Alex had a role in the deal.[54]

Albania was picked to produce a massive number of shells of ten different calibers, but there were obvious questions about how such a small country could fulfill the contract. Diplomatic sources said an American company would end up taking control of Albania's entire military and have specialists aid in the production—and that specialists from Ukraine could also be brought in. In other words, Albania would effectively be subcontractors, raising the question of why they're exactly needed in the first place.

---

52   "Skema si dy pika uji/ Ashtu si Rama sot, edhe Berisha kryeministër e ka patur "Sorosin" e tij!," Alfapress, February 29, 2024. https://alfapress.al/politike/skema-si-dy-pika-uji-ashtu-si-rama-sot-edhe-berisha-kryeminister-e-ka-p-i97856

53   https://www.instagram.com/alexsoros/p/C3_gO25xUrW

54   "Albania to Play Subcontractor Role in Major Arms Contract, with Alex Soros Key Figure," Oculus News, March 1, 2024. https://www.ocnal.com/2024/03/albania-to-play-subcontractor-role-in.html

Cooperation between the countries would further solidify in January 21, 2025, when Rama met with Zelenskyy in Davos and they signed the Agreement on Security Cooperation and Long-Term Support Between Ukraine and the Republic of Albania[55]— just days after Albania opened an embassy in Ukraine.

The agreement established a ten-year framework to strengthen ties between Albania and Ukraine amid the Russia conflict, and commits Albania to providing military, humanitarian, and technical assistance to Ukraine.

Rama and Alex were then photographed together two days later.[56]

In an interview with *The Financial Times*, Alex outlined his own vision for the future of the OSF, now that his father has officially handed him the keys to his kingdom. In response to Soros loyalists claiming he lacks his dad's Eurocentric agenda, Alex affirmed his identity as "a committed European," pointing to OSF's expanding operations in Ukraine, and was visibly animated when the conversation focused on foreign policy.[57]

As his hyperactivity on social media shows, Alex is equally as passionate about Ukraine and unabashedly documents his hobnobbing overseas, posting pictures rubbing elbows with world leaders, including heads of state in Europe[58] and beyond.[59]

Ukraine's not Alex's side gig, it's a war-torn proving ground where the Soros torch either blazes or gutters out. With Zelenskyy, Yermak, and others, he's not just meeting them; he's binding

---

55   "Ukraine and Albania Concluded Bilateral Security Agreement," Official Website of the President of Ukraine, January 21, 2025. https://www.president.gov.ua/en/news/ukrayina-ta-albaniya-uklali-dvostoronnyu-bezpekovu-ugodu-95585

56   https://www.facebook.com/photo/?fbid=1197681685053011&set=pb.100044335724180.-2207520000

57   Roula Khalaf, "Alex Soros: 'These people are bullies. And you fight back,'" *The Financial Times*, January 21, 2025. https://www.ft.com/content/fdde5d56-5dc1-4bd4-af43-b58ef969c1bb

58   https://x.com/AlexanderSoros/status/1591533253441241088

59   https://x.com/AlexanderSoros/status/1652017661004398592

them, threading OSF's billions into Kyiv's lifeline. While Russia snarls, George nudged Ukraine west with cash and coups; Alex's diving in.

Time will tell which direction Alex takes the OSF brand, but if his globetrotting exploits are any indication, he's venturing to be as ubiquitous as the Soros name.

(Chapter 6)

USAID and Other Overlooked Connections

For decades the US government had its own Sorosesque agency in the form of the United States Agency for International Development, better known as USAID. It wouldn't even be accurate to call it hiding in plain sight—there wasn't much of an attempt to hide.

USAID did attract criticism over the years and had been linked to Soros. But thanks to the "Elon Effect," the absurd programs USAID had been funding finally come under the scrutiny they deserved after Elon Musk singled out the agency for deletion. In February 2025, Musk blasted the agency as a "criminal organization...beyond repair." President Donald Trump agreed with Musk's assessment that the agency had to go, deriding it as run by "radical lunatics."

The projects being funded by USAID were the sort of ridiculous cases of government spending you'd see every year in Rand Paul's annual Festivus Report on government waste. This included funds for teaching Sri Lankan journalists to avoid "binary gendered language," sex changes in Guatemala, LGBT activism in Armenia, Jamaica, Uganda, and Latin America.[1] They read like public works programs for gender studies majors, because that's what they are.

---

1   Matt Palumbo, "Soros and USAID Have Been a Match Made in Hell," *The Daily Economy*, March 7, 2025. https://thedailyeconomy.org/article/soros-and-usaid-have-been-a-match-made-in-hell

Other hits included funding for Sesame Street in Iraq, drag show workshops for Venezuelan migrants in Ecuador, boosting tourism in Tunisia and Egypt, teaching Africans about climate change, and instructing the people of Kazakhstan about how to fight back against internet trolls.[2]

The creators of Mad Libs couldn't have written them better. Mafia-style "no show" jobs would be preferable to these kinds of jobs because it least they add zero value to society instead of negative value.

Entire volumes could be written on waste fraud and abuse within USAID. But amid the flood of reporting on the "most absurd of the absurd" programs being funded by the agency, what didn't get as much attention was how Soros fundamentally altered aid disbursement to benefit the left.

GEORGE SOROS MAKES USAID IN HIS IMAGE

George Soros had linked himself to USAID spending long ago. A quarterly performance report from The Soros Foundations in 1993 proves a relationship with USAID going back decades. The report details how the Soros Foundations Management Training Program signed an agreement with USAID on November 19, 1993. The program began advertising to recruit "professionals" in Poland, Bulgaria, Romania, Estonia, and Slovakia five countries.[3] The program was to train (translation: indoctrinate) thirty of them in public administration, business, telecommunications, environmental management, and more. At least, this was how Soros described what the aid was for—he was not going to admit something sinister in a document he knew would eventually be made public. But in reality, the goal was always to advance his ideology in those spheres he's recruiting into.

---

2   Ibid.
3   "The Soros Foundations: Management Training Program," USAID, December 1999. https://web.archive.org/web/20250204121425/https://pdf.usaid.gov/pdf_docs/pdabi206.pdf

According to their evaluation of the program, "all goals were met."

Notable early cases of Soros' involvement with USAID include his International Renaissance Foundation (explored in chapter five), partnering with them to support Ukraine's "Orange Revolution."[4] Another was the Organized Crime and Corruption Reporting Project (OCCRP), which, as you probably remember, was one of the groups cited in the Trump impeachment letter. USAID has the authority to veto appointment of "key personnel" to the OCCRP, which is odd for a supposedly independent anti-corruption NGO. OCCRP used to have a message on their website that read "OCCRP is made possible by" followed by the logo of USAID, but it was later removed, likely to try to conceal links between the two Soros-infested organizations.[5] Also, the East-West Management Institute—mentioned in chapter four as the Soros family's most influential group in Albania—had taken $270 million from USAID.[6]

In addition to using USAID to provide extra juice to projects advancing his interests, George himself has rewritten the rules to force USAID funding that *does* more legitimately meet the definition of "humanitarian aid" to become political.

Before USAID became a household name, the Heritage Foundation exposed George Soros as the "main implementor" of the agency's so-called aid since at least the start of the Obama administration. As they documented:

---

4   Andrew Wilson, "Ukraine's Orange Revolution, NGOs and the Role of the West," *Cambridge Review of International Affairs*, March 2006. https://commonweb.unifr.ch/artsdean/pub/gestens/f/as/files/4760/39746_173947.pdf

5   Yann Phillippin and Stefan Candea, "The Hidden Links Between a Giant of Investigative Journalism and the US Government," *Mediapart*, December 2, 2024. https://www.mediapart.fr/en/journal/international/021224/hidden-links-between-giant-investigative-journalism-and-us-government

6   Tiana Lowe Doescher, "USAID Gave $270 Million to a Soros NGO, but it Only Needed $9 Million to Doom Democracy in Albania," *Washington Examiner*, February 7, 2025. https://www.washingtonexaminer.com/opinion/3313896/usaid-gave-270-million-soros-ngo-only-needed-9-million-doom-democracy-albania

During the Obama years USAID was used to promote abroad policies that remain controversial within American society itself and that serve no clear national security interests. To achieve these ends, USAID has teamed up in some countries with groups funded by financier George Soros.

It was at this time that USAID started tying development money to countries taking progressive stances on gay/transgender rights, among other leftist causes including legalizing prostitution, and decriminalizing drugs. This happened to African countries, and European countries "from Ireland to Macedonia."[7]

And much of the money ends up directly in his hands:

It is Soros's right as a private individual to act on his convictions, but evidence is emerging that during the past eight years [leading up to 2017], Soros, his Open Societies Foundations (OSF), and their many smaller affiliates have received U.S. taxpayer money through USAID and that USAID has made the OSF the main implementer of its aid.

Joe Biden had requested nearly $30 billion for USAID in 2025, more than the OSF's lifetime spending.[8]

Max Primorac, the former acting chief operating officer at USAID, confirmed in an interview with the *Daily Signal* that "Biden's USAID and George Soros's Open Society Institute fre-

---

7   Mike Gonzalez, "State Department and Congress Should Probe USAID, Soros Promotion of Radical Agenda Overseas," Heritage Foundation, March 27, 2017. https://www.heritage.org/gender/report/state-department-and-congress-should-probe-usaid-soros-promotion-radical-agenda

8   "Budget of the U.S. Government: Fiscal Year 2025," Office of Management and Budget, pp. 106–109. https://www.whitehouse.gov/wp-content/uploads/2024/03/budget_fy2025.pdf

quently partnered by co-funding joint programs that promoted radical social agendas throughout the developing world."[9]

Soros and USAID have partnered on such a high volume of projects that OSF groups have sued USAID twice in cases that reached the Supreme Court.

The first case was after George W. Bush signed the United States Leadership Against HIV/AIDS, Tuberculosis, and Malaria Act, which provided federal funds to combat AIDS globally—with the only condition being that groups had to pledge to oppose "prostitution and sex trafficking." Alliance for Open Society International sued and the SCOTUS struck down the anti-prostitution pledge in 2013.

Following the ruling, this requirement was removed for NGOs operating in the United States, but not internationally, leading to Alliance for an Open Society suing again.

But sanity prevailed the second time, with the SCOTUS ruling that requiring the Open Society's affiliates to take an anti-prostitution pledge didn't violate the First Amendment. And why would it? Requiring money to be spent on anything requires value judgments to be made.

The irony here is that Soros sued the Bush-era USAID for tying aid to political positions on free speech grounds, while he's the man responsible for forcing USAID spending to be tied to left-wing political causes. When a leftist is acting hypocritically, it's always when they're winning.

What this all proves is that George had done a tremendous volume of work with USAID. How often is it that someone has two lawsuits with a government agency escalating to Supreme Court cases?

---

9   Tyler O'Neil, "Here's How Trump's Move on USAID Will Impact George Soros' Funding Empire," *The Daily Signal*, February 4, 2025. https://www.dailysignal.com/2025/02/04/trump-deals-huge-blow-lefts-funding-empire

USAID isn't just a government agency—it's a Soros amplifier, and it's a megaphone for his family's agenda that your tax dollars were paying for. George may have not created it, but he bent it and weaved the OSF's threads into its fabric since the '90s. The mechanics are slick—USAID's grants contain vague mandates like "promoting democracy," which is never the real goal.

OSF PLAYS DUMB AMID USAID REVELATIONS

Alex has tried to pretend that none of this has ever happened, even as his empire came under increased scrutiny from the USAID revelations.

In mid-February, as criticism of USAID was reaching its zenith, the OSF put out a statement on supposed "false claims" about their involvement with USAID. "The claims that the Open Society Foundations receive funding from USAID or direct the funding of a multibillion-dollar US government agency are manifestly false. These allegations are part of a broader effort to undermine international development work and delegitimize the independent funding of civil society organizations worldwide."[10]

Anytime the OSF puts out a statement to "debunk" claims against them, they read like they're deliberately written to insult our intelligence, as they don't even try to try to cover up the evidence against them.

Only a few months earlier, the OSF put out a press release boasting about one of their projects that was still taking USAID money.

"Alex Soros, chair of the Open Society Foundations, has outlined a new vision for the Foundations' higher education work, and reaffirmed Open Society's financial commitment to the [George Soros founded] Central European University (CEU)

---

10   "False Claims Regarding Open Society, George Soros, and USAID," press release, Open Society Foundations, February 12, 2025. https://www.opensocietyfoundations.org/newsroom/false-claims-regarding-open-society-george-soros-and-usaid

through 2032 and beyond,"[11] read the press release. As both this and the statement above, denying USAID funding, were being written, CEU was still receiving a $1 million grant from USAID. Due to the immense funding from George, CEU is one of the wealthiest per-student in Europe, but that hasn't stopped them from taking handouts.[12]

The USAID grant is administered through the American Schools and Hospitals Abroad program, which is for schools that "best demonstrate American ideas," a completely subjective criterion. Only an ideologue at USAID would agree that CEU meets this definition. USAID was funneling money to CEU at the same time as the Open Society University Network (co-founded by CEU) was hosting a webinar claiming that the reaction to 9/11 helped fuel attitudes of white supremacy and incite police officers to commit genocide against black people.[13] The Open Society University Network is a group of educational institutions that promote the "open society" agenda.

Even after stepping back from his OSF, George is still CEU's "honorary chair" of the Board of Trustees, and his heir, Alex Soros, is a member of the board.

Alex himself publicly protested the USAID gravy train drying up and has posted to X to fearmonger about USAID cuts hurting scientific research[14] and leading to outbreaks of disease.[15]

His true motivations are far more self-serving.

11   "Open Society Foundations to Explore New Model for Higher Education While Also Pledging to Continue Support for CEU," press release, Open Society Foundations, November 11, 2024. https://www.opensocietyfoundations. org/newsroom/open-society-foundations-to-explore-new-model-for-higher-education-while-also-pledging-to-continue-support-for-ceu

12   "Central European University—Vienna, Austria." The Global Faculty. https:// theglobalfaculty.com/central-european-university-vienna-austria

13   Joseph Vazquez, "USAID Granted $1M in Tax Dollars to George Soros's Radical Global University," Newsbusters, February 28, 2025. https://www. newsbusters.org/blogs/business/joseph-vazquez/2025/02/28/breaking-usaid-granted-1m-tax-dollars-george-soross-university

14   https://x.com/AlexanderSoros/status/1887939856388735173

15   https://x.com/AlexanderSoros/status/1898778869118967874

AND IT WASN'T JUST USAID

It wasn't just the USAID gravy train that the Soros' benefitted from.

The Open Society Institute and the Alliance for Open Society Institute (AOSI) received funding directly from the US government. Some sleuthing from Joe Vazquez uncovered that government funding was earmarked for the OSF to administer a foreign policy program for the State Department:

> The State Department and USAID committed $11,091,856 collectively in grant money split from 2007-2014 between the Open Society Institute and the AOSI, the "legal operating name" for Open Society Institute-Baltimore, which was later announced to be shuttering in 2023. Over $8 million of that figure was from the State Department to OSI for the purpose of administering the Edmund S. Muskie/ FREEDOM Support Act Graduate Fellowship Program on behalf of the agency. "MUSKIE GRADUATE FELLOWSHIP PROGRAM GRANT TO THE OPEN SOCIETY INST," the grant's description stated.[16]

An archived version of the State Department's website explained that the program "is part of the Department of State's public diplomacy effort to foster mutual understanding between the United States and other countries through educational and training programs."[17]

USAID specifically gave at least $1,959,606 to AOSI for the period 2007-2008, while the State Department gave at least $641,050.[18]

---

16   Joe Vazquez. "EXCLUSIVE: U.S. Government Committed Over $11 Million Directly to Soros's Open Society Groups," *NewsBusters*, April 28, 2025. https://www.newsbusters.org/blogs/business/joseph-vazquez/2025/04/28/ exclusive-us-government-committed-over-11-million-directly

17   Ibid.

18   Ibid.

ALEX GOES TO BANGLADESH

In another case of coincidental timing, at the end of January Alex met with Muhammad Yunus, the interim government chief of Bangladesh.

As has become standard for him, he made the meeting publicly known on his social media accounts. "Honored to be back in Dhaka to meet with [Muhammad Yunus], a champion of human rights and a longtime friend of [the Open Society Foundations]. This is a crucial time of transition for Bangladesh and we explored ways to deepen collaboration on critical reforms and investments."[19]

The timing of the meeting made it obvious what he was there to discuss. Trump issued a halt on nearly all foreign aid in his first days as president, and the White House has also moved to end or suspend all projects that the federal government had been supporting in Bangladesh. The only exception was aid to displaced Rohingya living in a refugee camp in the eastern part of the country.[20] This significantly impacted USAID projects there.

Bangladesh is just the latest chessboard for OSF.

The nation's chief advisor's office said that "The Open Society Foundations leadership on Wednesday met [Yunus] to discuss Bangladesh's efforts to rebuild the economy, trace siphoned-off assets, combat misinformation, and carry out vital economic reforms," but the foreign aid freeze was certainly a subject as well. How could it not be?

This visit also coincided with a period of significant political upheaval in Bangladesh, following the ouster of the comically corrupt former Prime Minister Sheikh Hasina in August of the previous year, an event some allege was driven by external forces,

---

19   https://x.com/AlexanderSoros/status/1884713271543955492
20   Joshua Kurlantzick, "Bangladesh Could Turn to China as Trump Pulls Aid from Country," Council on Foreign Relations, January 29, 2025. https://www.cfr.org/article/bangladesh-could-turn-china-trump-pulls-aid-country

including those linked to Soros's network. Hasina is accused of siphoning off roughly $234 billion during her sixteen-year tenure, and while this isn't meant to argue for her staying in power, it shows the role of the Soros family in picking her replacement.

Yunus has turned to Alex for help in recovering those siphoned off assets.[21] While it remains a mystery how he would do so, it does show Yunus believes it's something he has the power to do. He must be basing that off something.

Stopping corruption isn't a concern of the Alex, as Yunus himself has been plagued by corruption allegations—into which one of the Soros family's key allies, Hillary Clinton, has tried to stop investigations. Back in June 2017, Senator Chuck Grassley outlined in a letter to Secretary of State Rex Tillerson that former Secretary of State Clinton lobbied the government of Bangladesh and Prime Minister Hasina to end a corruption investigation into Yunus—a Clinton Global Initiative donor—and that State Department officials threatened Hasina's son with an audit if he didn't get his mother to terminate the investigation.[22]

As for Hasina's ouster, according to the *Sunday Guardian*, an Indian newspaper:

> When former Prime Minister of Bangladesh, Sheikh Hasina, was interacting with leaders of 14 parties in a closed-door meeting, the official residence of the Prime Minister of Bangladesh, on the evening of May 24, 2024, she warned them and perhaps as a reminder to herself of a "conspiracy" that was in play to remove her.
>
> ...

---

21   "Yunus Asks Soros for Help Recovering Stolen Assets," JagoNews24, January 29, 2025. https://www.jagonews24.com/en/national/news/80145

22   Letter from Sen. Chuck Grassley to Secretary Rex W. Tillerson, June 1, 2017. https://www.grassley.senate.gov/imo/media/doc/2017-06-01%20CEG%20to%20State%20(HRC%20Muhammad%20Yunus).pdf

Her concerns were proven right less than three months after her forecast.[23]

While the following isn't a smoking gun, there was Soros involvement in having Yunus be the successor to Hasina; so, it sure comes close, and shows that his relationship with the Soros family goes back decades:

> A report stated that in February 1999, Yunus secured a loan from the Soros Economic Development Fund and Open Society Institute, operated by the controversial businessman George Soros, to buy 35 percent of the shares of Grameenphone Ltd., with conditions tied to Grameen Bank's control.

Grameen Bank was founded by Yunus, and the loan was for $11 million. Grameenphone would then go on to become one of the leading telecom companies in the country. His bank was tied to another company called Grameen Telecom, a nonprofit that would use some of its profits to fund so-called "social and welfare projects" in Bangladesh after repaying its loan to Soros.

When Bangladesh's government announced it was forming a committee to investigate the bank, the long-time Soros family ally, then-Secretary of State Hillary Clinton, said the US government "would not endorse any action by the Bangladesh government to undermine Grameen Bank's achievements."[24]

Yunus was a donor to the Clinton Global Initiative at the time, and George Soros has donated heavily to the Clinton Foundation.[25]

---

23   "Bangladesh Coup Has the U.S. Written All Over It," *The Sunday Guardian*, August 11, 2024. https://sundayguardianlive.com/top-five/bangladesh-coup-has-the-u-s-written-all-over-it

24   Ibid.

25   Peter Overby, "Saudia Arabia, George Soros on Clinton Donor List," *All Things Considered*, NPR, December 18, 2008. https://www.npr.org/2008/12/18/98467642/saudi-arabia-george-soros-on-clinton-donor-list

In May 2017, Hasina confirmed that Hillary Clinton called her office in March 2011 and demanded that Yunus be restored to his position as chairman of Grameen Bank.[26]

Yunus' relationship with the Clinton family dates back decades to when Bill Clinton was governor of Arkansas. As Sen. Grassley noted:

> For decades, Yunus has been heralded by the Clinton Foundation and has been showcased at a number of foundation functions. Bill Clinton also personally lobbied the Nobel Committee on behalf of Yunus, and in 2006 he was awarded the Nobel Peace Prize. According to reports, Yunus' companies donated between $100,000 to $250,000 to the Clinton Global Initiative and $25,000 to $50,000 to the Clinton Foundation. Upon Secretary Clinton's appointment as Secretary of State, the Clinton-Yunus relationship deepened. Secretary Clinton's Department of State reportedly awarded more than $13 million in taxpayer funds to businesses aligned with Yunus.[27]

Yunus was removed from his position on the Grameen Bank board of directors in 2011, which was followed up by a concerted effort to interfere in the investigation into him, as evidenced by emails between Yunus's associates, the Clinton Foundation, Hillary Clinton, Cheryl Mills, and other State Department staff. Senator Grassley published many emails, many unfortunately redacted, between members of the Clintonsphere about Yunus.[28]

In one email from 2010 to Melanne Verveer, who was formally Hillary's chief of staff and then United States ambassa-

---

26 Madeleine Weast, "Clinton Pressured Bangladesh Prime Minister to Help Major Foundation Donor," *Washington Free Beacon*, May 12, 2017. https://freebeacon.com/national-security/clinton-pressured-bangladesh-prime-minister-help-foundation-donor

27 Letter from Senator Chuck Grassley to Secretary Rex W. Tillerson, June 1, 2017.

28 Ibid.

dor-at-large for global women's issues, she was sent an excerpt from an article about corruption allegations against Yunus. The sender was redacted. Verveer replied, "Just when we thought things had calmed down..."

In another email from January 2011, then-senior advisor to the Deputy Secretary of State Maya Seiden wrote to Thomas Nides, Cheryl Mills, Jacob Sulivan, and Piper Campbell that "the situation with Yunus and Grameen appears to be getting worse."

At the time, Nides was second United States deputy secretary of state for management and resources, Mills was third chief of staff to Hillary Clinton, Sullivan was twenty-sixth director of policy planning in the State Department, and Campbell was chief of staff to the deputy secretary of state.

Seiden also sent an email to the above group that same day as she bemoaned the worsening situation, that the US ambassador to Bangladesh is "heavily involved" and pushing for a meeting with Prime Minister Hasina.

Emails from March 2011 show Hillary Clinton communicating with Verveer through her private email HDR22@clintonemail. com, but all contents are redacted. The subject line was "Yunus Resignation Letter," and another was a forward of an email from Yunus titled "US Visit Cancelled," where he said the "Situation does not allow me to leave the country."

Hillary also was communicating with Cheryl Mills on her second secret email address, hrod17@clintonemail.com, but the contents are redacted.

No wonder she ended up deleting 30,000 of her emails.

Regarding her secret emails, Wikileaks does have some other emails regarding Hillary and Yunus going back to 2000, some of which are between her and Alex's now-wife Huma Abedin.[29]

---

29   https://wikileaks.org/clinton-emails/emailid/28530, and: https://wikileaks.org/clinton-emails/emailid/27996

In March 2011, Yunus wrote to Hillary to inform her that he was relinquishing the post of managing director of Grameen Bank.[30]

In May 2011, in an email with the subject line "Yunus Resignation Letter," Hillary wrote to Verveer that it was "sad, indeed"[31] that he'd be leaving.

Alex and Yunus previously met publicly in October 2024 ahead of the presidential election, where Alex referred to him as his "father's old friend."[32] This was less than two months after Yunus took power under suspicious circumstances.

UN Secretary-General António Guterres later pledged to help Muhammad Yunus during a visit in March.[33] Guterres is an associate of Alex, and at risk of sounding like a broken record, the two have been pictured together on Alex's social media.[34]

ALEX INHERITS INFLUENCE IN NORTH MACEDONIA

Another nation where George Soros and USAID have been highly active and that Alex has taken over is North Macedonia (formerly Macedonia). Soros had been involved in then-Macedonia since its independence, setting up the Foundation Open Society Macedonia (FOSM) in 1992.

With help from USAID often implemented hand and hand with Soros projects, FOSM was able to set up the first privately

---

30   https://wikileaks.org/clinton-emails/emailid/27959

31   https://wikileaks.org/clinton-emails/emailid/24245

32   Tirtho Banerjee, "Alex Soros Meets Bangladesh's Interim Leader Muhammad Yunus; What's the Connection?," *News Nine*, October 3, 2024. https://www.news9live.com/world/alex-soros-meets-bangladeshs-interim-chief-muhammad-yunus-whats-the-connection-2713131

33   Salah Uddin Shoaib Choudhury, "UN Secretary-General António Guterres Violates Rules by Pledging to Help Muhammad Yunus in Gauging Voice of Indian TV Channels and Newspapers," https://weeklyblitz.net/2025/03/26/un-secretary-general-antonio-guterres-violates-rules-by-pledging-to-help-muhammad-yunus-in-gauging-voice-of-indian-tv-channels-and-newspapers

34   https://www.facebook.com/Alexandersorospublic/posts/good-to-see-united-nations-secretary-general-antonio-guterres-during-the-paris-p/1403059096523102

owned media outlets in Macedonia, giving space to voices from their faction of the former Communist Party (now rebranded into the SDSM—Social Democratic Union of Macedonia). They quickly set up about eighty organizations covering various walks of life—institutes for analyzing corruption, economic think tanks, associations of journalists and media freedom groups, and groups promoting abortions, legal drugs and prostitution, and the Alphabet (LGBTQ) agenda.[35]

These media groups were weaponized against their main political threat, the right-wing nationalist (and anti-Soros) Internal Macedonian Revolutionary Organization—Democratic Party for Macedonian National Unity (VMRO-DPMNE party).

A movement called "Stop Operation Soros" in then-Macedonia called on USAID to be audited and accused them of contributing to the political crisis in their country. Among Soros's activities there included his foundation publishing and distributing a translated version of Saul Alinsky's infamous book *Rules for Radicals*.[36]

Just as Soros has done in Ukraine and many other countries, in 2015, the SDSM and George and potentially Alex (with the help of USAID) funded groups to start a Color Revolution to overthrow VMRO-DPMNE, which held power since 2006. This resulted in mass protests breaking out in 2016, and diplomats working for the Obama administration lending their support to the protests.

Unlike in America, where they want some plausible deniability, Macedonian Soros-backed activists brag about it. In America, Soros's lackeys will call you a conspiracy theorist—in Macedonia,

---

35   Interview with Macedonian journalist Cvetin Chilimanov, who has reported on USAID political and financial abuses in Macedonia since 2015.

36   Rod Dreher, "Saul Alinsky, A Gift from America?," *The American Conservative*, October 3, 2016. https://www.theamericanconservative.com/saul-alinsky-a-gift-from-america

they call themselves the "Soros Army." With the open support from the US administration and the US Embassy in Skopje, the protesters not only did not feel the need to disguise their activities, but instead they embraced the allegation. That is how we got to the images of USAID-funded pinko protesters wearing T-shirts with the logo "Soros Army."[37]

The fact that USAID directly gave millions of dollars to OSFM caused outrage in the country, considering the reputation of OSFM for staging violent protests and conducting regime-change operations. They even created clone organizations—Macedonian versions of groups like the Soros-funded or linked Media Matters and *PolitiFact*.[38]

The photos of protesters wearing "Soros Army" shirts was something so blatant that my first thought was they must be ironic, mocking people for calling them Soros-funded. And some of them did claim it was merely tongue-in-cheek after realizing how poor the optics were. But there was no joke here; a number have been proven to be part of organizations that took Soros and USAID money.

One protester pictured wearing one, Pavle Bogoevski,[39] was an LGBT rights activist for the Soros-funded Helsinki Committee of Macedonia—an organization that has received a $300,000 USAID grant for its "LGBT inclusion project." He was later elected as member of Parliament for the SDSM party, but his career was cut short when a taxi driver who was not a fan of SDSM recorded him during the drive as he was ordering cocaine.

Borjan Jovanovski, a journalist lavishly funded by USAID and Soros for his NOVA TV media project, and for the Kontravesti

37 "Macedonia Fights Back Against Soros Cultural Imperialism Machine," *Eurasia Review*, March 18, 2017. https://www.eurasiareview.com/18032017-macedonia-fights-back-against-soros-cultural-imperialism-machine-oped
38 Ibid.
39 https://x.com/arozgj/status/1888297807779369138

news program that was meant to be adapted for the color revolution, would also post pictures of himself with the same shirt.[40] As to leave no doubt, a USAID logo is displayed at the end of his show.[41]

In a staged PR move, an activist named Jasmina Golubovska working for the Soros-linked Legis, another organization facilitating the movement of migrants, was portrayed as the face of the color revolution after she applied her lipstick on a policeman's shield—a move that was afterwards copied in similar USAID-supported color revolutions across the world.[42] As students of history have learned by now, much of left-wing "history" in the twentieth century and beyond is just a series of photo ops.

Meanwhile, when questioned on if he was participating in the upheaval in Macedonia, George Soros outright denied it. "I have no answer, I am not committed to the destruction of the country, and I don't know how to answer, except to ignore it."[43]

His foot soldiers begged to differ.

The protests led to elections there in 2016 (that were initially planned for mid-2017), and to the chagrin of Soros and company, VMRO-DPMNE still won the most seats (fifty-one) as their party leader campaigned on "fighting for the de-Soros-isation of the country." But they were still short of a majority in the 120-seat parliament and needed to find a coalition partner.

To stop that, the Soros networks launched a pressure campaign against parties joining a coalition with VMRO-DPNE (thus giving them control of the government) so they'd join SDSM

---

40 https://x.com/She_MsA/status/1022102371638435841/photo/1

41 https://youtu.be/HudDtmp-T-Y?t=2051

42 Jessica Elgot, "Macedonia's Lipstick Protester: 'I Saw the Policeman Smile Very Slightly,'" *The Guardian*, May 13, 2015. https://www.theguardian.com/world/2015/may/13/macedonia-lipstick-protester-jasmina-golubovska

43 Emir Hamzai, "Soros: 'I Do Not Participate in the Destruction of Macedonia," *Telegrafi*, June 9, 2016. https://telegrafi.com/en/soros-une-nuk-marr-pjese-ne-shkaterrimin-e-maqedonise

(which won forty-nine seats) instead.[44] Two Albanian interest parties that won a combined thirteen seats ended up forming a coalition with SDSM, giving them a narrow majority. As a result, SDSM's Zoran Zaev would become the next prime minister following the elections, and he'd be photographed at a meeting with Alex and George the following year.[45]

This is when the SDSM-led government approved numerous historic concessions toward Greece and Bulgaria, which were blocking Macedonia's NATO membership and its first steps toward EU membership, including renaming the country.

George and Alex described the renaming of Macedonia to North Macedonia, due to a dispute with Greece about the regional history and the right to use this name, as "softening rivalries and someone opening a window of opportunity for leaders in Europe and the US to reshape the Balkans. In fact, the renaming alone presents a 'historic' opportunity."[46]

This was following the Prespa Accord between Macedonia and Greece, which ended the dispute on Macedonia's name (among other issues), and Macedonia's name officially changed to North Macedonia in February 2019.

Public opinion polling didn't show much support for the move. In fact, the name change was so unpopular that when a referendum was held on it in September 2018, most protested it so that the vote wouldn't reach the 50 percent turnout requirement needed for it to be a valid referendum. Voter turnout only

---

44   Ibid.
45   "Prime Minister Zaev meets with George Soros in Davos," *Telegrafi*, January 26, 2018. https://telegrafi.com/en/kryeministri-zaev-realizon-takim-george-soros-ne-davos
46   George Soros and Alexander Soros, "In the Balkans, a Chance to Stabilize Europe," *The New York Times*, June 18, 2018. https://www.nytimes.com/2018/06/18/opinion/northern-macedonia-rename-greece.html

amounted to an anemic 36.8 percent.[47] The ballot question asked: "Are you in favor of membership in NATO and the European Union by accepting the deal between the Republic of Macedonia and Republic of Greece?"

To counter this, the Soros propaganda machine painted a picture of a Macedonia eager to change their name. The prior February, a poll from the Soros-funded Institute for Democracy—Societas Civilis claimed only 33 percent opposed the name change.[48] Who knew 'there were pollsters worse than those tracking America's elections?

Despite the Soros rhetoric about "protecting democracy," the will of the people didn't matter, and the name was changed regardless. Protecting "democracy" just means protecting whatever the left supports at the time.

It can't be emphasized enough that the Soroses had enough control in Macedonia that he was able to change the country's name.

Alex was well-connected enough in the country to fly solo, having his own press conferences with Zaev near the end of his prime ministership, where the two discussed the North Macedonian government's "commitment to social and economic inclusion."[49]

Dimitar Kovačevski, the then-president of SDSM, was appointed prime minister of North Macedonia following the resignation of his Zaev in January 2022.

Wasting no time, Alex met with Kovačevski in February 2022, the month after he became prime minister of North Macedonia

---

47   Serena McMahon, "Low Turnout in Referendum Throws Macedonian Name Change into Question," NPR, September 30, 2018. https://www.npr.org/2018/09/30/653138345/low-turnout-threatens-the-result-of-macedonias-vote-on-whether-to-change-its-nam

48   Sinisa Jakov Marusic, "Most Macedonians Back 'Name' Deal, Survey Shows," *Balkan Insight*, February 5, 2018. https://balkaninsight.com/2018/02/05/survey-macedonia-majority-supports-name-deal-with-greece-02-05-2018

49   https://www.youtube.com/watch?v=UmnuCZ6d0DA

(he served until January 2024).[50] The last time the two were photographed together before this was in January 2024, ahead of "Western Balkan Meets EU" event before he left office.[51]

Like Albania's PM Edi Rama, Kovačevski would become a recurring character on Alex's social media in the years to come: pictured together on June 2022 at the Open Balkans Event with Rama himself,[52] pictured August 2022 ahead of the "Open Balkan Wine Fair,"[53] pictured March 2023 for an unspecified meeting,[54] and pictured lounging in May 2023 with a caption about how they're waiting for Rama.[55]

Kovačevski said they discussed European integration when they were pictured in September 2023 together.[56] Another photo showed Edi Rama with them in NYC. "The spirit of Open Balkans comes to NYC" Alex wrote.[57] And they were pictured together shortly after that, in November 2023. "Good to see Dimitar Kovačevski in good spirits and able to laugh as he has one of the hardest jobs of any Prime Minister in Europe."[58]

One picture (and caption) stood out from them all, once again providing strong evidence that Alex had already taken over the OSF empire before it was official. In a post from February 2023, Alex posted a photo of himself and his father meeting

---

50   https://www.facebook.com/photo/?fbid=521630555991464
51   https://www.facebook.com/Alexandersorospublic/posts/pfbid02BWGK4qhwfD
      MPwexmxdEnPmCSDz9e1sJVYtJaJFa1FFasjd3UxnR3Jry8FGp8AKYfl
52   https://www.facebook.com/Alexandersorospublic/posts/pfbid08Wd1spaSz1wPR
      qE4J4z7QZyxb7GbwFCdzpL8jrAt2MGCRmLcybhndRKhzfdXhBsbl
53   https://www.facebook.com/Alexandersorospublic/posts/pfbid0swSfSv9M4UZ5S
      fressiQgne5Q49wr8M1Rjg2beeeQBTATMqCcAJ5U1vRZr669VVVl
54   https://www.facebook.com/Alexandersorospublic/posts/pfbi
      d02BCgWSDCEBz3HjnAs7doidEEsnfWv9D4iMvYn2jV9xYagf9ZcT4NHC
      UG26CKm93BYl
55   https://www.facebook.com/Alexandersorospublic/posts/pfbid02ru3oHcspErkje
      5SSjHN8EPjLJxccLSNjW9fHejkBcVURRt7WbFSqBz6AQjqDrMwYl
56   https://www.facebook.com/Dimitar.Kovachevski/posts/pfbid02Q58fuSoobbN7
      DoSqRPpeXjiut6q15SgmvMjFi14auQdkCcHLMTBxpTty3RV5XNmGl
57   https://www.facebook.com/Alexandersorospublic/posts/pfbid02F93GSkhsaBW2
      ZhkM7EpdpksJgimATCk8Jf8nVQ56V5zv33xFsxtNay6jR5LoRJMYl
58   https://www.facebook.com/Alexandersorospublic/posts/pfbid0DsYRHafiDCGsnb
      NePzBTd6xTEEwo2LpWLZQqfLyVPJmHn9gJSktA3FgcMGbw6Mdpl

Kovačevski, with Alex giving him a hug and George shaking his hand. "Good to see Prime Minister of North Macedonia Dimitar Kovačevski *and introduce him to my father*," he captioned the post. [59] (Emphasis added.)

No longer was George introducing Alex to his allies, the son had become the father.

To the chagrin of the Soros family, VMRO-DPMNE would later regain power in 2024 with their coalition taking seventy-eight seats, and SDSM and its coalition partners would suffer its worst election performance on record, garnering only a third as much as they did in 2016. [60]

USAID's corpse is still warm, and Alex is left clutching a ghost. George turned it into his personal ATM, siphoning billions to grease OSF's gears until Trump and Musk torched it. With over five thousand programs axed, ten thousand jobs gutted, and $30 billion lifeline snuffed out, it's not a setback, it's a gut punch to the OSF. The machine has been unplugged.

THE WORKING FAMILIES PARTY: GIVING RADICALS THE KEYS TO LEGISLATIVE VICTORIES

Alex Soros has been aiding the Working Families Party (WFP), the most radical third party in the United States with representation in government.

Working Families Power (WFPower), the "direct action arm" of the party, received $6 million from the Soros machine. In addition, another $1 million from Alex's Democracy PAC was funneled into the WFP during the 2022 election cycle alone. [61]

---

59   https://www.facebook.com/Alexandersorospublic/posts/pfbid02pR11NJP5ikQG pEHDdciXAzuPpqy3bsygQDZNaXASuH7WzGW4DTY2C8xDkZCZwSLDl

60   https://en.wikipedia.org/wiki/Social_Democratic_Union_of_Macedonia

61   "Working Families Party PAC to PAC/Party," OpenSecrets. https://www.open secrets.org/political-action-committees-pacs/working-families-party/C006069 62/pac-to-pac/2022

The WFP is particularly notorious for being climate-obsessed, in addition to holding other far-left opinions even many Democrats in the twenty-first century won't touch.

Two elected officials on the Philadelphia City Council are members of the WFP. Councilmember Kendra Brooks had her photo prominently featured in a January 2021 story from Philadelphia's *Grid Magazine* headlined, "We've already laid the foundation for a Green New Deal in Philadelphia. We just need the will—and the cash—to make it happen." In the piece, Brooks bragged, "We are building the structure to create a Green New Deal that's community-led and community-driven, not something that's top-down," clearly following the policy path set in place by her party.[62]

Most of the WFP's power in legislatures isn't through officeholders bearing the "WFP" label, but instead through those holding office as Democrats who either hold dual membership in, or are endorsed by, the WFP.

The WFP has major influence over New York politics specifically and has de facto representation in their state legislature and the New York City Council through backing Democrats that also run under the WFP banner. New York has fusion voting, meaning that candidates can run representing multiple parties, and all votes count toward the candidate. So, Democrats who sign on to the WFP's platform, and have their blessing, can run as WFP candidates, too. Notable Democrats who also run as WFP include Andrew Cuomo, Kathy Hochul, Chuck Schumer, Hillary Clinton, and Joe Biden.

The WFP has scored notable victories for the left. In 2018, eight New York Democrats backed by the WFP flipped Republican

62   Alexandra M. Jones, "We've Already Laid the Foundation for a Green New Deal in Philadelphia. We Just Need the Will—and the Cash—to Make It Happen," *Grid*, January 4, 2021. https://gridphilly.com/blog-home/2021/1/4/m44jqdvt0xz19 dhglq7luuakyfpz6k

state Senate seats, turning the chamber blue.[63] The first member of the WFP to win office in New York State as a member of the party itself was Letitia James (who since changed to Democrat, and who would go on to become the radical state attorney general backed by Soros himself, notorious for unleashing a legal vendetta against Trump).

WFP helps keep the Democratic Party "accountable" (in the eyes of progressives), making the latter adopt further and further left-wing positions in order to earn their backing. In this sense, they're a left-wing equivalent of the Tea Party, while also being an actual political party. According to their website, they're currently fielding (in 2025) 461 candidates in New York, three in Ohio, ten in Oregon, and twenty in Wisconsin.[64]

The WFP is guaranteeing that the days of the moderate Democrat are over. Among their radical proposals includes free public college, in addition to the "cancellation" (taxpayer bailout) of all $1.77 trillion in outstanding student debt.[65] College graduates earn more than non-graduates, meaning their debt would be paid off largely by people who earn less than they do. They also back the weak-on-crime agenda, with policies that include paroling people age 55 or older that have served fifteen consecutive years in prison,[66] endorsement of "progressive" prosecutors (like George Soros has), and eliminating cash bail for nonviolent offenses. The week after George Floyd's death, the WFP called for defunding the police.[67]

63   "WFP-backed Democrats Flip New York State Senate!," Working Families Party, November 7, 2018. https://workingfamilies.org/2018/11/wfp-backed-democrats-flip-new-york-state-senate

64   "Our Candidates," Working Families Party. https://workingfamilies.org/candidates

65   Lyss Welding, "Average Student Loan Debt in 2025," BestColleges, February 11, 2025. https://www.bestcolleges.com/research/average-student-loan-debt

66   "Working Families Party New York: Legislative Agenda 2021," Working Families Party. https://workingfamilies.org/wp-content/uploads/2021/02/NYWFP_2021 LegislativeAgenda.pdf

67   https://x.com/WorkingFamilies/status/1267078490945437696

The party's organizing arm, WFPower, is primary focused on its cartoonish climate-change politics and ensuring the green policies it supports are incorporated at both the federal and state levels. WFPower lists itself as a co-leader that helped "build and steer" the Green New Deal Network (GNDN),[68] a project of the Soros-backed Tides Advocacy.[69] Soros seeded the Network with $525,000 in 2020 when the coalition was birthed.[70] The coalition claimed that it represents the culmination of a "decade-long campaign fighting to pump $1 trillion per year of federal climate justice investments into communities across the country."[71] Its goal, claimed the GNDN, was to "continue the fight for $10 trillion of federal investments by 2030" for eco-extremist policies.

One of the Network's major functions is gathering other climate-change activists to oppose the Trump administration. After Trump's 2025 inauguration, the GNDN organized a mass kickoff call with other climate hysterics to discuss how it planned to hamstring the president's "drill, baby drill" agenda. The speakers for the video call included leftists like Green New Deal legislation co-author Senator Ed Markey, Democratic Representatives Delia Ramirez and Yassamin Ansari, and climate extremist Bill McKibben, who is co-founder of the Soros-funded environmentalist organization 350.org.[72]

It's no wonder, then, why WFPower would proudly boast the fact that it is part of the GNDN's "Coordination Team." After all,

68 "Movement Power," Working Families Power. https://workingfamiliespower.org/movement-power
69 "How Green New Deal Network Drives Policy Solutions for Climate Justice," Tides Foundation. https://www.tides.org/case-study/how-green-new-deal-network-drives-policy-solutions-for-climate-justice
70 "Awarded Grants," Open Society Foundations. https://www.opensocietyfoundations.org/grants/past?filter_keyword=Green+New+Deal+Network+
71 "About Us: Coalition History," Green New Deal Network. https://greennewdealnetwork.org/the-coalition/about-us
72 "Climate Leaders and Elected Officials Host Mass Organizing Kickoff Call Following Donald Trump's Inauguration," Green New Deal Network, January 22, 2025. https://greennewdealnetwork.org/climate-leaders-and-elected-officials-host-mass-organizing-kickoff-call-following-donald-trumps-inauguration

its vision is that "it is in the interest of existing movement-aligned organizations to engage them to absorb as many new activists as possible into the permanent progressive infrastructure, while also working to maximize their effectiveness and impact in the moment." The GNDN is the perfect example of such extremist efforts put to work.

The Working Families apparatus's obsession with the Green New Deal is even more absurd, given its tenets. One study by the American Action Forum put its cost of implementation anywhere between $50 trillion and $90 trillion[73]—a cost that would still be massive even if it ended up being just 95 percent cheaper

Components of the Green New Deal include the absurd notion of retrofitting the nation's entire public housing stock for energy efficiency within ten years.[74] One 2020 analysis estimated that there are roughly one hundred million single-family homes in the United States, along with 5.2 million multi-family homes, 5.5 million commercial buildings, 350,000 industrial buildings, and 240,000 military buildings, for 111 million total. In other words, 30,410 buildings would need to be retrofitted *per day*.[75]

The Green New Deal is a Trojan Horse for further institutionalizing socialism within American policymaking. As former Chamber of Commerce executive director Thomas Donahue wrote in 2019, "No laughing matter, however, is the proposal's

---

73   Doug Holtz-Eakin, "How Much Will the Green New Deal Cost?," Aspen Institute, June 11, 2019. https://www.aspeninstitute.org/blog-posts/how-much-will-the-green-new-deal-cost

74   "Ocasio-Cortez, Sanders, Ramirez Reintroduce the Green New Deal for Public Housing Act," press release, US House of Representatives, March 21, 2024. https://ocasio-cortez.house.gov/media/press-releases/ocasio-cortez-sanders-ramirez-reintroduce-green-new-deal-public-housing-act

75   Brian Potter, "Every Building in America—an Analysis of the U.S. Building Stock," *Construction Physics*. November 2, 2020. https://www.construction-physics.com/p/every-building-in-america-an-analysis

ultimate objective: to give government unprecedented power over people's lives and our entire economy."[76]

Donahue also highlighted how the "authors of the Green New Deal intend to eliminate fossil fuels altogether. Good luck to the 3.4 million Americans who would lose their jobs as a result—not to mention anyone who drives a car." The GND's advocates like WFPower and WFP seem to be pushing for that same outcome.

In a 2024 podcast interview with WFP National Director Maurice Mitchell, *Convergence Magazine* analyzed that WFP "aims to become the leading political home for US progressives"—and the Soros empire is helping lead the charge.[77]

THE ALEX SOROS-CINDY MCCAIN CONNECTION

Have we been missing a Soros-McCain connection in front of our very eyes this entire time?

Alex Soros has posted numerous photos on his social media with Cindy McCain.

On May 6, 2024, Alex shared a photo with Cindy at the McCain Institute Sedona Forum. The topic of the forum was "Securing Our Insecure World," which used the "climate crisis" as a backdrop, and had a speaking roster of Democrats and RINOs including Mitt Romney, Janet Yellen, Arizona Governor Katie Hobbs, David Axelrod, and Secretary of State Antony Blinken. In a tweet with Senator Mark Kelly, Alex indicated that stopping Trump was a topic of discussion, referring to Kelly as "Inspiring as ever and attentive to the threat posed in November if Trump wins."

---

76   Thomas J. Donahue, "The Green New Deal Is a Trojan Horse for Socialism," U.S. Chamber of Commerce, February 18, 2019. https://www.uschamber.com/energy/the-green-new-deal-trojan-horse-socialism

77   William Lawrence, "How the Working Families Party Is Building Progressive Governing Power, with Maurice Mitchell," *Convergence*, February 21, 2024. https://convergencemag.com/podcast/how-the-working-families-party-is-building-progressive-governing-power-with-maurice-mitchell

Alex has posted photos with him, Cindy, and George at the Munich Security Conference,[78] he and Cindy discussing the World Food Programme,[79] and more. The earliest photo of them together is from 2020 at the Munich Security Conference.[80] The 2020 annual report for the Munich Security Conference lists Alex as part of the advisory council, and Cindy as a member of the board of an American partner group.[81]

It's no secret that the McCains were/are no fans of Donald Trump and the modern Republican Party, and that they've both been banished to RINO status.

The evolution of a George Soros-John McCain relationship has mostly flown under the radar, evading even me until I started researching Alex's relationship with Cindy. To understand that relationship, one must first understand the relationship between John McCain and George.

In 2001, John McCain founded the Reform Institute, a supposed nonprofit think tank that effectively acted as a loophole to allow McCain to take unlimited and unregulated donations. Most donors also contributed to his presidential campaigns (both in 2000 and in 2008), or his Straight Talk America PAC. Hypocritically, the Reform Institute has claimed it wants to "clean up" campaign finance—but years after its founding, in 2008, it sent out a fundraiser putting George Soros on blast as a Democrat mega donor.[82]

And just as they're hypocrites in claiming to want to see campaign finance cleaned up, while literally existing as a loop-

---

78   https://x.com/AlexanderSoros/status/1626619665848885251

79   https://x.com/AlexanderSoros/status/1747231929693278519

80   https://www.facebook.com/photo.php?fbid=1502193579942986&id=3781129
      89017723&set=a.482314728597548

81   "Annual Report: 2020," Munich Security Conference. https://securityconference.
      org/assets/02_Dokumente/01_Publikationen/MSC_Annual_Report_2020_
      190x250_96dpi.pdf

82   Jamie Amrhein, "Lining the Pockets of McCain's Reform Institute," The Center for
      Public Integrity, August 8, 2008. https://publicintegrity.org/politics/lining-the-
      pockets-of-mccains-reform-institute

hole to campaign finance laws, the institute was taking George Soros's money as they criticized others for doing the same.[83] The institute accepted multiple contributions from Soros, some up to $100,000, and from the Soros-funded Tides Foundation. The "maverick senator" also took money from Teneo, a company cofounded by Bill Clinton's "bag man," Doug Band.[84]

While not exactly a reliable source, Iran's intelligence ministry released an animated video in 2008 detailing a fictional conversation between Soros and John McCain, where the two discuss a conspiracy for "culture-building" and regime-change in Iran.[85] The truth aside, it's interesting that even they noticed the connection.

Alex and Cindy McCain's partnership could signal a broader coalition of establishment Democrats and RINOs uniting against populist conservatives, potentially influencing policy through forums like the Munich Security Conference.

What began as a subtle alliance between George Soros and John McCain has evolved into a visible partnership between their successors, Alex and Cindy, uniting two families with a shared disdain for Trump and a mutual interest in globalist causes—proof that the real power in politics often lies in the connections we overlook until they demand our attention.

---

83   Ken Silverstein, "McCain and the 'Reform' Institute," *Harper's Magazine*, April 11, 2008. https://harpers.org/2008/04/mccain-and-the-reform-institute

84   Richard Pollock, "Soros, Clinton-Linked Teneo Among Donors to McCain Institute," *The Daily Caller*, June 19, 2017. https://dailycaller.com/2017/06/19/exclusive-soros-clinton-linked-teneo-among-donors-to-mccain-institute

85   "Iranian Intelligence Ministry Broadcast Encouraging People to Snitch on Spies Features 'John McCain' Masterminding a Velvet Revolution in Iran from the White House," *MemriTV*, February 5, 2008. https://www.memri.org/tv/iranian-intelligence-ministry-broadcast-encouraging-people-snitch-spies-features-john-mccain

THE SOROS INFLUENCE OVER WIKIPEDIA

For someone of his background, Alex's Wikipedia page has always been short on details, only ever containing around twenty citations-worth of information at any point in its history, from when he was just a student playboy dabbling in philanthropy to when he became the head of a multibillion-dollar organization.

For whatever reason, Wikipedia's editors would like us to know the least possible about him. His page is "semi-protected," a status afforded to only 0.17 percent of pages.[86] The profile of the editor who changed his page to "protected editor status" identifies himself as a former journalist who has run for public office before representing the Democratic Party and Working Families Party. Not a single piece of negative information about Alex appears on his page in any form—not even in the form of framing it as being from "right-wing radicals" or "anti-Semites."

This isn't anything out of the ordinary, as Wikipedia has long been documented to be biased in favor of leftists with biographies on their platform.

A 2024 study from the Manhattan Institute that analyzed 175,205 emotional annotations found that Wikipedia articles favor left-leaning individuals, while painting right-leaning ones in a negative light.[87] The power of framing is powerful. For example, Wikipedia used to have a page on "Cultural Marxism," which presented the concept as an academic one. Once the political right began using the term, they changed course, and now anyone who searches "Cultural Marxism" on the platform will be redirected to the page "Cultural Marxism Conspiracy Theory."

---

86   https://en.wikipedia.org/wiki/Wikipedia:Protection_statistics
87   David Rozado, "Is Wikipedia Politically Biased?," Manhattan Institute, June 20, 2024. https://manhattan.institute/article/is-wikipedia-politically-biased

The former page has been replaced with one titled "Marxist Cultural Analysis."[88]

Amazingly, the Media Research Center in 2020 highlighted how one Wiki editor made five hundred biased edits to the pages of right-wing personalities, with no consequences—including one where he claimed that Mark Levin, who is Jewish, is an anti-Semite for criticizing George Soros.[89]

I mention all that to note that the elder Soros exerts an enormous influence over Wikipedia. In January 2016, Wikimedia launched an endowment as a "Collective Action Fund," with the Soros-backed Tides Foundation managing it.[90] Two years later, in October 2018, George Soros himself kicked in $2 million to the Wikimedia Endowment.[91]

When it comes to reliability, the oft-cited concern about how anyone can trust an encyclopedia that "anyone can edit" becomes irrelevant, because it's the editors really running the show. The editors wield immense power over what kind of information can and cannot be included on the site. This has given the left a virtual monopoly on "truth" on the platform—and it shows. Here are some more examples:

In 2021, Wikipedia's editors debated deleting the page on "Mass killings under communist regimes," with them raising concerns about the "verifiability" of claims made. One user com-

88   https://en.wikipedia.org/?title=Cultural_Marxism&redirect=no
89   Alexander Hall, "Report: Ex-Editor Calls Out Wikipedia for Its War Against Mark Levin," *NewsBusters*, July 14, 2020. https://newsbusters.org/blogs/free-speech/alexander-hall/2020/07/14/report-ex-editor-calls-out-wikipedia-its-war-against
90   "Wikimedia Endowment," Wikimedia. https://meta.wikimedia.org/wiki/Wikimedia_Endowment
91   Kaitlin Thaney, "George Soros, founder of Open Society Foundations, invests in the future of free and open knowledge," Wikimedia Foundation, October 15, 2018. https://wikimediafoundation.org/news/2018/10/15/george-soros-invests-future-free-open-knowledge

plained that the page pushes the "fringe theory" that "the ideology of communism is somehow inherently violent."[92]

Independent journalist Lee Fang reported in 2023 that Wikipedia allowed special consultants hired by Hunter Biden to manipulate his page with "stealth edits" to clean up his image.[93] You can bet that there are zero cases of a conservative getting that kind of treatment.

And as if there were any more questions as to where Wikipedia stands politically, their co-founder Larry Sanger has confirmed as much—that the site has gone woke. "You can't cite Fox News on socio-political issues. It's just banned now," said in an interview with *UnHerd News* in 2021. "It means that if a controversy does not appear in the mainstream center-left media, then it's not going to appear on Wikipedia."[94]

"If only one version of the facts is allowed then that gives a huge incentive to wealthy and powerful people to seize control of things like Wikipedia in order to shore up their power," he added.

Even the Wikipedia page "Ideological bias on Wikipedia" admits that "Multiple studies have found a left-wing bias at Wikipedia in both article content and editor sanctioning."[95]

And the Soros network won't let it get better anytime soon.

Research from reporter Ashley Rindsberg documented that the Soros link is more than just financial. Just look at the high-

92   Jessica Chasmar, "Wikipedia Page on 'Mass Killings Under Communist Regimes' Considered for Deletion, Prompting Bias Accusations," Fox News, November 29, 2021. https://www.foxnews.com/politics/wikipedia-page-mass-killings-communist-regimes-deletion-bias

93   Luis Cornelio, "Wiki WOW! Damning Emails Reveal Manipulated Biden Wikipedia Entries," *NewsBusters*, August 16, 2023. https://www.newsbusters.org/blogs/business/luis-cornelio/2023/08/16/wiki-wow-damning-emails-reveal-manipulated-biden-wikipedia

94   "Wikipedia Co-founder: I No Longer Trust the Website I Created," *UnHerd*, December 14, 2021. https://unherd.com/newsroom/wikipedia-co-founder-i-no-longer-trust-the-website-i-created

95   "Ideological bias on Wikipedia," Wikipedia. https://en.wikipedia.org/wiki/Ideological_bias_on_Wikipedia

er-ups at Wikimedia and their (mostly direct) ties to Soros, as well as various left-wing organizations.[96]

Eileen Hershenov served as general counsel at the Wikimedia Foundation from 2017–2018—and was also general counsel and associate general counsel at the OSF. In addition, she served as general counsel for Central European University, which was founded by Soros in 1991.

Zack Exley was chief revenue officer of Wikimedia from 2010–2013 and was also a fellow at the OSF. His involvement in Soros-backed projects didn't end there, having also been co-founder of the Soros-funded New Organizing Fund, and director of organizing at MoveOn.org. Exley helped co-found the Justice Democrats, along with the Young Turks' Cenk Uygur and Saikat Chakrabarti, who would later go on to be Alexandria Ocasio-Cortez's chief of staff. Justice Democrats was a PAC founded to get progressive Democrats elected.

Katherine Maher served as executive director & CEO of the Wikimedia Foundation from 2016–2021, and previously as chief communications officer 2014–2016. She was also a board member of Soros-funded Center for Democracy & Technology, and founder of the Soros-funded Sharek961. As of this writing she's CEO of NPR, which has received donations from Soros, and made headlines for her prior "woke" comments on assuming the role, including publicly branding Trump a racist.

Lisa Seitz-Gruwell is president of the Wikimedia Endowment, and has been chief advancement officer from 2015 to the present. Previously she was a consultant at Gruwell and Associates (among their largest clients was Soros-founded Democracy Alliance), and board member at the Soros-tied Progressive States Network.

---

96   Ashley Rindsberg, "How Soros-Backed Operatives Took Over Key Roles at Wikipedia," *Pirate Wires*, January 6, 2025. https://www.piratewires.com/p/george-soros-wikipedia

Among other positions, Gruwell was previously appointed by then-San Francisco Mayor Gavin Newsom to the city's civil service commission.

Ethan Zuckerman, a Wikimedia advisory board member since 2007, has also served as a head, chair, and member of various OSF boards, and was once advisor to then-OSF President Christopher Stone

Rebecca MacKinnon, Wikimedia's VP for global advocacy since 2021, also founded the OSF-funded NGO Ranking Digital Rights. MacKinnon had previously been a journalist for CNN.

Cameran Ashraf has been Wikimedia's head of human rights since 2021, served as OSF's deputy director of internship for rights and governance, and is currently a professor at CEU.

Lastly, Melissa Hagemann was a Wikimedia advisory board member from 2007–2018 and has been employed by the OSF for over twenty-two years. She was also a steering committee member of the now-defunct Open Climate Campaign.

So next time a Wikipedia article tries to guilt-trip you into donating to them during their seemingly never-ending fundraising efforts, remember that they already have a billionaire backer pulling the strings—and truth is a casualty of it.

Chapter 7

Year One—Examining Alex's Biggest Grants

To demonstrate that Alex Soros is funding the same kind of radical groups as his father, I tracked all US-based groups that received grants from Alex in 2023 (the most recent year for which the OSF has data) that total $500,000 or more per grant.

I chose the $500k threshold for two main reasons; that it would only include groups the OSF unquestionably has significant influence over due to it usually comprising a significant percentage of their total funding, and because examining every grant would take up more than the length of this book, as the OSF gave 2,166 total grants in 2023.

In total, there were 148 grants in this category, some of which were grants for the same organization over differing time periods (so the number of organizations in this chapter won't total 148). There were also a few that didn't seem significant enough to bother including.

I divided the groups into four main categories.

The first is "fund of funds," a term I borrowed from the financial world. The OSF itself funds both thousands of groups and groups that fund other groups. It seems to make little sense at first glance, do they think other groups are better at making grants than they are? That's one interpretation, but it's more likely that it's to give themselves a degree of plausible deniability in the groups they want to fund. As was explained earlier in the book,

OSF has tried to deny funding individuals like Chesa Boudin and Alvin Bragg with this sort of illogic.

The next are think tanks and research organizations that are active in crafting left-wing policy to then be advocated to legislators.

Then there are "get out the vote" organizations that mobilize voters, usually based on a specific geographical region or ethnicity, to turn out. Fortunately, they didn't have much luck in 2024.

After that are a handful of media organizations OSF funds, which adds to a legacy of media influence that Alex inherits from his father.

Lastly, I categorized the remaining groups in a more general "civic engagement" category.

Individually linking each source for this chapter would result in footnotes taking up half of the page (I opt for footnotes over endnotes in all of my books so sources are easier to read). Every group's description is from their website, or the *InfluenceWatch. com* profile of them, and any financial data is from *ProPublica*'s "Nonprofit Explorer," which provides each group's filings.

One thing that's impossible not to notice in reading through the descriptions of the groups is how they're packed with the sort of word salad buzzwords you'd see the corporate version of on a LinkedIn profile. (For anyone who doesn't get the reference, profiles on the job-seeking website LinkedIn are notorious for exaggerating credentials and minor accomplishments. It's the only place a dishwasher will unironically refer to themselves as a "bacterial disarmament specialist."). It often feels like the groups here copying and pasting each other's mission statements and then rearranging a few words.

I attempted to merge their mission statements into one sentence and come up with the following, and came up with "The Blah Blah Blah Collective aims to build a radically inclusive mul-

tiracial equity-driven democracy for LGBTQIA2S+ black/native/
latinx/indigenous/AAPI/POC/low-income communities to break
the shackles of systematic oppression through building resilience,
while mobilizing intersectional voters by organizing them to challenge structural systems, amplify collective power, and reimagine
a just, sustainable future for all."

As you'll see in the pages to come, that's not far off.

THE SUSPICIOUS

But before diving into all those, which are listed in tables, there
were a number of organizations I came across that were suspicious when it came to the obvious question of what exactly it was
that they did. This included groups that provided no information
on their operations, had social media accounts inactive for years,
were registered to PO boxes, hadn't updated their websites in
years, or had abnormal financials. All while receiving millions of
dollars. How does such an organization receive a grant that presumably has a vetting process?

It would be irresponsible to deem them fraudulent simply by
analyzing them from behind a computer screen, but they warrant
a look at by regulators.

They are as follows.

The Asian American Advocacy Fund, Inc. received $1,425,000
and vaguely claims to advocate for the rights of Asians in Georgia
without explaining what those rights are. The "advocacy" section of their website only lists pro-Palestine and pro-Black Lives
Matter advocacy. A documentary featured on their home page for
over a year has barely racked up over 300 views. No events are
listed on the "events" tab on their website.

The Black Male Initiative Fund received exactly the same
amount. Their website says they "seek to create effective outcomes

for our communities by empowering black men economically and civically through the use of direct action, advocacy, and grassroots organizing," to create a "healthy, just, and equitable society." Their website doesn't give any information about any activism they've done, and there are no news reports on their activities. The only tabs on their website ask people to donate.

The Black Male Voter project, a group that supports ending cash bail and qualified immunity, received $900,000 despite their website not being updated since August 2022. Their website gets little traffic; a YouTube video that appears near the top of their website that was posted 3 years ago has only 650 views as of writing. Again, there's no news reports on their activities.

The Black Organizing for Leadership and Dignity (BOLD), which received $2,250,000, had the oddest website of them all. It's merely a single paragraph of text over a photograph of people appearing to do some sort of Tai chi, which states that they're a "catalyst for transformative leadership. Through training, project incubation, and network cultivation BOLD supports the infrastructure of deeply impactful, powerful, and coordinated movements" next to a donate button.

Their address is registered to a PO Box and they have no social media presence. No information whatsoever explaining what they actually do is available.

Future Forward USA Action, which wants to "to help rebuild America's middle class—and American democracy—by advancing new ideas and fresh perspectives," got an astronomical $15 million, and their revenue and expenses suspiciously almost track each other one for one. This is the only group I looked up on the entire list that had financials that tracked like this. Expenses are easier for organizations like this to project because they have control over them, while revenues are more variable. This doesn't necessarily mean anything fraudulent is occurring, it's just an oddity that every dollar raised seems allocated for spending the moment it comes in.

Most of their funds go to PACs that support Democrat politicians, and a third goes to Waterfront Strategies, an advertising purchasing firm.

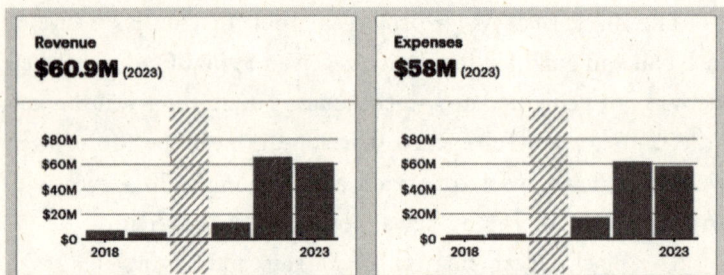

The most suspect of all was also the one that received the largest amont of money; One American Future Action, which took in a whopping $18,055,000.

They champion three issues: lowering costs for families, increasing access to health care and abortion, and civic engagement. No examples of activism are given on the website, and the "In the News" tab on their website includes a single article. It's unclear what this group does operationally, the answer appears to be close to nothing.

Their financials are truly bizarre. In 2023 they booked nearly $13 million in revenue but only had $1.3 million in expenses, and $11.4 million in assets, 100% of which is in cash. For a tax-exempt organization to only spend 10% of its revenue in a single year is unheard of, and begs the question of how such a minor organization could raise so much money.

Exactly $1 million of their expenses were grants to only four groups, while the rest were management, legal, accounting, and "other." They recorded only $104 in office expenses, no expenses for information technology (computer related expenses), advertising, or travel. Their directors, treasurer, and president all report working 1-hour workweeks, while their CEO reports a fifteen-hour workweek, and they all report no income.

The organization seems to be a passthrough to other liberal groups, as it has no operations or expenses associated with operations, and no directors who take a salary. To speculate, the massive cash pile could be on hold to be deployed in coming years to fund other causes that Alex backs.

Ultimately, nobody knows (yet).

As for the rest, here they are.

Fund of Funds		
Organization	**Grant Amount**	**Notes**
Amalgamated Charitable Foundation	$10,925,000	Funds groups "working to build an inclusive, multiracial democracy that is open, just, resilient, and trustworthy."
Civic Nation	$2,000,000	Funds a number of other left-wing groups. Previous board members have included six high-ranking members of the Obama administration, and Michelle Obama is featured on their homepage.
Hopewell Fund	$10,850,000	Left-wing group managed by Arabella Advisors. One of the five largest non-profits associated with the Democratic Party.

Organization	Grant Amount	Notes
National Urban Indian Family Coalition	$600,000	Distributes grants to "voter engagement" projects.
NEO Philanthropy, Inc.	$1,500,000	Fiscal clearinghouse for left-wing causes.
Possibility Labs	$10,000,000	Envisions a "just world where "where Black, Indigenous, People of Color and systemically oppressed communities have the power of self-determination."
Proteus Fund, Inc.	$600,000	Founded with goal of abolishing the death penalty.
Rockefeller Philanthropy Advisors, Inc.	$3,750,000	Manages over $500 million annually in "charitable giving." Generally supports left-wing views on climate change and supposed "human rights" issues.
Sixteen Thirty Fund	$13,665,000	The "hub of dark money spending on the left." Administered by Arabella Advisors.
Social and Environmental Entrepreneurs, Inc.	$769,265	Fiscally sponsors start-up organizations that promote climate advocacy and far-left views on the justice system and culture.
Solidago Foundation	$3,000,000	Funds "grassroots groups that are led by people most directly affected by structural inequities working to protect and reform our democratic systems."

Organization	Grant Amount	Notes
State Democracy Project	$1,000,000	Sponsors left-wing voter mobilization groups and left-wing organizations.
State Engagement Fund	$3,300,000	Dark money group that funds left-wing groups.
Michigan Civic Action Fund	$1,200,000	Makes grants to left-wing groups in Michigan.
New Venture Fund	$1,250,000	Gives grants to left-wing organizations. Focuses mainly on social and environmental change. Largest nonprofit created and managed by Arabella Advisors.
Tides Advocacy	$1,800,000	A favorite of the OSF that itself is similar to the OSF.
Tides Center	$1,000,000	Same as above.
Tides Foundation	$2,100,000	Same as above.
Way to Rise	$5,000,000	Works to direct funding from donors and grantmaking institutions to local activists and political organizations.
WorkMoney, Inc.	$15,000,000	Left-wing dark money group, possibly a union-backed venture. Has targeted moderate Democrats like Krysten Sinema and Joe Manchin (who left the party in 2022 and 2024, respectively).

Think Tanks and Research Organizations		
Organization	Grant Amount	Notes
ASO Communications	$600,000	Works with left-wing groups to help with messaging through research, surveying, and campaigning. Has worked on messaging for campaigns related to climate change, transgender issues, and race and class.
Center for American Progress	$3,000,000	A favorite of the OSF discussed earlier in this book.
Center for American Progress Action Fund	$2,000,000	A favorite of the OSF discussed earlier in this book.
Constitutional Accountability Center	$750,000	Advocates a leftist interpretation of the US Constitution.
Independent Strategic Research Collaborative	$1,500,000	"Research, strategy, messaging, and collaborative convening hub for progressive national, state and local organizations working to realize the promise of a truly equitable, multi-racial democracy."
New America Foundation	$5,000,000	Liberal think tank that focuses on national security, technology, health, gender, energy, education, and the economy.

Organization	Grant Amount	Notes
North Carolina A. Philip Randolph Educational Fund	$1,275,000	Advocates for left-wing legislation, regulation, and government programs, and "intends to develop technical and policy solutions for the growing problems of voter disenfranchisement, lack of voter participation."
Open Markets Institute	$600,000	Think tank that focuses on monopolies and how to break them up.
Reset Tech	$550,000	Works to "support a realignment of digital media markets with democratic values" through research, policy analysis, and supporting organizations with shared values.
The Movement Cooperative	$2,055,000	Project of the Tides Foundation. They vaguely claim to provide "shared tools, trusted data, engineering expertise, research support, and collaborative space that help our members organize more efficiently, campaign more effectively, and build power that lasts."

Get Out the Vote		
Organization	**Grant Amount**	**Notes**
America Votes	$4,400,000	Founded by former Planned Parenthood head Cecile Richards. Works with over four hundred state and national partner organizations to win elections.
Ballot Initiative Strategy Center	$1,250,000	Aims to boost voter turnout by working with local, state, and national leaders. Using the most LinkedIn style language I've seen on this list, they describe themselves as "leveraging ballot measures across the United States to strengthen democracy; center people of color, queer, low-income, immigrant, Indigenous, and other marginalized communities; advance racial equity; build and transform power; and galvanize a new progressive base."
Battleground Texas Engagement Fund	$1,200,000	Pushes left-wing advocacy with goal of making Texas a swing state.
Black Progressive Action Coalition	$1,500,000	Tries to mobilize black voters to turn out for Democrats. Also supports a leftist agenda on criminal justice reform, voting eligibility, and economics.
CASA in Action	$1,600,000	Has 155,000 members, mobilizes "Black, Latine, Afro-descendent, Indigenous, and Immigrant voters."

Organization	Grant Amount	Notes
Forward Action Fund	$600,000	"Increase the participation of working-age people in democracy, enabling the next generation to thrive" in New Hampshire
NCAAT in Action	$900,000	Primary goal is voter mobilization in North Carolina, specifically among Asian Americans. Promotes information on how to vote, registration deadlines, and tips on how to get friends and family to vote.
New Rural Project	$750,000	Promotes voter turnout in rural counties in North Carolina.
Our Voice, Our Vote—Arizona	$1,050,000	Runs campaigns to boost black voter turnout in Arizona.
PODER	$750,000	Looks to increase "Latinx" voter turnout
Poder NC Action	$750,000	Same as above
Power to the Polls, Inc.	$900,000	Trains poll workers for elections.

News and Media		
Organization	**Grant Amount**	**Notes**
Courier Newsroom	$15,000,000	Discussed earlier in book.
In Union USA Action	$1,000,000	"Provides working people with monthly newsletters and information online about the issues facing working people across the country." Slush fund for the Democrat Party supported by nine top labor unions. Their social media accounts have been active since election day 2022 (midterms) and phrasing on the website also indicates it hasn't been updated since 2022.
Texas for All	$750,000	Creates videos about left-wing issues in Texas. As of writing, the 11 videos on their YouTube page have under three hundred views combined—amounting to $2,500 from the OSF per view. They've also organized protests at the Texas State Capitol. A photo of the most recent protest on their X account showed that only twenty people showed up. Their tax-exempt status was revoked in 2011 after not filing a Form 889-series return notice for three consecutive years. Their most recent financials (2018) showed only $150k in revenue.

Organization	Grant Amount	Notes
The National Trust for Local News	$6,387,708	Supports local news by buying organizations in "news deserts" instead of giving them grants, which gives them complete influence over their operations. Claims to be the primary source of local news for six million Americans.

Civic Organizations		
Organization	Grant Amount	Notes
Accelerate Action Inc.	$12,600,000	Catalyzes digital media networks to "increase civic engagement with BIPOC and low-income communities."
Accelerate Change	$2,400,000	Clone of Accelerate Action, their website has the same mission statement.
Advancement Project Education Fund	$2,700,000	Focuses in "racial justice" issues and envisions a future "where people of color are free." From what exactly remains a mystery.
Arizona Wins	$750,000	Coalition of progressive advocacy orgs and labor unions to advance left-wing policies in Arizona.

Organization	Grant Amount	Notes
Center for Racial and Gender Equity	$600,000	"Grassroots policy and electoral campaigns, engaging Black voters and building Black women's leadership to advance a legislative agenda and candidates that explicitly support Black women's liberation." Amusingly, their website has a "key victories" section that ends in 2021.
ColorOf Change.org Education Fund	$1,300,000	Part of Color of Change, which claims to be "nation's largest online racial justice organization." Their site lets people create online campaigns for left-wing causes. Their homepage features a series of petitions people can sign.
Committee on States	$1,500,000	Part of the left-wing donor conglomerate "Democracy Alliance," which has given over $1 billion to liberal organizations. This grant is equal to 60% of the Committee on States' total assets in 2023.

Organization	Grant Amount	Notes
Community Change Action	$4,000,000	Advocacy and grantmaking organization that supports left-wing causes and promotes voter engagement. The press releases tab on their website leads to a 404 error. Their social media accounts (some of which are inactive) have anemic engagement, and a YouTube video on their homepage explaining their "Vision for Racial Justice" has garnered under 200 views in over three years.
Down Home North Carolina	$1,200,000	Builds "multi-racial power for working people in North Carolina's small towns and rural places."
Emgage Action	$750,000	Muslim-American organization that "supports and advocates for just policies that strengthen our pluralistic democracy and protect human rights at home and abroad."
Equality Federation	$1,500,000	Advocates for LGBTQ+ issues.
Four Directions Native Vote Inc	$600,000	"Native-led national voting rights organization dedicated to advancing equality at the ballot box across Indian Country."

Organization	Grant Amount	Notes
Freedom Action Now	$750,000	"Black and Southeast Asian Wisconsin based political organization creating change for most impacted communities through voter education, leadership development, community organizing, and policy advocacy." Vision is to "advance the feminist abolitionist agenda."
Fund for Educational Excellence	$995,000	"Working to close the equity and opportunity gaps for all students in Baltimore City Public Schools." Their website's homepage only lists their mission statement (above), and a link asking people to "call your members of Congress" to demand action "on the issues that matter most to you." No address or any information is provided.
GLAHR Action Network	$600,000	"Educates and organizes the Latino community in Georgia to defend and promote their civil and human rights."
Indivisible Project	$3,000,000	"Fights for democracy, combating fascism, preserving rights, values, and communities. It promotes collective action and organizes protests, events, and campaigns to advocate for educational equality, criticize government policies, and ensure accountability from elected officials."

Organization	Grant Amount	Notes
Institute of International Education, Inc	$900,000	"Focuses on international student exchange and aid, foreign affairs, and international peace and security."
International Refugee Assistance Project	$1,100,000	"Advocates for systemic changes that benefit broader refugee populations."
Latino Victory Project	$1,500,000	"Dedicated to building political power in the Latino community so that the voices and values of Latinos are reflected at every level of government and in the policies that drive our country forward."
Leaders Igniting Transformation Action Fund, Inc.	$900,000	"Building political power for young people of color." Supports abolishing ICE and detention facilities and supports a "path to citizenship" (amnesty). Calls for abolishing police and prisons.
Leadership Conference Education Fund, Inc.	$750,000	"Provide a powerful voice for human dignity and equality—and a bulwark against discrimination." Opposes Trump immigration agenda and echoes Black Lives Matter style rhetoric.
League of Conservation Voters	$750,000	Environmental advocacy. "Builds political power for people and the planet." Advocates "Stopping the Elon Musk takeover."

Organization	Grant Amount	Notes
Living United for Change in Arizona	$1,800,000	Supports abolishing ICE and once sent a tweet in Spanish that translates to "f*** border patrol." They also once followed Senator Kyrsten Sinema into a bathroom and harassed her.
LUPE Votes	$600,000	Supports amnesty and socialized medicine. Targets Hispanic voters in South Texas.
Make the Road Action Fund Inc.	$1,650,000	Opposes enforcement of immigration laws at the border and US interior. Supports amnesty and abolishing ICE and supports ending or reducing incarceration of illegals and all criminals from ethnic minority backgrounds.
Michigan People's Campaign	$750,000	Organizes to support Democrat candidates in Maryland.
More Perfect Union Action	$700,000	Pro-labor union advocacy group that's part of the More Perfect Union media organization.
MOVE Texas Action Fund	$975,000	Works "to build power in underrepresented youth communities through civic engagement, leadership development, and issue advocacy." Founded to increase participation in local elections.

Organization	Grant Amount	Notes
National Employment Law Project, Inc.	$995,000	Lobbying arm of the labor-union-funded advocacy research organization National Employment Law Project and part of the Tides Advocacy Fund.
NEO Philanthropy Action Fund, Inc.	$3,000,000	Lobbying arm of NEO Philanthropy. Supports far-left lobbying and election-related advocacy groups including Asian Americans Advancing Justice, NextGen Climate Action, and Make the Road Action.
Nevada Advocates for Planned Parenthood Affiliates, Inc.	$750,000	Supports Planned Parenthood.
New Georgia Project Action Fund	$1,800,000	Works to increase civic participation of "Black, Latinx, AAPI, and young Georgians—and other historically marginalized communities by building grassroots political power in support of progressive leaders, policies, and issues."
New Left Accelerator	$900,000	Helps left-wing activist group increase their outreach.
Oficina Legal del Pueblo Unido, Inc.	$1,200,000	Supports police abolition and advocates for illegal immigration.
Ohio Organizing Campaign	$1,000,000	Organizes about "racial, economic, and social justice" issues in Ohio.

Organization	Grant Amount	Notes
Ohioans United for Reproductive Rights PAC	$3,500,000	Advocates for abortion access in Ohio.
One APIA Nevada	$1,050,000	Advances interests of American Pacific Islanders in Nevada.
Organize Pennsylvania	$1,275,000	"Movement for racial, economic, and social justice in Pennsylvania" that endorses candidates and claims to educate voters. They've only endorsed two candidates, one of which is the George Soros-backed Philadelphia DA Larry Krasner. Nearly all the group's revenue in 2023 was from the OSF and Tides Foundation.
Pennsylvania United	$1,575,000	"Works to connect communities of color with white working-class communities in counties across Western PA."
People for the American Way	$1,000,000	Founded in the 1980s to fight the Christian right. "A national progressive advocacy organization that inspires and mobilizes Americans to defend freedom, justice, and democracy from those who threaten to take them away."
Planned Parenthood Action Fund Inc.	$3,000,000	Activist arm of Planned Parenthood.

Organization	Grant Amount	Notes
Planned Parenthood Advocates of Michigan	$900,000	Same as above.
Planned Parenthood Votes! South Atlantic	$1,050,000	Same as above.
Protect Democracy Project	$750,000	Uses "litigation, legislative and communications strategies, technology, research, and analysis to stand up for free and fair elections, the rule of law, fact-based debate, and a better democracy for future generations."
Race Forward	$625,000	Works to "dismantle structural racism by building collective community power and transforming institutions."
Rockwood Leadership Institute	$560,000	Provides training and fellowship programs to empower nonprofit and social change leaders with skills in leadership, collaboration, and equity to drive "systemic change."
Run for Something Action Fund	$1,000,000	Recruits and supports young, diverse, progressive candidates, to run for state and local offices. Provides education, outreach, and resources like candidate training and fundraising support.

Organization	Grant Amount	Notes
Siembra NC	$600,000	Works to defend illegal aliens in North Carolina from ICE.
State Democracy Defenders Action	$1,000,000	Left-wing lobbying organization. OSF provided over a third of the group's funding their first year in existence (2023).
State Voices	$1,500,000	"Pro-TLGBQIA+, pro-BIPOC, pro-immigrant justice and pro-disability justice," and pro-word salad.
Texas Freedom Network	$1,200,000	Opposes school vouchers and removing overly sexualized books from school curricula. Also supports abortion and claims to be a "watchdog of the religious right."
Texas Organizing Project	$1,575,000	Organizes black and latino people in Texas, organizes around issue-based campaigns and tries to boost voter participation.
The Center for Empowered Politics	$1,650,000	Lobbying arm of the Chinese Progressive Association that was founded by CCP-linked individuals, and created the Black Futures Lab, which is run by Black Lives Matter co-founder Alicia Garza (who was responsible for creating the group's name).

Organization	Grant Amount	Notes
UNITE HERE Action Fund	$2,850,000	To "assist hospitality workers and their families to achieve economic, social, and racial justice in workplaces and communities through education and advocacy, leadership development, and promoting full participation in civic life."
Upwardly Global	$554,000	Helps immigrants, refugees, and asylees fund jobs to help displace the native born and drive down wages.
Vera Action, Inc.	$1,500,000	Fights to end mass incarceration and end bail. Fights ICE detentions and deportations.
Voces de la Frontera Action	$1,200,000	Claims to be the "driving force behind Wisconsin's most expansive statewide Latine, immigrant, and BIPOC youth political engagement network." Supports amnesty and driver licenses for all. Also makes candidate endorsements.
Voter Registration Project	$5,000,000	Mobilizes black, latino, native American, and low-income voters.
VoteVets Action Fund	$600,000	Uses current and former members of the military to promote left wing causes related to the environment, LGBT rights, immigration, and labor.

Organization	Grant Amount	Notes
We the People Action Fund	$975,000	Identifies as an "engine for learning," fostering "stable, long-lasting alliances, and building "long-term deep organization infrastructure."
Western Native Voice	$600,000	"Montana-based nonprofit organization dedicated to empowering Native communities and addressing issues that impact Indigenous people...our mission is to nurture and elevate Native leadership, amplify Native voices, and advocate for policies that create positive change for Indigenous communities."
Worker Power	$1,425,000	"A multi-racial, multi-generational organization dedicated to preserving democracy and improving the lives of working families across the United States through voter engagement and strategic policy interventions." Their first campaign was to unseat Arizona Sheriff Joe Arpaio.
Working America	$2,250,000	Political organizing arm of the AFL-CIO.
Working Families Organization	$5,150,000	Documented earlier in book in length.

Chapter 8

Miscellaneous—More on The Empire Alex Inherits

Most of this book takes the form of explaining how George Soros set the stage for Alex Soros in one area or another, and then what Alex did with the influence he was gifted with. There were some that there wasn't enough details on to make entire full chapters out of but were still worth mentioning in the interest of being comprehensive.

I've written on some of these already in *The Man Behind the Curtain*, and thought they'd be worth repeating here in a condensed format, with information about Alex included. I decided to put this at the end of the book because some percent of readers have already read some of this information and would be re-reading what they already know, and because the topics here are mostly unrelated with no way to weave them together.

Most of this chapter has to do with Europe. Since Alex "took over" operations there in 2015, the information is especially relevant.

EUROPEAN PARLIAMENT

George maintained hundreds of relationships with politicians in Europe, including country leaders and members of the European Commission and European Parliament, that Alex likely benefitted from for years before officially taking over the OSF.

In 2018, a 177-page document titled "Reliable Allies in the European Parliament (2014–2019)" that numbered hundreds of MEPs who were judged by George and his network as reliable allies was leaked.

The document revealed that OSF's allies during the 2014-2019 legislature spanned eleven committees and twenty-six delegations, with a total of 226 Members of European Parliament (MEP) being named "likely allies," out of 751 total MEPs at the time. [1] If "Soros Allies" were their own political party within EU parliament, they would've been the largest that session. [2]

The document begins by naming allies in EU bodies, their bodies of work, and potential allies within them. Among the European Parliament bodies includes the Conference of Presidents, which is parliament's highest decision body, the bodies that run EU parliament, implement and monitor EU foreign policy, assist on "democracy, rule of law, and human rights" issues, and deal with monetary and economic policy, including financial activities of the European Investment Bank.

Others included the committees responsible for human rights protections and the development of "gender mainstreaming in all policy sectors," including many, many others.

The EU is represented globally through over 140 delegates and offices around the world.

The document outlined how the OSF boasted six allies in the delegation to Albania, thirteen to Bosnia and Herzegovina and Kosovo, eight to the then-Macedonia, ten to Moldova, twelve to Montenegro, eleven to Serbia, fourteen to Turkey, four to Belarus, sixteen to Russia, seven to Ukraine, ten to Israel, nineteen to the Palestinian Legislative Council, among many others.

---

1   "Leaked Document Reveals Soros' Potential Allies at the European Parliament," *European Post*, August 18, 2016. http://europeanpost.co/leaked-document-reveals-soros-potential-allies-at-the-european-parliament

2   And by an even larger margin than it appears had they given up their prior party status in this hypothetical.

EUROPEAN COURT OF HUMAN RIGHTS

In addition to outsized influence over the European Union's parliamentary assembly, George is entrenched in Europe's legal system through the European Court of Human Rights (ECHR).

The ECHR is the highest judicial body in Europe and is thus the "final word" legally.

French constitutional lawyer Grégor Puppinck reviewed the CVs of over a hundred justices that worked with the ECHR from 2009 to 2019 to see which NGOs they were affiliated with. After, he published a report outlining George's network of NGOs and its infiltration of the ECHR. Overall, twelve judges out of forty-seven were found to have collaborated to varying degrees with the OSF and NGOs associated with the OSF.[3]

Each judge is elected for a nonrenewable nine-year term.

The collaborators are a mix of judges who directly worked for the OSF and those who worked for NGOs heavily supported by Geroge. Most of the NGO-linked judges are from Alex's new hub, Eastern Europe, and the causes they support include liberalization of drug policy, legalization of prostitution and abortion, and the rights of (i.e. "special treatment for") refugees and sexual minorities.

The report found that three ECHR justices have collaborated with Amnesty International, which Soros funds. Five judges have worked with the International Commission of Jurists (ICJ), which received $1.9 million from Soros from 2017 to 2018. Seven of the judges have collaborated with the Soros-funded Helsinki Committee.

As for advancing the Soros agenda through the courts, the report explains that:

---

3   Grégor Puppinck and Delphine Loiseau, "NGOs and the Judges of the ECHR 2009-2019," European Centre for Law & Justice, February 2020. https://static.eclj.org/pdf/ECLJ+Report%2C+NGOs+and+the+Judges+of+the+ECHR%2C+2009+-+2019%2C+February+2020.pdf?

The favorite mode of action of [Soros-linked] NGOs before the Court is through third-party interventions. This procedure is a practice by which a private or legal person submits to the attention of the Court elements of assessment on a case in which it is not a party to the initial proceedings. The author of the third intervention then becomes a "third party" in the case. This procedure is very beneficial, even if the neutrality and the exterior- ity of the participants are often only a facade. Indeed, the ECHR often has to judge complex and important ques- tions with strong social consequences.

The Court is then placed above national authorities, even legislative ones. The intervening NGOs then have the role of expert, of intermediary body, but also of lobby. In addition to factual information, NGOs can also present the Court with a plurality of ideological or philosophical approaches to the issue in question. By intervening in a case, the objective of NGOs is to enlighten the Court and in doing so to convince it to adopt its own position, and thus to contribute to the development of its case-law, and through it, of that of the European law.[4]

George has directly benefitted from this influence.

When Hungary began cracking down on George it was the ECHR that he appealed to. In a press release in 2018, the OSF called on the court to "act against Hungary over its so-called Stop Soros laws, which criminalize and tax the work of independent civil society groups, under the pretext of controlling migration."[5]

---

4   Ibid.

5   "Open Society Foundations Call on European Court of Human Rights to Defend Hungarian Democracy," Open Society Foundations, September 24, 2018. https:// www.opensocietyfoundations.org/newsroom/open-society-foundations-call-european-court-human-rights-defend-hungarian-democracy

The European Court of Justice ended up taking on cases related to Hungary's anti-NGO laws, and laws against foreign funding of universities.

In 2020 George got what he wanted when the European Court of Justice struck down Hungary's anti-NGO law in June and their ban on foreign-funded universities, ruling that it was incompatible with EU law. [6]

As is usually the case, his meddling pays off.

Despite the evidence presented, the ECLJ's report was initially dismissed. The ECHR promoted its most controversial judge, Bulgarian Yonko Grozev, to the position of "section president" two months after it was published.[7] Grozev spent his career as a lawyer and activist with Soros-affiliated NGOs and was himself an executive with the OSF until he joined the court in 2015. There was already controversy surrounding his nomination back in 2014 because three members of the Bulgarian selection committee were his NGO fellows. He became a judge despite having no experience as a magistrate (which the majority of ECHR justices do).[8]

As section president, Grozev heads one of five sections of the Court, and sits in on the most important cases. He is the judge of deontology (right and wrong) in his section and has authority to decide on a case-by-case basis whether to invite, allow, or refuse the intervention of NGOs he's linked to in cases.[9]

---

6   "Open Society Welcomes Court of Justice of EU Ruling on Hungary Anti-NGO Law," Open Society Foundations, June 18, 2020. https://www.opensocietyfoundations.org/newsroom/open-society-welcomes-court-of-justice-of-eu-ruling-on-hungary-anti-ngo-law

7   Grégor Puppinck, "Soros's Hold on the European Court of Human Rights: the ECHR Persists and Signs," ECLJ, May 2020. https://eclj.org/geopolitics/echr/emprise-de-soros-sur-la-cour-europeenne-des-droits-de-lhomme--la-cedh-persiste-et-signe-

8   Ibid.

9   Ibid.

Court rules state that a judge can't participate in a case if "his or her independence or impartiality may legitimately be questioned." Despite George's NGOs long-standing support for assisted suicide and euthanasia, Grozev was still allowed to decide on a case of an unnamed Polish man hospitalized in a vegetative state, effectively sentencing him to death. The family of the man had initially lost their case to keep him alive when British High Court Judge Sir Jonathan Cohen ruled in favor of the University Hospitals Plymouth National Health Service Trust (he was being treated in the UK) to "lawfully discontinue" his treatment. Appeals to the ECHR were unsuccessful, and Grozev may have made his decision without even looking at the patient's case file.[10]

After discovering Grozev's ties to George, the Polish man's family wrote to the president of the Court Robert Spano to request a review of the case, which was officially rejected on January 19, 2020, with the allegations simply being dismissed as "unfounded." The patient died a week later.[11]

Not until over a year after the ECLJ's report did the Council of Europe (of which the ECHR is its best-known body) concede that there was a problem. Ambassadors of the forty-seven member states of the Council of Europe adopted an official text admitting the credibility of the ECLJ's report on NGOs influencing the ECHR and announced that they'd reevaluate the effectiveness of their current system of selection by the end of 2024.[12]

---

10   Grégor Puppinck, "A 'Soros-Judge' Abandons a Polish Patient to His Death," ECHR, January 2021. https://eclj.org/euthanasia/echr/echr---a-soros-judge-abandons-a-polish-patient-to-his-death

11   "RS Dies of Starvation, Condemned to Death by a Soros Judge," *Daily Compass*, January 19, 2021. https://newdailycompass.com/en/rs-dies-of-starvation-condemned-to-death-by-a-soros-judge

12   Grégor Puppinck, "The Council of Europe Concedes the Veracity of the Report on Ngos and the Judges of the Echr & Rejects the New "Soros-Judge" Candidate," ECLJ, April 2021. https://eclj.org/geopolitics/echr/le-conseil-de-leurope-admet-la-veracite-du-rapport-sur-les-ong-et-les-juges-de-la-cedh-et-rejette-la-candidature-dune-nouvelle--juge-soros-

Unfortunately, George has already made his mark, and Alex inherits influence over a key ally in the ECHR.

CENTRAL EUROPEAN UNIVERSITY

In a world where you thought colleges couldn't possibly move any further to the left, Alex inherits full control of Central European University (CEU), where he is and already was a member of the board.

The creation of CEU represented George Soros' first journey into institution building.

George's idea for an "independent" university in Central Europe was spawned during a meeting at the Inter-University Centre in April 1989. George recalled of the meeting, "At that time I rejected [the idea of CEU] in no uncertain terms. 'I am interested not in starting institutions but in infusing existing institutions with content,' I declared. After the fall of the Berlin Wall, I changed my mind. A revolution needs new institutions to sustain the ideas that motivated it, I argued with myself. I overcame my aversion toward institutions and yielded to the clamor for a Central European University."[13]

On the eve of the Soviet Union's dissolution, George published "Underwriting Democracy," in which he emphasized the importance of building institutions to advance his leftist agenda, and CEU would be his first project.

George and his advisers considered Bratislava, Prague, Warsaw, Budapest, Vienna, Trieste, Krakow, and Moscow to host the University. George said he was "anxious not to start the university in Hungary. Since I am myself Hungarian, the university

---

13   "George Soros and the Founding of Central European University," Center for Strategic Philanthropy and Civil Society, April 9, 2007. https://cspcs.sanford. duke.edu/sites/default/files/SorosCEUOriginsfinal.pdf

would immediately become a Hungarian one," but that would quickly change.[14]

George initially wanted to create a university with "three legs" in Warsaw, Prague, and Budapest, but this plan would never materialize.[15]

In June 1990, Czechoslovakia's government agreed to provide buildings in Prague and Bratislava, pay for operating costs, and give them 50 million crowns in funding. Working in his favor, George had a personal friendship with Czechoslovakian President Václav Havel. The government of Hungary promised to make a building available in Budapest for use as a third campus, which they never fulfilled, so Soros privately rented out a building in Budapest.[16]

After being offered a ten-story building by then-Prime Minister Petr Pithart, CEU's Prague campus opened in April 1991 with four departments: economics; environmental sciences; politics and sociology; and history. [17] CEU heavily focuses on the social sciences over hard sciences, and both campuses offered roughly the same number of programs. Eventually, the early curriculum would be expanded to include European studies, international relations, nationalism studies, and art history at Prague, and legal and gender studies at Budapest.[18]

At the school's opening ceremony, George committed to funding CEU $5 million per year for five years. A third foundation was established later in the year to serve as an umbrella for the two other campuses.[19] In 1992, George committed to a permanent endowment.[20]

14   George Soros, *Soros on Soros: Ahead of the Curve* (J. Wiley, New York, 1995), p. 134.
15   "Central European University (CEU)," *Influence Watch.* https://www.influencewatch.org/non-profit/central-european-university
16   "George Soros and the Founding of Central European University," Center for Strategic Philanthropy and Civil Society.
17   George Soros, *In Defense of Open Society* (PublicAffairs, 2019), p. 96.
18   Ibid., p. 101.
19   Tereza Pospíšilová, "Transnational Philanthropy and Nationalism: The Early Years of Central European University." *Monde(s) 2, no. 6.,* 2014, pages 139–140.
20   Ibid.

George outlines his vision in CEU's statement of intent:

Everyone in Central Europe today wants a high-quality Western-style education. The CEU will provide for the region the academic equivalent of the best Western education, and thereby attract students of the highest caliber. It will also aim to provide a window of opportunity for some of the most able students whose studies should lead to a period of further study at a leading Western university.[21]

As Tereza Pospíšilová, a professor whose research areas include philanthropy, writes in a paper of CEU's early years, CEU is not just a network but perhaps an "international social movement."[22] CEU wasn't established solely as an educational institution, as it also investigated and held public discussions on their preferred political topics at conferences they held in the region. Many early conferences and workshops featured participants from George's inner circle.

CEU has had a number of notable faculty members, including former minister of foreign of affairs of Hungary Péter Balázs, former president of the Supreme Court of Israel Aharon Barak, former minister of finance of Hungary Lajos Bokros, and former minister of culture of Hungary András Bozóki.

The emphasis on research (to support Soros-backed and Soros-adjacent causes) could explain why the student-teacher ratio is so low. Today CEU is located in Vienna, Austria, and reports employing nearly as many staff as students. For the 2019–2020 year, CEU employed 367 faculty, ninety-three researchers, 395 permanent administrative staff, and 355 short term admin-

---

21   "George Soros and the Founding of Central European University," Center for Strategic Philanthropy and Civil Society.
22   Pospíšilová, "Transnational Philanthropy and Nationalism," *Monde(s)*.

istrative staff,[23] all for a student body of 1,299.[24] In America, the national average student-teacher ratio is sixteen students per faulty member.[25] CEU officially boasts a ratio of three and half students per faculty (only counting full-time faculty).[26]

CEU has since graduated nearly twenty thousand students from nearly 150 different countries, most of whom went on to work in business, research, education, and government.

Recent courses offered since 2020 show how the school molds progressive activists. They include "Black Skin, White Masks: Decolonization through Fanon," "Confronting the Crisis: Refugees and Populism in Europe," "Gender and Sexuality in the Middle East," "Environmentalism of the Poor," "A History of Modern Police," "Capitalism and Slavery," and much more. Even in something as seemingly apolitical as an architecture degree has course offerings that include "Architectural Entanglements with Labor" and "The Politics of Infrastructure."

The Soros family flag and their US sphere of influence have firmly been planted in the university. George' son Robert Soros was elected to the CEU board of trustees in 2012.[27] Other current and former members of the board include the OSF's London director, William Newton-Smith; the OSF's New York president, Christopher Stone; Bard College's president, Leon Botstein;

---

23   "Faculty and Staff," Central European University. https://www.ceu.edu/about/facts-figures/staff

24   "Students," Central European University. https://www.ceu.edu/about/facts-figures/students

25   "What is a Good Student-to-Faculty Ratio for U.S. Colleges?" Best Value Schools, August 11, 2020. https://www.bestvalueschools.com/faq/what-is-a-good-student-to-faculty-ratio-for-u-s-colleges/#:~:text=The%20national%20average%20of%20students,Center%20for%20Educational%20Statistics%20report

26   "Schools and Departments," Central European University. https://www.ceu.edu/academics/schools-departments#:~:text=Students%20come%20from%2036%20countries,faculty%20ratio%20is%203%3A1

27   "Robert Soros Elected to CEU Board of Trustees," Central European University, October 30, 2012, https://www.ceu.edu/article/2012-10-30/robert-soros-elected-ceu-board-trustees

Harvard Law School's Benjamin Heineman Jr., and Harvard Professor Patricia Albjerg Graham.[28]

CEU is well entwined with Harvard. CEU's business school celebrated its twenty-fifth anniversary with the publication of a new book *Free Market in Its Twenties: Modern Business Decision Making in Central and Eastern Europe*, for which George wrote the intro. Soros also hosted a book launch event in Budapest, which featured Harvard Business School Dean Nitin Nohria.[29]

Notable CEU alumni include former president of Georgia Giorgi Margvelashvili, former Georgian minister of defense Tina Khidasheli, Members of European Parliament Lívia Járóka and Monica Macovei, Chairman of the Slovakian Party of the Hungarian Coalition József Berényi, and former Croatian Minister of Justice Orsat Miljenic.

Alex reaffirmed OSF's commitment to CEU after officially taking over in 2023, and announced that he was planning a "new model for higher education."[30]

THE OPEN SOCIETY UNIVERSITY NETWORK

Like all his influence campaigns, George' influence over other universities is global. In the words of the Open Society Foundations, George launching his "global network" was to "transform" higher education.

---

28 "Central European University, Annual Report 2015," Central European University, 2016. https://www.ceu.edu/sites/default/files/attachment/basic_page/15437/ar 2015final.pdf

29 "CEU Business School Marks 25th Anniversary with Book Launch with Soros, Harvard's Nohria," Central European University, June 23, 2014. https://www.ceu.edu/article/2014-06-23/ceu-business-school-marks-25th-anniversary-book -launch-soros-harvards-nohria

30 "Open Society Foundations to Explore New Model for Higher Education While also Pledging to Continue Support for CEU," Open Society Foundations, November 11, 2024. https://www.opensocietyfoundations.org/newsroom/open-society-foundations-to-explore-new-model-for-higher-education-while-also-pledging-to-continue-support-for-ceu

As he said in an OSF's press release upon announcing the creation of his Open Society University Network (OUSN) in January 2020: "I believe our best hope lies in access to an education that reinforces the autonomy of the individual by cultivating critical thinking and emphasizing academic freedom. I consider the Open Society University Network to be the most important and enduring project of my life, and I should like to see it implemented while I am still around."[31]

George endowed the global network with $1 billion and asked other philanthropists to contribute.[32]

CEU and Bard College were named as the "core" of the new network partnered with Arizona State University and other global institutions such as American University of Central Asia in Kyrgyzstan and BRAC University in Bangladesh.

Bard College President Leon Botstein was named as chancellor of OSUN and described it as one of the "most transformative initiatives in higher education I have witnessed in my career" before expressing his gratitude toward George.

Just days before the announcement, George spoke to the World Economic Forum where he railed against the rise of nationalism in the US, UK, Hungary. Nationalism is, in his words, the "great enemy of the open society." He blasted Trump in the speech as the "ultimate narcissist," which is rich coming from him, considering he wrote in his 1987 book *The Alchemy of Finance* "I have always harbored an exaggerated view of my self-importance…to put it bluntly, I fancied myself as some kind of God."[33]

31   "George Soros Launches Global Network to Transform Higher Education," Open Society Foundations, January 23, 2020. https://www.opensocietyfoundations.org/newsroom/george-soros-launches-global-network-to-transform-higher-education#:~:text=DAVOS%2C%20SWITZERLAND%E2%80%94George%20Soros%20announced,asking%20other%20philanthropists%20to%20contribute

32   Ibid

33   George Soros, *The Alchemy of Finance* (John Wiley & Sons, New York, 2003), p. 372.

"I believe that as a long-term strategy our best hope lies in access to quality education, specifically an education that reinforces the autonomy of the individual by cultivating critical thinking and emphasizing academic freedom" he told the audience. "30 years ago I set up an educational institution that does exactly that (cultivating critical thinking and emphasizing academic freedom). It is called the Central European University and its mission is to advance the values of the open society."[34]

Excluding Bard and CEU, CEU's global network includes twenty-four colleges and universities and fifteen research and educational institutions. Their objective is to leverage the resources of universities around the world to provide a common curriculum for teaching and facilitating partnerships to research global issues.

Most of the universities the OSUN partners with espouse the typical progressive lingo we're all accustomed to, but one that stands out for its radical ties is Al-Quds University in Jerusalem. Al Quds Bard College (in association with Bard College) also opened on a campus in 2009.

Al-Quds previously had partnerships with Brandeis University and Syracuse University that ended in 2013 after members of the Hamas-allied terrorist organization Islamic Jihad held a march on campus where they performed Nazi salutes and the University did nothing in response.[35]

Later in 2016, the university's own administration organized an event to honor terrorist Baha Alyan, who months earlier with an accomplice boarded a bus in Jerusalem and murdered three Israelis with a gun and knife before being shot and killed by an

---

34   Christian, "The Open Society University Network (OSUN)," AALEP, January 25, 2020. http://www.aalep.eu/open-society-university-network-osun
35   Henry Rome, "Syracuse Follows Brandeis in Halting Ties With Al-Quds," *The Jerusalem Post*, November 22, 2013. https://www.jpost.com/diplomacy-and-politics/syracuse-follows-brandeis-in-halting-ties-with-al-quds-332650

Israeli security guard. One of the victims the terrorist shot and stabbed in the chest was a 78-year-old man.[36]

A Palestinian TV station called *Wattan* reported on the event that "More than 2,500 male and female students participated in the chain, and it included the reading of books and letter-writing by the participants, all of this in the presence of the martyr's father, the lawyer Muhammad Alyan." This involved the students writing letters "to the souls of martyr Baha Alyan and the other martyrs and their relatives... Participants in the activity wore shirts with a picture of martyr Baha Alyan." The dean of student affairs at Al-Quds confirmed that the university supported it.[37]

Students affiliated with the Marxist designated terrorist organization Popular Front for the Liberation of Palestine set up a monument on campus called the "Monument to the Martyrs of Al-Quds University" bearing the inscription "Beware of natural death; do not die, but amidst the hail of bullets"—a quote from the organizer of a 1972 terrorist attack that killed 26 travelers, including 11 Americans.[38]

Another terrorist group that Al-Quds allows on their campus is the "Sisters of Dalal Mughrabi," which honors the terrorist who led the massacre of 37 Jews in the 1978 "Coastal road massacre" that was the deadliest terrorist attack against Israel until the October 7, 2023 attacks.[39]

If this is something Alex has a problem with, he's had more than enough time to kick them out of the OSUN. Despite any attempts to moderate his rhetoric on Israel relative to the rest of the left, he remains in bed with universities like this.

---

36   "Read Like A Murderer: Pa Honors Killer Of Three As Role Model To Encourage Reading," *Jewish News Service*, June 21, 2018. https://www.jns.org/read-like-a-murderer-pa-honors-murderer-of-3-as-role-model-to-encourage-reading
37   Ibid.
38   Ibid.
39   Ibid.

THE SOROS MEDIA INFLUENCE EMPIRE

Alex takes the stage in a media environment overwhelmingly sympathetic to the left and his causes without Soros influence. Their influence serves as another layer of protection in a world where his father has been entrenched in the same media that will be covering Alex in the decades to come.

As is standard for George, his influence began in Europe before America. By 1994 he had thirty supposedly independent radio, TV stations, and publications under his influence just in Eastern Europe, and that's a drop in the bucket compared to his modern American influence.[40]

From 2004 to 2011 George spent nearly $50 million funding about American 180 media organizations, and "news infrastructure" such as journalism schools and industry organizations. The funding figures are derived from tax forms and news stories and understate the true extent of his funding, because they don't include indirect funding (Soros funding an organization that then donates to media).[41]

The Media Research Center has found links between Soros at over thirty mainstream news outlets. Publications and news companies represented by journalists that serve on Soros-funded boards include ABC, NPR, *New York Times*, *Seattle Times*, *LA Times*, *Baltimore Sun*, CNN, *Atlanta Journal-Constitution*, Sunlight Foundation, *Fortune Magazine*, among others.[42] Not a single one of these has published a story critical of Alex.

The list of publications that have or have had staffers that serve on the board of George Soros-funded media outlets includes

---

40   Dan Gainor, "George Soros: Media Mogul," Media Research Center, August 15, 2011. https://web.archive.org/web/20210708020915/https://www.mrc.org/special-reports/george-soros-media-mogul

41   Ibid.

42   "Over 30 Major News Organizations Linked to George Soros," Media Research Center. https://web.archive.org/web/20210513132805/https://www.mrc.org/commentary/over-30-major-news-organizations-linked-george-soros

Arizona Daily Star, Associated Press, CBS, *El Nuevo Herald, Fortune,* Gazette Communications, Hearst Newspapers, *Houston Chronicle, New York Times,* PBS, *The New Yorker, Sacramento Bee, Seattle Times, Toronto Star,* USA Today, Vista, *Washington Post,* HuffPost, *St. Louis Beacon, Voice of San Diego,* the National Federal of Community Broadcasters, and Poynter Institute, among many others.[43] Once again, not a single one of these publications above has published anything critical of Alex,

To give one example of how these outlets protect the Soroses, *The Washington Post* has been quick to run to George's defense. *Post* writer Emily Tamkin penned an article in 2017 on the "Five Myths about George Soros," attempting to convince us that he's not "plotting a revolution or paying people to protest." In it, she provides cover for George aiding the Nazis in Hungary, denies that he pays people to protest by naming protests that he didn't fund and ignoring the ones that he does, claims the fact that George broke the Bank of England is a myth, and says that he isn't "plotting a destructive resolution in America" because he's "simply a large political donor."[44] The piece reads as if Soros himself handed the author a list of the most common criticisms of him and asked them to play defense.[45]

Later in 2020 she published a glowing biography of George titled *The Influence of Soros: Politics, Power, and the Struggle for an Open Society,* which reads like it was commissioned by the OSF itself. Interestingly, in 2023, Alex's Chief of Staff Laura Silber published a lengthy thread on Twitter criticizing my writings on George in the New York Post that was shared far out of proportion with her small number of followers.[46] In going through the

43   Ibid.
44   Emily Tamkin, "Five Myths About George Soros," *The Washington Post,* August 25, 2020. https://www.washingtonpost.com/outlook/five-myths/five-myths-about-george-soros/2020/08/06/ad195582-d1e9-11ea-8d32-1ebf4e9d8e0d_story.html
45   Ibid.
46   https://x.com/laurasilber/status/1620796777405513728

users who shared the post, it was a "who's who" of OSF linked individuals that I'd recognized from researching for past writings, as if they were all sent an email to promote her thread. Among those sharing it was Tamkin.

Just an amusing aside; in Siber's thread she complained that I apparently "passed up the opportunity for reasoned discourse and healthy debate, preferring to demonize, dehumanize, and stir up hate instead" by publishing a series in the *New York Post* criticizing her then-boss George. In preparation for this book I asked her if I could send over a list of questions about Alex for her to answer and she refused. Go figure.

More recently there are George's newer investments discussed earlier in this book, including the purchase of Audacy, and his investment in Crooked Media, which produces the popular podcast Pod Save America, and Alex has since invested heavily in groups like Courier Newsroom.

Soros media influence ranges from local to national and has greatly impacted the national narrative when it comes to the latter.

With friends everywhere in the media, George has been able to create and fuel countless high-profile narratives, and now the torch has been passed on.

POLAND

As was explained in the first chapter, Alex refocused the OSF's efforts in Europe by moving them eastward. In the *Politico* reporting this, Alex said that "the rise of Poland as a leading economy will eventually make it a net contributor to the EU."

Those comments (from 2023) came amid looming elections in Poland. Law and Justice (PIS),[47] a right-wing populist party with close ties to the Catholic Church, had ruled the country for

---

47   The abbreviation is PIS because its name in Polish is Prawo i Sprawiedliwość.

eight years, and is diametrically opposed to the "open society" vision. Among their polices include implementing a near total ban on abortion and fought a crusade against LGBT ideology.

George had handed over to Alex the media apparatus he needed to launch an assault on PIS.

Previously, in 2019, ahead of the crucial Polish parliamentary election, publisher Agora, which owns the major daily *Gazeta Wyborcza*, partnered with a George Soros-backed fund, SFS Ventures, to acquire a 40% stake, and a 60% stake in Eurozet, Poland's second-largest radio station, for $34 million. The move was widely seen as an effort to attack PIS, which failed as PIS was able to remain in power through their "United Right" coalition that won majorities.

Pluralis, a Dutch investment fund backed by George, purchased 40% of the leading Polish publisher Gremi Media for the equivalent of roughly 21 million Euros in January 2022. Among Gremi's publications include the second-biggest non-tabloid daily paper in the country. Shareholders include the Soros Economic Development Fund (17.41%), King Baudouin Foundation (28.46%), and Mediahuis (25.39%).[48]

Pluralis is managed by the Media Development Investment Fund, which George is also a funder of.[49]

The empire expanded the month of the 2023 parliamentary election when Pluralis purchased a controlling stake in Rzeczpospolita, one of the most prestigious news outlets in Poland, in a move widely seen as being to influence the upcoming elections. Rzeczpospolita is generally a right-leaning paper, and Law and Justice officials criticized the takeover.[50]

---

48   "Soros-backed Investor Completes 40% Purchase Of Leading Polish Media House." *Notes From Poland*, January 10, 2022. https://notesfrompoland.com/2022/01/10/soros-backed-investor-completes-40-purchase-of-leading-polish-media-house
49   Ibid
50   Thomas O'Reilly, "Soros Network Grows Media Empire Before Key Polish Election." *The European Conservative*, October 4, 2023. https://europeanconservative.com/articles/news/soros-network-grows-media-empire-before-key-polish-election

PIS would go on to lose control in the 2023 election after winning a sizeable percent of seats that fell below a majority and failing to find a coalition partner. The OSF had to settle for a center-right alternative, as the overwhelmingly Catholic country only has two left-wing parties with representation in government that held a combined 5.4% of the seats in their lower house, and 9% in their upper house (PIS has 41% and 34% respectably) post-election. While hardly a perfect analogy considering the differences in both our countries, this could be analogous to someone like Alex settling for Lisa Murkowski and Susan Collins over Donald Trump.

Fast forward to 2025, and Alex was in Poland just days before its presidential election for the Impact CEE conference, the biggest business conference in Europe after Davos, where he said he was there to discuss the reaction to Trump's second term.[51] Alex is close with one of the leading candidates, Rafał Trzaskowski, who identifies as a centrist but is regarded as being more progressive. Barack Obama was also at the conference.

Fortunately it was to no avail.

In a close 50.89%-49.11% victory, Donald Trump-backed nationalist Karol Nawrocki defeated Warsaw Mayor Rafał Trzaskowski in Poland's presidential election.

Nawrocki officially ran as an independent but was backed by Law and Justice. Trump hosted Nawrocki at the White House the month prior to the election in a sign of support, and Department of Homeland Security Secretary Kristi Noem gave a speech endorsing him and encouraging people to vote for him at CPAC's first conference in Poland a week before election day.[52]

---

51   https://x.com/AlexanderSoros/status/1922743662489883133
52   Matt Palumbo, "Trump-backed Nationalist Defeats Soros-backed Candidate in Polish Presidential Election," *Silverloch, June 2, 2025. https://silverloch.com/ trump-backed-nationalist-defeats-soros-backed-candidate-in-polish-presidential-election*

MOLDOVA

Leaked OSF documents revealed that from July 2013 to February 2015, the OSF secretly paid the salaries of three staffers to Moldovan Prime Minister Iurie Leancă (who was in office from May 2012-February 2015). Documents detailed that money was funneled through a German nonprofit to evade the law,[53] which is interesting considering the suspicious payments discussed early in the prior chapter on where the "big money" went during Alex's first year running the show.

The leaked document explains that "Due to the constraints in the Moldovan legislation, OSF cannot directly pay staff members of the Prime Minister's office. The advisors will be paid as research consultants within a project run by a German think tank—the Institute for European Policies."

One document dated July 3, 2014, reveals that $141,750 was disbursed to "support" PM Leancă." As the *Daily Caller*'s Peter Hasson reported:

> At Leanca's request, OSF began paying salaries to three of his staffers in July 2013: chief of staff Eugen Sturza, economic adviser Valeriu Prohnitchi and political affairs adviser Vlad Kulminski. A fourth staffer, Liliana Vitu, was added to the payroll with the July 2014 proposal. Vitu, it's noted, previously served on the board of OSF's Moldova branch.
>
> The proposal was approved by Leonard Benardo, who is now OSF's regional director of Eurasia.

---

53   Peter Hasson, "Soros Organization Secretly Paid Salaries for Staffers of Moldovan Prime Minister," *Daily Caller*, August 24, 2016. https://dailycaller. com/2016/08/24/soros-organization-secretly-paid-salaries-for-staffers-of-moldovan-prime-minister

OSF paid each of the four staffers $33,750 for the eight months of work between July 2014 and February 2015. The Institute for European Policies received a $6,750 administrative fee for channeling the money to the staffers.[54]

For reference, Moldova is the second-poorest country in Europe, and per-capita income in US dollars today is below $10,000.

The proposal explained that the purpose of the payments was to coordinate the government's focus on its reform agenda, assigning task to advisers to make sure that strategic priorities are addressed, leading work with the IMF and European Bank for Reconstruction and Development, and making the goal of drawing Moldova closer to Europe.

According to the proposal, PM Leancă was "very satisfied with the quality of expertise and the support his advisors provided," describing their contribution as "crucial."

Those bribes overlap with Alex taking over European affairs, and he's been more public with the current leadership.

Alex has met with Maia Sandu, who has been President of Moldova since 2020, at least four times. All that have been made public by Alex has been at public events, not private meetings.

---

54   Ibid.

Alex's Meetings With Moldovan President Maia Sandu	
Date	Location
September 22, 2021[55]	UN General Assembly
February 22, 2022[56]	Munich Security Conference
January 19, 2023[57]	World Economic Forum
September 20, 2023[58]	UN General Assembly

He's also met with Moldova's Prime Minister Dorin Recean at least once in January 2024 at the World Economic Forum.[59]

Sandu is on the center-right of the political spectrum by Moldovan standards and defeated a member of the Party of Socialists of the Republic of Moldova. This makes sense in light of Sandu's pro-EU views, a key part of the Soros agenda, while Moldova's Socialist Party is anti-EU. PM Leancă has also been in various center-right political parties, showing that the Soroses will work with anyone they think they can use to advance a particular aspect of their agenda.

The Socialist Party also has pro-Russian views, which are at odds with Alex's. And, in a rarity for a far-left party, has strong socially conservative views, including opposing gay marriage, opposing abortion, and opposing anti-discrimination measures supposedly to protect sexual minorities, which is at odds with the Soros ideology. The party's leader, Igor Dodon, holds an annual "World Congress of Families" that has attracted a largely

---

55   https://www.instagram.com/alexsoros/p/CUIrBIiLIiE
56   https://x.com/AlexanderSoros/status/1495097383998431235
57   https://www.instagram.com/alexsoros/p/CnmumkDO-QC
58   https://www.instagram.com/alexsoros/p/CxbJmZARIWH
59   https://x.com/AlexanderSoros/status/1749099925558747336

right-wing showing, including George's top opponents such as Hungary's Viktor Orban as speakers.[60]

Weeks after Alex took over the OSF, the Soros Foundation Moldova put out a press release assuring everyone that everything would continue as usual, quoting Alex to reiterate their goal of creating conditions for "Moldova to become an open society, and become a member of the European Union."[61]

Fast forward to April 2022 and the Soros Foundation Moldova pledged to invest $500,000 to improve the efficiency of Moldovan state-owned enterprises to expand their influence over them. In a project expected to take two years, the Foundation signed a memorandum to cooperate with the Moldovan Public Property Agency (PPA) and Expert-Group analytical center to improve relevant legislation, digitalization, transparency and professionalism in the PPA and other state enterprises.[62]

The director of Moldova's National Anticorruption Centre (CNA), Iulian Rusu, met with various non-governmental representatives, including a delegation from the Soros Moldova Foundation, to discuss streamlining the Criminal Assets Recovery Agency. Rusu mentioned that CNA was interested in greater communication with the public and NGOs.[63]

60   Madalin Necsutu, "Moldova to Host Global Christian Right-Wing Congress," *BalkanInsight*, January 23, 2018. https://balkaninsight.com/2018/01/23/moldova-to-host-world-congress-of-families-before-elections-01-23-2018

61   "Alex Soros: The Moldovan Foundation Has Always Exceeded Expectations." *Soros Funds Moldova*, June 27, 2023. https://soros.md/alex-soros-fundatia-din-moldova-intotdeauna-a-punctat-peste-asteptari

62   "Soros Foundation Moldova Invests US$500,000 in Enterprises With State Capital," *InterPressNews*, April 19, 2022. https://web.archive.org/web/20220421071512/https://ipn.md/en/soros-foundation-moldova-invests-us500000-in-enterprises-with-7966_1089266.html

63   "IPRE Has Developed A Guide That Aims To Strengthen The Capacities Of Investigative Journalists And Integrity Verification Analysts In The Field Of Justice." *CIVIC.MD*, February 28, 2024. https://www.civic.md/stiri/ong/77242-ipre-a-elaborat-un-ghid-care-are-drept-scop-consolidarea-capacitatilor-jurnalistilor-de-investigatie-si-analistilor-de-verificare-a-integritatii-din-domeniul-justitiei.html

Rusu said, "We count on the support of Soros Foundation Moldova in developing the program for the recovery of criminal assets, a process that will involve all national authorities. Thus, we will have a synchronized approach and communication, which will generate the necessary synergy between the National Anticorruption Center, the Ministry of Justice, the Parliament and the representatives of the civil society."[64]

We all know how the OSF's "anticorruption" efforts have been abused in Albania and Ukraine, and now it's coming to Moldova.

Collaboration between the CNA and Soros Foundation Moldova was further supported by the Department of Good Governance's director, Natalia Camburian, and Program Coordinator, Adrian Staver, proposing further dialogue between the Foundation and the CNA's subdivisions.[65]

Later in October 2022, Moldovan President Maia Sandu met with representatives of the OSF and Soros Foundation Moldova to discuss democracy, social and economic issues, and the country's "European aspirations." The occasion of the meeting was the 30th anniversary of the Foundation's presence in Moldova. President Sandu expressed appreciation for the OSF's supposed promotion of democracy, independent media, and development of education and science programs in her country, while also hoping for further support in anti-corruption, justice, and education reforms.[66]

In October of 2023, the Soros Foundation Moldova launched several activities to support the Moldovan Ministry of Energy. According to Petru Culeac, Executive Director of the Soros Foundation

---

64   Ibid
65   Ibid
66   "President Maia Sandu Met With Representatives Of The Open Society Foundations." *Presidency of the Republic of Moldova*, October 12, 2022. https://presedinte.md/eng/comunicate-de-presa/presedinta-maia-sandu-s-a-intlnit-cu-reprezentantii-fundatiilor-pentru-o-societate-deschisa

Moldova, the initiative was to "support the authorities in their efforts to ensure the country's energy security, so that, as a result, everyone living in Moldova will have access to energy, the environment will be protected and public resources will be managed transparently and efficiently."[67]

Part of the initiative involved producing seven public policy studies to improve the "corporate governance" of energy industries in the country.[68]

Additionally, the Soros Foundation Moldova aimed to assist the Ministry of Energy in combatting Russian disinformation related to energy in Moldova.[69]

Starting in February 2024, the project was scheduled to be implemented over thirty-six months by the Soros Fund of Moldova along with IP Keystone Moldova and the Association of Social Innovation Fund of Moldova.[70]

In February 2024, The Institute for European Politics and Reforms and Institute for Reporting War and Peace co-produced a pamphlet guide for investigative journalists to assist them when investigating corruption and integrity in judicial institutions. The project was funded by the EU and Soros Foundation Moldova. The guide includes practical recommendations and procedures for collecting and evaluating information on individuals suspected of corruption, such as noting that a judge who legally favors his brother-in-law in a legal proceeding is not upholding the appearance of incorruptibility. The guide also includes infor-

---

67   "The Soros Foundation Moldova Provides Support To The Ministry Of Energy In Improving Corporate Governance Of Enterprises, Financing Interns And Solutions For Gas Distribution Networks Under Moldovagaz Management." *Ministry of Energy of the Republic of Moldova.* October 20, 2023. https://energie.gov.md/en/content/soros-foundation-moldova-provides-support-ministry-energy-improving-corporate-governance

68   Ibid

69   Ibid

70   Ibid

mation on the legal boundaries of information access and use, as well as potential risks to journalists when investigating corruption cases.[71]

In March 2024, the Moldovan "Local Partnerships for Energy Efficiency in Social Services" project, co-funded with the European Union, announced that it would award 35 grants to social civil organizations March 6, 2024. Each grant is approximately €87,000, and the project's total budget is over €4.8 million, with €4.3 million provided by the EU and €500,000 by the Soros Foundation Moldova.[72]

The goal of the project funds civil society organizations to improve energy efficiency in social service buildings that the country may better "align with EU standards, especially regarding climate neutrality," according to Jānis Mažeiks, the Ambassador of the European Union to the Republic of Moldova.

And in return, Soros influence will increase, as the project also aims to elevate the importance of civil society organizations in "social policy dialogue and building inclusive communities for vulnerable groups.[73]

BELARUS

Alex has shown support for the opposition to the dictatorship ruling the Russian client state of Belarus and met numerous times with Opposition Leader Sviatlana Tsikhanouskaya. Including

---

71   Chyzhyk, Halyna and Dawid Sześciło. "Independent Investigations of Cases of Grand Corruption and Integrity Checks of Justice Sector Actors." *Soros Funds Moldova* (among others), February 2024. https://ipre.md/wp-content/uploads/2024/02/Ghid-Investigatii-independente-ale-cazurilor-de-mare-coruptie.pdf

72   "The European Union And The Soros Foundation Moldova Launch A Grant Program For Energy Efficiency In Social Services." *EU4Moldova*, March 6, 2024. https://eu4moldova.eu/the-european-union-and-the-soros-foundation-moldova-launch-grant-program-for-energy-efficiency-in-social-services

73   Ibid

Belarus in this chapter simply serves the purpose of being comprehensive in documenting Alex's influence, not to act as a defense of Belarusian Dictator Alexander Lukashenko.

Belarus' legislature is a rubber stamp with no official opposition parties, and she leads the opposition through the United Transitional Cabinet, a government in exile she created in 2022 following a rigged election.

Her husband announced his intention of running for presidency in 2020 against President Lukashenko, who has "won" every election since Belarus became an independent country. Her husband was arrested two days after the announcement, leading to her running in his place, which Lukashenko allowed under the belief that a female candidate wouldn't be able to form an opposition. In the election she only took in 10% of the vote in results that weren't accepted by the European Union and various other countries, and they sparked widespread protests in Belarus that were far out of proportion than what you'd expect for a candidate that only got 10% of the vote.

One country, Lithuania, recognizes her as the legitimate head of Belarus.

Alex met with Tsikhanouskaya at least twice in February 2023 at the Munich Security Conference,[74] and in January 2024 at the World Economic Forum,[75] where he's praised her as his "fellow Davos do-gooder" and an "incredibly brace leader" of the opposition.

In February 2025, Tsikhanouskaya visited Alex's favorite country, Albania, where she was photographed with PM Edi Rama (among other members of the socialist leadership).[76] In

---

74   https://www.instagram.com/alexsoros/p/Coz_QASO1ug

75   https://www.facebook.com/Alexandersorospublic/posts/with-my-fellow-davos-do-gooder-the-incredibly-brave-leader-of-the-belarussian-op/961853668635815

76   https://www.facebook.com/S.Tsikhanouskaya/posts/pfbid0GjTq6h2P4Fk2cbmwUZrdz7DQ1wwnSiHv3YY39ugUCJd2eYRbbfUf4b5cKcG84YfGl

a social media post, she said the Albanian government doesn't recognize the election results of Belarus, the legitimacy of its first and only President Alexander Lukashenko.

Other issues she reported they discussed launching of internship programs for Belarusians in government institutions of Albania, legalizing Belarusians in Albania, supporting Lithuania's lawsuit to the International Criminal Court against the Lukashenka regime, and ways to expand contacts and cooperation with other Balkan countries, as well as relations with the second Trump administration.

Alex's opposition to the Lukashenko dictatorship is hardly objectionable, but if he is to have success, it will be important to keep an eye on Belarus as a country he looks to infect with his ideology with after it becomes a democratic country.

When it comes to change within Belarus specifically, it's virtually impossible that the OSF will ever have an impact there as long as Lukashenko is alive.

Restrictions on NGOs in Belarus followed tightly on the heels of Lukashenko's seizure of power in 1996. The largest NGO to be targeted was the Belarusian Soros Foundation, which was fined $3 million in a move to bankrupt the foundation and eliminate it from the country. The Soros Foundation, which additionally funded many other NGOs in Belarus, closed the following year.[77]

George denied the accusations of the Belarusian government, saying that the fine would not be paid, and that it was a "blatant attempt to close the foundation by imposing an exorbitant penalty for nonexisting infractions." The Soros Foundation had spent

---

[77]   Mark Lenzi, "Lost Civilization: The Thorough Repression of Civil Society in Belarus." Demokratizatsiya, 2002. https://web.archive.org/web/20190801163918/https://www.demokratizatsiya.pub/archives/10-3_Lenzi.PDF

over $13 million in Belarus, allegedly to support "education, science and civic groups" since its inception.[78]

In addition to the foundation stopping its spending in Belarus with its closing, the United States suspended $40 million in aid in retaliation for Lukashenko's political crackdown on similar organizations throughout the country.[79]

78   https://www.nytimes.com/1997/05/02/world/belarus-fines-soros-foundation-3-million-in-apparent-crackdown.html

79   Miller, Judith. "Soros Closes Foundation in Belarus." *New York Times*, September 4, 1997. https://www.nytimes.com/1997/09/04/world/soros-closes-foundation-in-belarus.html

Conclusion

Alex Soros may try to present himself differently from his father, but he's only done that in one single way: by *declaring* himself to be different from his father. The new Soros is just like the old Soros, and the only ways they differ are the ways in which Alex is even more radical, and that, unlike his father, he's openly boasting about his influence. The Soros agenda is still globalism. In many ways, his public swagger is a self-inflicted weakness his father never had. Every photo op he posts provides more ammunition for conservatives to expose him with, and tips them off to where they should be looking. It's as if he's dropping clues.

And Alex is just getting started. By the time this manuscript is published, he will have been in power for over two years. In the decade to come, it'll be possible to make a much more comprehensive overview of the Alex Soros agenda—which I will write.

Alex won't match his father's efficacy unless we let him. George's empire grew in an era when his influence was a background murmur, passively tolerated by a public too distracted to connect the dots. That era's gone with alternative media's rise, from X to independent journalists, and leaders like Trump, Musk, and Bukele, who aren't shy about calling it out.

The script has been flipped.

Acknowledgments

This book wouldn't be possible without Post Hill Press's Anthony Ziccardi, for being on board with my idea for this book, and Dan Bongino, with whom I co-authored the book *Spygate* in 2018, which opened the door for me to Post Hill (and to basically every other political opportunity I've had).

The Media Research Center's Joe Vazquez helped more than any other person with the immense original research in this book. We spent dozens of hours together researching and authoring two original studies that were, in part, intended to help write this book (and, in part, to help him meet his writing quota). His prior research on George and Alex Soros was also an immense help.

When it came to my hundreds of pages of notes and printed articles, the dream team of Dan Perrucci (also known for taking great author photos), Greg Matechak, and Martin Kariuki saved me many hours by helping me organize them all and identify any duplicate or redundant information.

Townhall's Mia Cathell helped a great deal with suggestions on which parts of the then nearly completed book should be "beefed up" with more content, and she provided useful ideas, all of which I incorporated.

About the Author

Daniel Perrucci

Matt Palumbo is the content manager of BonginoReport.com and the bestselling author of nine books.